THE HABIT OF LABOR

THE HABIT OF LABOR

Lessons from a Life of Struggle and Success

STEF WERTHEIMER

Overlook Duckworth
New York • London

This edition first published in hardcover in the United States and the United Kingdom
in 2015 by Overlook Duckworth, Peter Mayer Publishers, Inc.

NEW YORK
141 Wooster Street
New York, NY 10012
www.overlookpress.com
For bulk and special sales, please contact sales@overlookny.com,
or write us at the above address

LONDON
30 Calvin Street
London E1 6NW
info@duckworth-publishers.co.uk
www.ducknet.co.uk

Copyright © 2015 by Stef Wertheimer

All rights reserved. No part of this publication may be reproduced or transmitted
in any form or by any means, electronic or mechanical, including photocopy,
recording, or any information storage and retrieval system now known or to be
invented, without permission in writing from the publisher, except by a reviewer
who wishes to quote brief passages in connection with a review written
for inclusion in a magazine, newspaper, or broadcast.

Disclaimer: The events and conversations described in this book are derived
solely from the author's recollections. The author has made every
attempt to verify all facts against existing records, but any errors
are the product of misremembrance rather than ill intent.

Library of Congress Cataloging-in-Publication Data

Wertheimer, Stef, 1926- author.
[Ish leyad mekhonah. English]
Stef Wertheimer and the building of a nation / Stef Wertheimer.
pages cm
Includes index.
1. Wertheimer, Stef, 1926- 2. Industrialists--Israel--Biography. I.
Title.
HC415.25.W46713 2015   338.092--dc23 [B]   2015023974

Book design and typeformatting by Bernard Schleifer
Manufactured in the United States of America
ISBN US: 978-1-4683-1086-3
ISBN UK: 978-0-7156-5014-1
FIRST EDITION
2 4 6 8 10 9 7 5 3 1

To all of my loved ones and friends.

"*Tearing us from our roots, from our natural soil, from the Land of Israel, and the subjugation and persecution in the exile, which first of all alienated us from all nature, from all natural life, from all productive work, turned us into a parasitic people . . . our national spirit, our national identity, had been sustained solely by the remnants of the past or from the table of others. . . .*

"*Now, in our aspiration to return to life, for national revival, both human and personal, we must correct all this and to a great extent create all this from the beginning. We must return to nature, to independent work and to our own language. First of all, of course, we must aspire to return to our land, to strike roots in the Land of Israel through our own working of the soil and to revive our national language.*"

—A.D. Gordon, from *"The Nation and Work"*
Special edition, 1956, published by the Haifa Workers Council,
the Zionist Library, edited by S.H. Bergman and L. Shohat,
p. 263. Translation by Anett Daffan

CONTENTS

EDITOR'S FOREWORD *ix*
PREFACE *xiii*
AUTHOR'S NOTE *xix*
1. Childhood *1*
2. Adolescence, Bahrain, and the Palmach *25*
3. Independence *45*
4. A Vision for Education *77*
5. Branching Out to Turbine Blades *95*
6. Home *103*
7. Public Service *113*
8. Founding a Village *135*
9. The Great Breakthrough *145*
10. Industrial Parks: A Way to Ensure the Future *155*
11. On Entrepreneurship *177*
12. Life's Unexpected Turns *183*
13. Expanding Markets *195*
14. A New Kind of Export: The Tefen Model *207*
15. A New Marshall Plan for Industrialization of the Middle East *211*
16. The Deal *221*
17. Summing Up, and a Look to the Future *225*
    ACKNOWLEDGMENTS *233*
    TIMELINE *235*
    LIST OF PRIZES, AWARDS, AND HONORARY DEGREES *239*
    INDEX *243*

EDITOR'S FOREWORD

This autobiography, which Stef Wertheimer narrated to the Israeli journalist Yitzhak Ben-Ner, was published in Hebrew in January 2011 under the title *A Man Next to the Machine*. It was on the best-seller list for half a year. Ira Moskowitz skillfully translated the book to English.

This English version of the book is an adaptation, not a strict translation. While it follows much of the original text, it also updates the book and covers more of the projects Stef Wertheimer undertook outside of Israel that English-speaking readers might find of interest. It now includes several entirely new chapters. One discusses his concept for a new initiative for the Middle East that is akin to the Marshall Plan; Stef and I worked very hard to advance this project in Washington, DC, from 2001 to 2004. Another includes a broader discussion of his collaborative technical education initiatives with the government of Baden-Württemberg in Germany, and another is a chapter that outlines Stef's suggestions for budding entrepreneurs. Yet another new feature is a timeline at the end of this book that shows Stef's life in context with the international and domestic events that have shaped Israel.

THE HABIT OF LABOR

This version also brings readers up to date on what I consider to be Stef's most remarkable skill: his ability to transform former foes into allies. He has been honored for his outstanding service to his country, for his firm's innovative products, for his vision in advancing entrepreneurship and exports through his industrial parks, for promoting crucial foreign investment in Israel, and for the inspiration he has provided to the next generation. By using both his hands and his head he has become one of the wealthiest individuals in Israel. But in this achievement-filled life, one quality stands out above all: his ability to reverse history, turning tragic events into constructive projects.

In 1936, shortly before the Nazi regime began its most malevolent practices, ten-year-old Stef and his family fled their small village of Kippenheim in the southwestern corner of Germany near Switzerland and France, where the Wertheimers had lived since the end of the eighteenth century. It was a time of trauma, of dislocation and relocation in the austere and demanding landscape of Palestine, then under British control.

By 2009, however, things were very different. In the intervening decades Stef had built firms in Germany and had eventually become partners with that government to introduce their successful system of education into Israel. The boy who had fled for his life, now a successful man, returned to a standing ovation in the parliament of Baden-Württemberg, the seat of government for the region he'd lived in as a young boy. A day later, in an official ceremony, he was awarded Baden-Württemberg's highest honor, the Verdienstmedaille, or Order of Merit Medal. And in May 2012, German president Joachim Gauck bestowed on him that nation's highest honor, the Grosse Verdienstkreuz, the Order of Merit, Grand Cross, at a ceremony at the King David Hotel in Jerusalem; this large, red enameled ornament, sus-

Editor's Foreword

pended from a red striped grosgrain ribbon, embodies the unexpected course that a life can follow.

In the Middle East, Stef has also made peace with former enemies. In 1952—less than five years after the Israeli War of Independence ended—he began to include Arabs and those from other minority sectors within his workforce. The enormous success of the precision cutting tools firm that he built, ISCAR, is due in part to his insistence on using the talents of all sectors of this country. He has also conferred with local Muslim leaders from Jordan and Turkey and in the Palestinian Authority to promote a more secure future through industrialization.

Certainly Stef will always remember the tragic fate of his fellow Jews under the Nazi reign of terror, and he will never forget his many young friends who fell in the war for Israel's independence. Nonetheless, he has been able to extend his hand in fruitful partnership with a new generation of Germans and Arabs, an act that should serve to inspire others in any region that struggles for a peaceful settlement to ongoing ethnic conflict.

—*Lynn Holstein*

PREFACE

I have led a complex life in an extremely challenging era, full of obstacles and detours, dreams that came true, and disappointments in my efforts to help to realize a national dream. When the State of Israel was established in 1948, I never believed that the ensuing years would be so challenging.

Israel is a country with two narratives. It encompasses an area that is about the size of New Jersey; within this limited space live primarily two groups, the Jews and the Arabs, both of which longed for a state of their own in the early decades of the twentieth century. It is a place where, in fact, both were promised just that. The British who ruled here under from 1917 to 1948 raised hopes on both sides. Commissions were formed, wars were fought, and the State of Israel came into being.

Zionism—the Jewish movement that began in the late nineteenth century in hopes of returning the Jews to their ancestral home in the Land of Israel—is a work in progress; we have completed two stages, and a third remains. The first stage was agriculture and building, a working of the land we had so yearned for during our many centuries of exile. As we thrust our hands into the soil to plant new orchards and build schools and roads, we started to heal ourselves from the persecution we had

THE HABIT OF LABOR

endured in faraway lands. Through hard manual labor we became like citizens of any other country of the world, free to engage in productive activities and proud of what we produced. No longer were we confined to pursuing the occupations that had been dictated to us by others, such as moneylending or the peddling of merchandise. Agriculture and building began to heal the Jews and to restore our sense of confidence.

The second stage was defense. It was inevitable that the two peoples who resided in this land in the early twentieth century, the Jews and Arabs, would clash. We Jews, with our dispersed and tortured history, longed for a land where we could be self-sufficient and carve out our own future. The Palestinians, after years under Ottoman rule, yearned for self-determination as well. Creating an army that would protect us in the major war that ensued in 1948 and others that followed was a critical need.

In addition to that complex situation arose another: the discovery of oil in various countries of the Middle East. What looked like a bounty at first was a mixed blessing that brought vast wealth to a few in the region while leaving most of the population in poverty. It distracted leaders, who saw no need to democratize or industrialize their countries in light of the gushing flow of oil revenues. As a result, generations of Arabs were left behind as the world moved forward.

For the past seventy years I have been working for a transition to the third stage of Zionism—export industry—to fulfill our personal and national identity here in Israel. As agriculture and building helped to heal the Jews, so can industry help to repair our relations with our neighbors. Industry can provide people with a productive and meaningful purpose in life. It can bring Arabs and Jews together in the workplace and promote our common interests instead of focusing on our differences. It can usher

Preface

in a better way of life for all sectors of our society. It can help us to achieve our most important goal: to live in peace with our neighbors.

My idea to make the Middle East a better place is a simple one: educate both the Jews and Arabs within Israel for skills in industry so that they can be successful and, in parallel, offer technological and entrepreneurial training to our Jordanian, Palestinian, and Lebanese neighbors so that they too can create a strong middle class and become competitive in the world market.

As I write this to our south the Arab Spring has unseated President Hosni Mubarak's long-term rule of Egypt, and his successor, Mohamed Morsi, has been deposed as well. In Gaza, Hamas has demonstrated its ability to launch missiles into Tel Aviv, as was painfully demonstrated in August 2014. To our north, President Bashar al-Assad is using brutal means to retain power in Syria, while a new and even more violent regime, the Islamic State of Iraq and al-Sham, commonly known as ISIS, states that it wishes to dominate the region and force on it a twisted interpretation of Islam. And to our east, Jordan's King Abdullah II is struggling to tend to more than 1,300,000 Syrian refugees who have fled there from their nation's conflict, as the BBC online News Business reported on February 2, 2015. As always, security remains high as a national concern for Israel.

Israel was founded so that Jews could assume a more natural life. In a place of their own, early Zionist leaders like A. D. Gordon, a philosopher who revered manual labor as a means of Jewish redemption, showed that we could put down roots, work in areas that were previously forbidden to us (such as industry and agriculture), and protect our own borders.

Sadly, though, more than sixty years after the establishment of the State of Israel, emigration and survival still are at the forefront of our concerns. It is not only at our borders that one senses a threat; there are internal issues that are imperiling us as well.

We here in Israel underestimate the importance of manufacturing as a vital component of any successful country. It is important on the national level, where it helps to ensure a dynamic economy for the nation. It is also significant on the personal level, giving people skills that will make them proud of the products they create and providing jobs that will enable them to raise their families with dignity. We must provide training so that our people, like others in the world, will have the skills to produce products for the export market.

The future of the Jewish nation will be determined by our ability to abandon old habits acquired from our centuries-long history as a minority in other countries. We have been engaged in nation building for more than six decades now, but that has not been long enough to change our mind-set and those rigid ideas of survival. In the early years of the state we embraced a healthy attitude toward manual work. We had no choice; we had to build roads, infrastructure, and cities. Today, however, that love of working with one's hands has been replaced by what is often an overemphasis on a university education and a disdain for skilled labor.

An effective program of industrialization can benefit this entire region, as has been the case in countries such as South Korea, Singapore, and Japan; through industry they experienced rapid development and ushered in a higher standard of living and greater social and economic stability.

Warren Buffett's two-stage purchase of my precision cutting tools company ISCAR is only part of this story. The book outlines in some detail how an initiative, what I call a new Marshall Plan, could resolve some of the most crucial problems of this region. Such a program could incorporate my Tefen Model

Preface

for industrial parks, which could prove as successful for our neighbors as it has been in Israel and Turkey.

At the moment, Israel's economic situation is strong. We have a Western standard of living and are growing like an emerging nation. The entire world admires the entrepreneurial nation we have built in recent years. This is a world based on innovation, small companies founded by young people who develop original ideas in a wide range of fields. I'm happy to see this development, but with reservations. For example, the fact that the system is exit-oriented is very problematic. Almost before a start-up company is formed it begins looking for someone who might want to acquire it. The ideas are born here in Israel, but unfortunately all too often the development and manufacturing is conducted in other places where there is a greater quantity of skilled workers. Israel then misses out on the many jobs thus created—jobs that could have helped to foster peace.

It was just a few years ago that people thought it possible to divide the world between those who think and those who manufacture. Factories in the West shut down, and manufacturing moved to countries such as China and India. Only recently have we come to realize what a mistake this was. America is returning to work, seeking to retrain its workforce, rebuild its factories, and reverse the practices of the era in which everything seemed to be made abroad. The recovery of the automobile industry is a great American success story, and the ability to rehire many workers is the new American hope. Germany, which had the foresight not to give up its production lines or its superb dual educational system that combines classroom study with apprenticeships, finds itself today at the forefront. It is suffering the least in the European economic crisis, with all of the weaker states in the EU looking to it for assistance.

THE HABIT OF LABOR

A healthy society needs to ensure a certain level of manufacturing. A young person should be able to decide between a vocational track and an academic track, and to know that his or her success will be accorded the same level of esteem in either area. I want a society in which those who engage in manufacturing will take no less pride in their work than those who appear in court to defend their clients.

I am writing this book because I have not realized some of my dreams. I dream that our children will be able to earn an honorable living in Israel and will not leave the country to try their luck abroad. I dream that a "Made in Israel" stamp on a product will have the same cachet as one that reads "Made in Switzerland." I dream that our government will be poorer and the citizens richer. I dream that security will no longer command such high national priority for us and for our neighbors. And I dream that our neighbors will live alongside us in peace, with equality of rights, with political and economic independence, and with a similar standard of living.

AUTHOR'S NOTE

The name of this book, *The Habit of Labor*, comes from A. D. Gordon (1856–1922), who inspired Zionism through labor. "We [Jews] lack the habit of labor," he wrote, "for it is labor which binds a people to its soil and to its national culture."

The notes, quotations, and testimonies on my approaches to educational issues are taken from the collection *The Educational Vision of Stef Wertheimer*, edited by Dan Prat. Notes written about me by my friends are taken from a booklet produced for my eightieth birthday, edited by Ruti Ofek. Notes by my late wife Miriam are taken from a booklet produced in her memory, edited by Erez Harpaz.

THE HABIT OF LABOR

CHAPTER 1

CHILDHOOD

What is the first sight etched in a person's memory?

The road to the train station was long, and our maid held my hand and hurriedly dragged me there on foot, in the mud, probably to meet her boyfriend. I was about three years old then. Later, at home, my mother scolded the young woman for taking me with her. Maybe I just recall what they told me years later. But the image of the long road endures—perhaps because I never let anyone drag me along again.

Kippenheim: a tranquil village, surrounded by fields and forests. It lies in the Black Forest region of Germany, ten kilometers from the Rhine River and Alsace, the French border, and one hundred kilometers from the Swiss border. Albert Einstein and Kurt Weill were born not far away. White lace curtains in the windows, and lots of flowers. Courtyards immersed in shadows. The residents are deep-rooted farmers, some of whom have switched to commerce and small industry. Cuckoo clocks are produced in the region.

I was born in Kippenheim at 1:45 on the afternoon of July 16, 1926, in the house where my father was born. It is a stone house with three floors, a small courtyard and thick climbing plants on the back wall.

THE HABIT OF LABOR

My aunt, Dr. Selma Wertheimer, delivered me, with the help of three assistants. I lived there until the age of ten. We were three children at home: me; my brother Zvi (Peter), two years younger than I; and Doris, four years younger than I. Both of them were good kids. On the other hand, I was a rebellious child, a troublemaker.

Twenty years after I left this home, I reluctantly returned to it, alone, and then again years later, with friends. The house has hardly changed at all; only the plum and apple trees are gone from the yard.

On this street, Bahnhofstrasse, which leads to the train station, every sixth house was the home of Jews during my childhood. At the end of our house, where the minimarket is today, there was a grocery store that belonged to my family and was sold to a German named Dorner. Aunt Erna lived at the end of the street. On the main street, adjacent, was the home of Uncle Hermann, and across from him was the home of Uncle Richard, which stood next to the Rathaus, the town hall. A minute's walk from there, across from the synagogue, lived Aunt Fanne and Uncle Max. Max and Richard worked in the tobacco business. In the records of the Jews of Baden, eight members of the Wertheimer family appear as business owners in Kippenheim: the butchers Abraham Wertheimer, Hermann Wertheimer, and Julius Wertheimer; Leopold Wertheimer and David Wertheimer, in the livestock business; another Hermann Wertheimer, who operated a market for metal materials; Poldy Wertheimer, who ran a textile store; and my father Eugen Wertheimer, who operated a market for grain, flour, and animal feed.

Uncle Jonas lived in a house opposite the well-tended Rathaus. He was chronically ill and usually sat at the window, looking out. The next building, the home of Aunt Fanne, which now houses a local lottery agency, is where my parents would send me when I misbehaved too much. My cousin Erich would help me with my math and French lessons during my last school year in Germany.

On my second trip here, fifty-three years later, my friends urged me to go in as we stood next to the three-story house where I was born. Reluctantly, I knocked on the door of our home, where the Allen family now lives. I answered the voice that emerged from the intercom at the entrance. I said: "It's Wertheimer. I was born here." The man recognized my connection to the place. On the old wooden steps, whose carpet absorbs every creak, I went up to the second floor. The owner—about forty years old, mustached and pleasant—welcomed me. He had heard the name Wertheimer from his parents, who had purchased the home. "Your brother from the United States already visited us here," he said to me—as if it were obvious that we would all return sooner or later. Everyone in Kippenheim and the surrounding villages—Schmieheim, Ettenheim, Lahr—knows the name Wertheimer and the other Jewish names; they cannot free themselves from these names. I looked around; everything remained as it was, almost, except that the furniture had changed. A typical residence of a typical German family in a typical German village. I mumbled a few words of farewell and hurried to leave the house.

My friends were surprised that the village and my boyhood house left me completely apathetic, indifferent to the sights, the beauty, the warm welcome, and the childhood memories. I do not like this village. I do not feel any sense of belonging to it, and I have no pleasant memories associated with it.

In the street where we once walked in the snow to the nearby school, a plump and red-faced man came up to me and asked politely what I was looking for and who I am. When I told

THE HABIT OF LABOR

him "Wertheimer," his face lit up like someone who had found a long-lost brother.

"Stefan?" he called excitedly, gripping my hand tightly and shaking it relentlessly. "You don't remember me? He said his name, which did not ring a bell, and said that we had learned in the same classroom for three years. I felt none of the same excitement, but he did not notice as he enthusiastically told me about our schoolmates. "You know," he said with a pained expression, "so many good friends from the class were killed on the Russian front during the war . . ."

Mother's parents lived farther down the street, on the third floor, above their inn, the Badischen Hof on Poststrasse 7, which still bears its original name. Celebrations and wedding receptions were held in the inn's restaurant. Mother's brother Hermann managed the hotel with the restaurant and the butcher shop below. They continue to kill the livestock in the paved courtyard—though it is no longer kosher slaughter as it was then—and the snorting of the pigs can be heard in the air.

Nearby lived Hilde Wachenheimer, who was a few years younger than me. She and her parents did not escape, went through the concentration camps, and survived. In America, she became a poet. She sent me her poems, which all deal with the Holocaust. I wrote back to her, "I don't occupy myself with the past."

But, in fact, there is no way I can avoid addressing the past.

Kippenheim had about two thousand people when I was a child. The village's population has more than doubled today, but now there are no Jews. Jews were permitted to settle in Kippenheim in the mid-seventeenth century after the Thirty Years' War as "protected Jews." The first documented Jew was Jud Lowe, who came in 1654. Other Jewish families followed, and by 1793 there is a record of one of my ancestors, Hirschel

Childhood

Wertheimer.¹ In 1871 the Jewish population reached its peak with a total of 323.²

During my boyhood, about ten large extended Jewish families made up about 15 percent of the population. They were engaged in the usual occupations of Jews—butchers, merchants, bankers. There were no farmers among them, as the laws prevented Jews from owning land.

My family's roots may go back to Meir of Rothenburg, who was also known as Rabbi Meir Ben Baruch (ca. 1215–93) and Maharam of Rothenburg. The name Maharam is an acronym for the Hebrew words Morenu ha Rav Rabbi M . . . and was used for many rabbis. "Our" particular maharam was a commentator, rabbinic authority, and spiritual leader of German Jewry. He was well known for his school at Rothenberg ob der Tauber, which he maintained at his own expense. He was also famous for his protest against Kaiser Rudolph I, who imposed heavy taxes on the Jews. The maharam was imprisoned for his stance and apparently refused to be released in exchange for the high ransom the kaiser demanded so as not to encourage additional arrests. After seven years of captivity, he died in his cell.³

My paternal grandfather was a flour and grain merchant, like his father and grandfather before him, and he was known as the Baron of Flour. My own father continued in this business.

---

¹ Allemania Judaica: Arbeitsgemeinschaft fuer die Erforschung der Geschichte der Juden im suedeutschen und angrenzenden Raum, "Kippenheim (Ortenaukreis): Jüdische Geschichte/Betsaal/Synagogue," http://www.alemannia-judaica.de/kippenheim_synagoge.htm.

² Mitgliedergruppe Ettenheim Historischer Verein für Mittelbaden, *Schicksal und Geschichte der jüdischen Gemeinden: Ettenheim—Altdorf—Kippenheim—Schmieheim—Rust—Orschweier* (Ettenheim, West Germany: Historischer Verein fuer Mittlebaden e.V. Ettenheim 1988), p. 441.

³ Nissan Mindel, "Maharam of Rothenburg, circa 1220–1293," http://www.chabad.org/library/article_cdo/aid/111856/jewish/Maharam-of-Rothenburg.htm.

For three years he studied the grain business in Mannheim with the father of Dr. Reuven Hecht, who later built the Dagon granaries in Haifa. He met my mother Karolina, or Lina, in the village; he was about three and a half years her senior. Mother, who was also from the Wertheimer "tribe" but not a direct blood relation, studied music at the nearby Freiburg Conservatory for several years and continued teaching piano after marrying my father. I remember her playing and singing songs by Franz Schubert with Father. The home was full of books, which I explored with great curiosity as a child.

Her family, and Father's family, like all the Jewish families in the village, were not assimilated and strictly observed *kashrut*, the Jewish dietary laws, though they were not particularly religious. On every Sabbath or for every Jewish festival, everyone would go to the village synagogue, which was the center of the Jewish community. The synagogue was built in 1850, a large, elegant building with reddish bricks. Above its doors the inscription "This is none other than the house of God" was carved in large Hebrew letters. The children would play in the paved courtyard and in the narrow lane that climbed the shoulder of the grassy hill. In the house behind the synagogue lived the local *hazan* (cantor), Schwab, who taught me and the other children a bit of Hebrew. On Friday nights we would all congregate there, adults and young people alike. After Saturday morning prayers the entire family would come to Uncle Hermann's home for a second breakfast.

I first returned to the village only in 1956, twenty years after leaving it as a child. And when I returned it was not because of nostalgia; I felt nothing but anger. I wandered around the streets; I saw my parents' home, and the homes of my uncles, but I did not go inside. I did not speak with anyone. Later, in 1963, when I lived for over a year with my family in the Nether-

Childhood

lands, where I started the first Israeli factory overseas, we would sometimes travel for a ski weekend in Switzerland and pass by Kippenheim. My wife Miriam did not understand my aversion for the place. She was also born in Germany, but her attitude toward Germany was more tolerant. I would exit highway 5 toward Basel, stop near the village, and say, "Wait for me in the car. I'll be back in half an hour."

I would enter Kippenheim by myself, now a place devoid of Jews. Those who did not leave in time died in the camps. Only in the local Jewish cemetery, in Schmieheim, can you find many familiar names. With 2,500 graves it is the largest Jewish cemetery in southern Baden. Established in 1682 by the Jewish community of Ettenheim, today the cemetery is a forgotten site. But a sign at its entrance states that it was not overlooked by the Nazis. According to the sign, it suffered massive damages during the "pogrom days of 1938," including the burning of its mortuary.

Some of the tombstones are from the seventeenth or eighteenth centuries; many are dark with age. Time has erased the names from many of them. On some gravestones, names are carved in Hebrew letters only. You find there a lot of Weil, and Auerbacher, Dreyfus, Durlacher, Wachenheimer, and Wertheimer. There lie both of my grandfathers and grandmothers, my Uncle Siegfried, my father's brother who was killed as a soldier in World War I, and other relatives: Benno Wertheimer, Leopold Wertheimer, Paulina Wertheimer, Samuel Wertheimer, Siegfried Wertheimer, and Sophie Wertheimer.

The gravestones attest to generations of Jews—physicians, merchants, and intellectuals—who were part of the heart and soul of the region for centuries, until one day their neighbors sought to erase them. A tombstone erected in memory of the Jews who fell fighting in World War I calls out in Hebrew letters,

THE HABIT OF LABOR

"Peace, peace to the near and far."

Another vestige of the Jewish community in Kippenheim, the old synagogue, was also pillaged by the Nazis, and local residents before the war, and it was turned into a granary for animal feed. I have never been a religious person—but here, angrily, I decided to embark on what became a protracted battle. As a member of the Knesset, in dozens of long letters to members of parliament in what was then West Germany and with the help of Erich Lehman (one of my longtime employees), I called upon the village council of Kippenheim to renovate the building so that it could reclaim its honor. I also provided some money for the initial restoration work. The authorities in the region and the Kippenheim village council were not enthusiastic; they even became angry. But the persistent pressure—twelve years of heated correspondence and numerous trips—finally paid off.

My demand received publicity in the local media, and the pressures there intensified—especially among young Germans, who felt driven by their sense of shame. In the end, the authorities acquired the building and renovated its exterior with typical German precision. It is now recognized as a preserved memorial.

Father was a tough and hardy man. He lost his older brother, Siegfried, in World War I, and he himself lost a leg in the fighting near Verdun in France and was decorated with the Iron Cross for bravery in the German Army.

Years after his death, we found Father's diary outlining his experiences in the war: the march to France via Belgium, his injury and the amputation of his leg while in French captivity. He wrote most of the diary at the military field hospital in Ettlingen. My daughter Ruti and my grandson Erez translated it into Hebrew. Father wrote,

Childhood

Many around me are wounded, one has his whole left cheek hanging down in rags, another has a stomach wound, everyone is shouting but only the medic can help because the crisis of the attack had arrived! Our company commander pops up, praises us for holding out so bravely, since the 12th Company next to us had already retreated! . . . Here was the enemy break-in point, and this was to be held if we were to hold the section of the trench. . . . It went on like this for some time longer, our ammunition was used up and only 2 men were left unwounded, one of them [being] myself.

It might have been 5 o'clock already, we could no longer count on reinforcements, we were surrounded on all sides and attacked with hand grenades when we both retired to the nearby medical shelter, where our comrades were lying with a few medics. It still took some time before the Frenchman dared to come near, his hand grenades were already crashing in front of the shelter, suddenly one falls down the trench steps and explodes with unspeakable noise! . . . Soon there is a second—a third—I drop to my knees and feel the warm blood dripping down my left knee! I gather my utmost willpower and nimbly hurry up the steps, straight into the arms of the furious Frenchman!

Three [to] four hold a pistol to my head, direct me from one end to the other . . . then an older French officer ran up . . . and I beg him to save me for my dear parents. He . . . handed me over to another, who finally brought me through the German barrage back into the valley to the French battalion shelter. And now began for me the hardest time of my life so far! In captivity!

Ten days later a French doctor recommended amputating Father's wounded leg. Father relates that the thought put him through "a terribly hard mental struggle," but that after the surgery was performed he was "happy to feel a weakening of the unspeakable pains."

For the rest of his life Father walked with a wooden leg, which did not deter him from conducting himself as a regular person, without demanding anything of others because of his disability. He was good at riding a bicycle with his one leg, even during his old age. If he had pains, he did not talk about them. He always kept everything inside him. All of the extended family greatly admired Father as a man of integrity. He was intelligent, an autodidact, a lover of books, someone who was interested in all subjects, and a person of uncompromising principles.

But he and I did not get along very well. I was stubborn and spiteful. He was strict and punishing, and I would respond by doing the opposite of what he asked. When Mother baked a cake for my eighth birthday, I ate a piece of it before the birthday party. I received a spanking and a severe scolding. Thereafter, prior to each of my birthday parties, the traditional cake would vanish from the table as if by magic. Everyone knew who did this—but no one said a word to me. If they punished me, I would punish them back—for example, refusing to go with them on a visit. There were constant clashes between Father and me. Mother, who was softer, always tried to mediate. "You have a stupid face, child," she affectionately told me once. "Protect it."

When the trouble I made for my parents would become intolerable, they would send me to Aunt Fanne, my mother's sister. Mother had five sisters and four brothers; most of them lived nearby.

But Father and I also had good days, taking trips together on Sundays in the forests around Kippenheim, during which we had interesting conversations. I think that he did not expect much of me. Occasionally I would come to him, full of enthusiasm, to tell him about a new idea, and he would quickly douse my enthusiasm. "Oy, Stefan," he would sigh, "nothing will come of you."

And yet, there are some indications that I had a certain sense of responsibility even as a child. The proof resides in the red book titled *Das Leben unseres Kindes* (The Life of Our Child), in which Mother chronicled her first child's progress. I keep it in my mother's tall secretary that now occupies a central place in our living room. Like many new mothers, she had time to fill in only some of the printed entries. Under the chapter title "Besondere Ereignisse im fünften Lebensjahre" (Special moments in the fifth year of life) she wrote about my birthday party. She listed the six children whom she invited and then, at the bottom of the page, she seems to have written something that I dictated to her: "Mit 5 Jahren habe ich meiner Mutter alle Besorgungen gemacht" (At age 5, I helped my mother with all of the shopping).

And then a later entry appears in my own, childlike handwriting. It falls under the printed title "Besondere Bermerkungen ueber die ersten drei Schuljahre" (Special remarks about the first three years of school). Even then it seemed that school held no interest for me, for I wrote about work instead: "Mit 9 Jahren besorgte Ich allein das Geschaeft" (At 9, I took care of the shop alone). The shop I referred to was our family's small grocery store at one end of our house.

In the red book my mother also recorded my first word, claiming that it was "Fedora," the name of a fine German chocolate company. The love of good chocolate has remained with me all my life.

Grandmother Paulina, Father's mother, lived one floor above us. Her beautiful apartment was filled with soft rugs, old pictures, and lots of books. Grandmother pampered me, and I spent many hours with her until her death, one year before we left Germany. I read a book a day, at least. I loved a wide range of books, from scientific and technical works to the boyhood adventure series of Karl May, that trickster who was imprisoned for a total of eight years for theft and fraud. I was not alone in my admiration for his books; his work garnered several generations of young fans across the world, including Albert Einstein, Hermann Hesse, Adolf Hitler, and Albert Schweitzer. With published works numbering 200 million volumes in thirty languages, he is said to be one of the most widely read German authors.[4] Many of his stories were set in the Wild West, in the Middle East, and the Far East—all places, with a few exceptions—that he had never visited.

I was not an introverted loner, however. I had a few German friends among the neighbors, but my real friends were my cousins in the village, who were close in age to me.. For a few years, my partner Lynn Holstein planned a dinner for all the cousins at the Carlyle Hotel in New York City; except for one who lives in Baltimore, they all reside in the New York area. I had not seen some of them for years. Our conversation focused on what "the spirit of Kippenheim" instilled in our lives. For children, there was not much to do in this small village. I was the youngest, and I was not invited to kick the ball on the field, so I found my refuge in reading.

Even when fears arose with Hitler's rise to power, we were insulated by the protective family. We were children in a closed Jewish society that did not prepare us for the world at

---

[4] Jan Fleischhauer, "Germany's Best-Loved Cowboy: The Fantastical World of Cult Novelist Karl May," *Spiegel Online International*, March 30, 2012, http://www.spiegel.de/international/germany/marking-the-100th-anniversary-of-german-cult-author-karl-may-s-death-a-824566.html.

Childhood

large and for social integration. But we all learned to be survivors.

At age ten I was exposed to the world beyond Kippenheim for the first time when I went to visit my uncle in Nuremberg, a big city that stirred the curiosity of a child. Perhaps the fact that my nice uncle, aunt, and cousins accepted me just as I was is also what made the vacation so wonderful, because at home I was not accepted—period. That is how I felt. In Nuremberg I visited the German National Museum, with its collections focusing on Germany's history, science, craftsmanship, and nature. I felt I could stay there forever. I went there every day, fascinated by the endless characters, events, ideas, research, and revolutionary technical inventions displayed there—for example, models and illustrations of the inventions of Leonardo da Vinci. It was a formative event for me, an initial opening of a door to the world, and I returned to Kippenheim a different person.

At about the same time, a major surge in the Nazi movement began in Nuremberg. My parents did not conceal their concern. While we Jews were not cherished in our village, I do not remember encountering blatant anti-Semitism there. But during my year in secondary school in nearby Ettenheim, one teacher harassed me all the time. I was the only Jewish child in the class, and I waited impatiently to leave that school.

At the beginning of the 1930s it was not certain what the future would bring, but Adolf Hitler's voice could already be heard more and more frequently. Men in brown uniforms with red armbands already appeared in the village, and Germans greeted one another with the Nazi salute. In various places swastika flags were seen. One time, when the car of Reichsmarshall Hermann Goering passed through the village, local residents stood on the sides of the road and waved flags. In 1933, one of the main streets of Kippenheim was renamed Adolf-Hitler Strasse.

THE HABIT OF LABOR

The tranquility of the Black Forest villages was not shaken by such signs of things to come. But I remember the worried faces of my parents when they listened on the radio to news about the Nazi racial laws enacted in Nuremberg in 1935 and when German Jews were subsequently stripped of their citizenship. Even earlier, in 1933, emergency regulations were issued, and a boycott of Jewish businesses was declared. Father could not bear the revocation of his citizenship. Yet he, who had fought for Germany and lost his leg in the war, had superb instincts. He decided, "The man is crazy. We need to get out of here."

Our family was not Zionist. In 1935, when Father decided to leave Germany, he considered emigrating either to Palestine or to America. He chose the former because, unlike the United States, the English government, which then controlled Palestine under what was known as the British Mandate, allowed factories to be transferred there. The liquidation process lasted for nearly two years. Father was wealthy, with a variety of businesses, and he insisted on investing most of his money in acquiring a large flour mill, including all the equipment, with German Jewish partners who were also about to leave Germany.

Several days before Christmas in 1936, Father, Mother, my sister, my brother and I said farewell to relatives and friends and set off on our way. I do not remember feeling emotional about leaving Kippenheim. Perhaps I also did not fully realize the significance of the departure. During the two years of preparations, I had read a lot about the Land of Israel, and I was full of curiosity. Most of the extended Wertheimer family subsequently emigrated to America or Latin America, and those who did not leave in time were exterminated in the Holocaust. In an elegant memorial book titled *Jewish Fate*, published in memory of the Jewish community in the Kippenheim region by young

Childhood

Germans of conscience from this area, I can find the pictures and names of many members of the extended family and their places of death: Aunt Fanne Valfer, whose home I would frequent on Saturdays, was taken to Gurs in France and there, apparently, she was murdered together with her husband Max. Others were killed at Theresienstadt and Sobibor.

We got into our vehicle, crossed the nearby border into Switzerland and reached Basel, where we stayed with relatives for a few days. We then departed by train for Italy. I still have a picture I took in Milan with my box camera: my family standing by the magnificent Duomo.

From Milan we traveled to Venice and from there to Trieste, where we boarded a beautiful ship, the *Marco Polo*, which took us to Palestine via Alexandria. We arrived at Haifa on February 10, 1937. The journey lasted a month and was quite enjoyable. But when the *Marco Polo* laid anchor at Haifa, a difficult problem arose: How would father, with his prosthetic leg, disembark from the rocking ship to the teetering boats that ferried the passengers to the shore? He managed the challenge nonetheless, and we proceeded by train to Tel Aviv.

At first we stayed at the Sheinkin Hotel at 8 Sheinkin Street. I looked totally foreign, a small village boy with three-quarter pants and a cap, eagerly anticipating the surprises that awaited me. I did not know Hebrew, except for the prayers I had learned back in my German village.

After a month my parents found an apartment at 7 Frishman Street in Tel Aviv, near the seashore. They lived there until their dying days, in a neighborhood of German émigrés like themselves. The singer Yosefa Schocken lived across the street from us. Yosefa and Mother quickly became friends and every Saturday morning Mother would open the window that faced the window of Mrs. Schocken's apartment and ask in German,

THE HABIT OF LABOR

"Yosi, we'll do a round?" Mrs. Schocken had a grand piano; she would sing, and Mother would accompany her. Sometimes Father, who played a bit of violin, and Zvi, who played the accordion, would join them, while my sister Doris, her friend Uli (Yosefa's daughter, who would later become a well-known singer in her own right), and I would sing. I had joined the choir of the Shivat Zion Synagogue on Ben Yehuda Street.

After learning basic Hebrew for about four months in an intensive language program (*ulpan*) with other immigrant children, I went to the nearby Tel Nordau Elementary School. It was not easy for me to learn the language. In general, I do not pick up languages quickly. Hebrew is the language in which I now think and dream, but my Hebrew is not as expressive as my English, which I enriched over the years through extensive reading. I maintained my fluency in German because we spoke German at home and read German newspapers such as *Blumenthal* or *Aufbau*.

When I started fifth grade at the Tel Nordau School, everything seemed foreign and incomprehensible. I met the rough local boys for the first time. I suffered insults; they laughed at my appearance, my clothing, my heavy German (known here in Israel as *yekke*) accent. But as a strong kid, I did not suffer this quietly and would get into fights with those who insulted me.

I established several friendships: Gidon Bachman, who later became a prominent filmmaker and theorist and completed books and films about Federico Fellini and Pier Paolo Pasolini; Edgar Santo, who left the country before the establishment of the state, leaving no trace (and I would be happy to know what happened to him); and Ernst Halperin, who became a world-renowned professor of nuclear physics.

It was not a coincidence that the four of us, European immigrants—from Austria, Czechoslovakia, Germany, and Hungary—became friends. The established Jews (known as *sabras*

Childhood

after the local fruit that is prickly on the outside but sweet on the inside) did not accept us. We felt rejected even though the country was then flooded with new immigrants. In our class, about a third of the pupils were new immigrants. Nonetheless, some pupils and teachers, and even the principal, Mr. Feller, tried to make us feel like foreigners.

I was a fairly weak pupil. I did not like most of the teachers, but there were also some good teachers, like Mr. Posnanski, who taught literature and instilled in me a fondness for Sholem Aleichem, Mendele Mocher Sforim, and others. I spent my time with friends during recess in the school courtyard and at the nearby stand that sold pressed dried fruit (called *Leder* because in its pressed state it looked like leather) and falafel, or would take a daily swim in the sea, even on cold winter days. We would wander together on Ben Yehuda Street, where pine trees were planted in those days, or we would sit like good kids at Ernst's home and listen to classical music; his parents had hundreds of fine records.

Our house on Frishman, near the corner of Hayarkon Street, still stood until 2011, though by then it was quite dilapidated. We lived on the second floor, and my room overlooked the street. There was a lending library on the first floor, with many books in German. It was a pleasant neighborhood, with the nearby Harlinger Café, the Logos bookstore, and the Scala record shop, where I purchased my first records. In the building next to us lived a photographer, and he once had me pose for a margarine advertisement. I never liked margarine, and my lack of enthusiasm seems to be evident in the photo.

The wonderful beach was nearby, and we spent many hours there, swimming and playing games with a medicine ball. The promenade was then just being paved. On Saturdays the adults from the neighborhood would also come to the seashore, some of them in bathing suits and bathrobes, and some in pajamas. For me, the beach was a second home, and I would help the lifeguards Emil and Yoska, who were kind enough not to send me away.

On the corner of Ben Yehuda and Frishman streets stood the synagogue where I had my bar mitzvah. Across Frishman lived Mr. Kaufman, Father's business partner, who ultimately bought Father's share in their flour mill. At the corner of Mendele Street, an elderly optician had a small shop. When I started to work as his apprentice, he would give me eyeglasses to repair, and I would work on them at home during the evening to earn extra money.

One of my first girlfriends lived on the other side of Ben Yehuda Street, on the third floor My friend Gidon Bachman lived on the next street, and Edgar Santo's family was also not far away. Tichon Hadash High School was around the corner, and on Hayarkon Street, near today's Sheraton Hotel, was the headquarters of the Palmach, the strike force division that had been created in 1941 within the Haganah (the Jewish underground army that preceded the Israel Defense Forces). Today there is a parking lot there. Next to it was the Red House, which served as headquarters for several of the central prestate institutions: the Histadrut labor federation, the Haganah, and Mapai, the precursor of the Israel Labor Party.

Our family's economic situation at that time was not yet secure. During the first year after our arrival, Father set up his large flour mill, called the Kaufmann Milling Company, in the Nahlat Yitshaq neighborhood: four stories, about forty workers, and two partners, M. M. Kaufmann and J. J. Dreifuss, who likewise came from Germany. After a year of preparations and construction, the mill began to operate and was actually successful. Occasionally, when I was kicked out of class at school, I would

Childhood

come to help with the construction work and painting. Once, as I sat in the office—I was about twelve then—a good and quite rare conversation developed between Father and me about the mill. I told him that he should improve efficiency—for example, he should bring machines from the top floor down to the ground floor so workers would not have to haul sacks down the entire stairway from above. I advised him about his resources and objectives, and suggested ways to plan suitable housing for the workers—a twelve-year-old economic adviser.

Later I also sat and drew him a sketch, in which I tried to organize the essential factors: the mill building in the center, with paths branching out to all of the areas of know-how, production, and marketing. One path led to the Research Division at the Weizmann Institute, which I thought would be useful in upgrading some of my father's grain products and introducing new ones, such as new baby foods that the institute was working on. A second path led to the AKA packaging plant, which handled the packaging of the products, and a third path led to the port of Tel Aviv, to the ships that transported the products overseas. I did not forget that credit lines and improved living conditions for the workers were a prerequisite for boosting efficiency. In the drawing, the smoke emerges from the factory's chimney in the form of sterling banknotes, as a reward for enhancing production efficiency. Near the factory, I sketched living quarters and shopping centers for workers. Without realizing it, I was already developing plans as an industrialist; it was an early vision of what I would much later build in Tefen. At the top, I also included Tel Aviv's most beautiful house, which was known as the Pagoda House because of its upturned roof. It had no meaning for me then, but it did years later: there, on the third floor, lived a young woman named Miriam who would become my wife.

THE HABIT OF LABOR

I still have this drawing, sketched in pencil, with explanations in German, framed in my study at home. I do not remember whether Father took my proposal seriously at all, but when I look at this faded drawing, it seems to me that already at age twelve I had crystallized my mission in life.

In 1939, when World War II began in Europe, there was a recession in Palestine. Father and his partners tried to switch to producing feed for animals, with the assistance of scientific research from the Weizmann Institute—bran, ground carob, and so on. The products were good, but the market was weak. Father hastily sold his share in the mill, losing most of his property and money there, but he did not blame anyone; he simply accepted it as reality. Had he held on for another year, the factory would have experienced great demand because of the war, but I suppose he did not really like working with his partners and decided to cut his ties. Maybe my early and persistent drive to succeed was brought on by my Father's failure.

At home we entered a period of belt tightening. A wealthy family became one barely able to make ends meet. Years later my cousin Erich told me that my parents had to sell our German oven to pay for my bar mitzvah. They started to sell home-baked cookies to earn a living, and I devised several machines for them for mixing dough, frosting, and baking. At first they baked sweet cookies; but Father had severe diabetes, and it was difficult for him to check the products by tasting them. Mother came up with the successful idea of baking crackers with caraway seeds. Everything they baked was sold in tins, and they managed to make an honorable living from their work.

While they created a life in Palestine, my parents were unable to dislodge their native land from within them—they hated it and longed for it at the same time. They spoke German, read German, and clung to the world of German culture that

Childhood

shaped them; and they maintained a circle of friends who, like them, were German émigrés uprooted from their natural surroundings. The home was also a German home, with heavy furniture from over there. But Father was a man of principles; he refused to stay in contact with anyone in Germany. Mother, on the other hand, corresponded throughout the years with a few friends there. After the war, my parents returned for a visit to West Germany and Kippenheim once or twice, they but felt a bit of disdain for everyone who remained there.

In seventh grade I had the first of a long series of confrontations with ruling bureaucracies. The principal, Mr. Feller, expelled me from school after I hit a teacher named Dubnikov, who would aggressively pinch the students in his class. He harassed me in particular and regularly made fun of my clothes and imitated my accent in front of the other children. One day, when he pinched Vera, the girl who sat next to me, I got up, a thirteen-year-old gentleman, to defend her honor. I was still a child, but a strong child. I punched him, and my life took a different turn as a result. The administration adamantly refused to allow me to return to school. Father was angry, Mother was very sad, and I felt hurt. The sense of being the black sheep of the family intensified. My parents, who had already despaired of my inability to obey authority, did not look for another school, instead deciding it would be better for me to learn a vocation. "There's no money at home," Father said. "So if you're not succeeding at school—go work and help support the family!"

I started working as an apprentice in an optician's shop on Allenby Street. Between running errands, I learned to grind lenses in the store's workshop. I worked there for about two years; I liked the work, but when I reached the age of fifteen and a half, both my employers and I felt that I had already outgrown working

THE HABIT OF LABOR

with eyeglasses. They also took in cameras for repair, and I was sent to deliver them to Mr. Auerbach in the apartment around the corner, on Geula Street, where he worked with his wife.

Auerbach accepted me as an apprentice in the repair of cameras, a field that I saw as more challenging than optics. He was a superb professional, a perceptive person and a natural pedagogue who worked alone at his machines, which included a planer, a lathe, and a miniature grinding workshop for precision mechanics; he produced small metal parts for cameras. I worked at his side for nearly a year and enjoyed every moment.

I suppose that this man recognized my technical aptitude and knew how to stir my interest in this work. He systematically introduced me to the secrets of precision mechanics. I learned to discover the vitality and warmth in metal in comparison to cold and lifeless glass. There, for the first time, next to the simple lathe, I took pleasure in the work of turning metal.

From Auerbach I learned the educational value of this combination of mentor and pupil: an experienced employer, who teaches his apprentice the secrets of the trade, makes demands of him, corrects him, and guides and supports him. Though the joint mission of the two individuals is to create a final and flawless product, there is also another mission that is no less important: to bestow knowledge upon the apprentice. A good mentor is equipped with the skill for creating a good product, as well as the ability to pass on this know-how to others.

Auerbach understood that I did not come to him just to look for work but also to learn a profession. After about a year, he recommended that I learn with Professor Emanuel Goldberg, a renowned optician who had immigrated from Germany, where he had developed the Zeiss Contax camera; in Tel Aviv he opened an optics laboratory at the Engineers' House. Professor Goldberg, who wanted to start a training workshop, was

Childhood

looking for German-speaking students because he did not know Hebrew. I went with Father to his laboratory and was accepted, together with five other students selected from among many. We worked there in the professional atmosphere of a development department, at a level comparable to that of Germany at the time.

Along with my work as an apprentice, I continued to pursue high school studies for two years at the Haskala School, three and a half hours every evening—and this was after a workday of about ten hours. I also continued to read voraciously. I was eager to learn, but in my own way. I always resisted conventional, banal classroom studies, with the teacher instructing the class and the pupil receiving instruction.

After my brother Zvi began working (he followed in my tracks as a lathe operator and became a superb machinist of precision metalwork), we would bring our salary envelopes home every Friday afternoon and give them to Father. Sometimes I would ask for a bit of spending money for something—I started to appreciate music, and would often go to concerts with my friends—but if Father said "not this week" I would not argue. I decided to save a little money and buy a record player, and occasionally I would enrich my collection with a few new records.

When World War II broke out, we in Palestine did not yet understand the repercussions of this historic tragedy. The horrors of the Holocaust were still unknown to us, and young people in prestate Israel were not yet called upon to serve in the British Army or its Jewish Brigade. Tel Aviv was, in the meantime, a distant and peaceful place. As teenagers, my friends—Gidon, Edgar, Ernst—and I would concoct various strange ideas and send letters to the king of England with sage advice on how to win the war against Hitler. These were methodical letters, full of innovations we devised, such as how a British pilot could blind his opponent, the German pilot, so the latter would not be able to see him as he aimed his plane's machine gun at him. The king for some reason did not bother to respond to our many letters. Perhaps the war kept him too busy.

Unlike most of my friends, I did not join a youth group. I sometimes visited the clubhouse of the Blau-Weiss (the Blue-White), one of the first European Jewish youth movements. Founded in 1912 in Germany, it had about three thousand members at the end of World War I.[5] It was banned by the Nazis, but made its way to Palestine, where it brought young German-speaking immigrants together. Yet I regarded these organizations as closed clubs for the chosen. Such clubs were foreign, arrogant, and restrictive in my view, while I wanted to be independent. I was not a lone wolf, however; I had a group of friends, both boys and girls. We spent time together boating on the Yarkon River, at the seashore, or listening to classical music on the second floor of the Nusbaum Café, opposite the beach. The owner would play the records we requested, which were nearly worn out from overuse.

During my free time I would often go to the seashore, where we would play *hakafot*—a type of stickball. I was a valued player because of my strong throws. My sister Doris, who became quite a tomboy, was also a regular player in our group. Besides this, I did some boxing and later also served, in the summer, as an assistant to the lifeguards. I spent a lot of time on the *hasaka*, a surfboard on which one stands and paddles with a long oar. The world war was already raging, but it was far away; here, life was good and pleasant. For the time being, at least.

---

[5] NS-Dokumentationszentrums Köln, "Jugend! Deutschland 1918–1945," http://www.jugend1918-1945.de.

CHAPTER 2

ADOLESCENCE, BAHRAIN, AND THE PALMACH

In Professor Goldberg's optical laboratory I worked and learned in a scientific atmosphere alongside four engineers of optics, mechanics, and physics, including Goldberg's daughter, Chava. This group later comprised the core of the advanced optics company El-Op. They produced aircraft navigation instruments, devices for measuring blood sugar levels, and many scientific instruments used by the Weizmann Institute, the Haganah, the British Army, and others.

In 1940, the British approached Professor Goldberg about producing compasses for the army. A compass has a piece of hard, magnetized stone that must be sharpened so that a needle can be attached to it very precisely. I assisted one of the laboratory workers in searching for a good way to create the right point at the end. We tried for three months, and read lots of how-to books, but we did not succeed. About thirty years later, during a visit to a factory in Czechoslovakia, I saw how they solved this problem in a very simple way—with a thin wire, a stabilizer and diamond dust—and I was very angry that I had never thought of this.

I learned a lot in Goldberg's laboratory, but I started to realize that my basic lack of education was holding me back. I was just a teenager, but I wanted to advance more quickly. I began to read difficult professional material and to study on my own.

I left Goldberg to work as a lathe operator for about six months at the American army base at Tel Litwinsky where they produced parts for fuel containers ("jerry cans") using new and wonderful lathes. I also worked as a lathe operator for a while at the Hadaikan factory. I went through five different places of work in two years. I was full of energy, and curious, but lacking in patience, too unwilling to waste time in a place that had nothing more to teach me.

Gradually the awful reality from the outside began to penetrate our lives. The boats carrying illegal immigrants, refugees from the devastation in Europe, started to arrive. I occasionally brought clothes to these immigrants who clandestinely disembarked from the boats—*Patria* on Frishman Beach and *Tiger Hill* on Gordon Beach—to help them look like local residents.

I also met Miriam during this time. Our first meeting was when I came to visit her sister, Ruth, at their apartment in the Pagoda House on Nachmani Street. It was a beautiful *yekke* home with lots of books and oil paintings. The family had immigrated from Andernach, near Cologne, and her father was a good family doctor. When I knocked on the door Miriam opened it and said, "She's not home." I looked at her and liked what I saw; I said, "That's okay. I'll stay!"

When we met, Miriam was thirteen and I was about sixteen. She was completely different from her older sister: skinny and beautiful, with black eyes and black hair. It was love at first sight, at least on my part. She was still a child then, but I announced to my friends, "She will be my wife!" At least this is what one of the girls in our group, Ruth, claimed. They laughed at me, saying, "You're robbing the cradle."

Adolescence, Bahrain, and the Palmach

Miriam's childhood memories in Germany included anti-Semitic incidents. She and her sister Ruth would play in their large garden and were not permitted to go out into the street, because a woman had once approached Miriam on the street and said to her, "Jesus died because of you!" Little Miriam was shocked and had responded apologetically, "It's not me; I wasn't there!"

On Kristallnacht in November 1938, Nazi rioters broke into the home of the Jewish neighbors and the two Wallach sisters saw from their window how the hooligans were destroying the nearby synagogue. With their mother the girls fled to the home of non-Jewish friends. The rioters stopped their rampage two houses away from the family home. But Dr. Wallach was taken to Dachau and spent five weeks there. Miriam's mother traveled to Berlin, paid a lot of money, and managed to obtain an immigration visa for the whole family. They were then smuggled via a petroleum truck into Belgium, where they remained until their arrival in Palestine several months before the outbreak of World War II. Miriam was nine years old. In Tel Aviv, Miriam attended the Balfour School,[6] participated in the Scouts, and was also a member of a group that planned to help settle a kibbutz.

Miriam initially took little interest in me because I was not a member of any youth movement. Most of the time she was

---

[6] The Balfour School was named after an individual who was pivotal to Israel's existence, British foreign secretary Arthur James Balfour. On November 2, 1917, Balfour wrote to a leader of the Jewish community, Lord Rothschild, stating, "His Majesty's government view [sic] with favour the establishment in Palestine of a national home for the Jewish people . . . it being clearly understood that nothing shall be done which may prejudice the civil and religious rights of existing non-Jewish communities in Palestine or the rights and political status enjoyed by Jews in any other country." Robert John, "Behind the Balfour Declaration: Britain's Great War Pledge to Lord Rothschild," http://www.ihr.org/jhr/v06/v06p389_John.html.

busy with her friends, and I worked every day and prepared to leave for Bahrain.

At that time, the British Royal Air Force (RAF) issued a tender for an expert to perform maintenance work on navigation instrumentation in fighter aircraft at the RAF base in Bahrain. Apparently the RAF couldn't recruit British technicians for this mission because of the very hot desert climate. The British asked Professor Goldberg to recommend someone. Though barely seventeen years old, I was apparently the only one who met the essential requirements: professional qualifications and the ability to work in the desert heat. The year was 1943, and the Allies were already preparing for a large attack on Japan. Bahrain became a central base for this planned assault.

I passed the qualification tests and was recruited under a civilian contract with the British Ministry of Defense. I did not wear a uniform. I flew to Baghdad, where I waited a month at the British military base until a flight to Bahrain became available. I arrived at Bahrain's military airfield on a stifling hot day and presented my letter of recommendation to the base commander, Captain Thompson. The base was still under construction, but planes landed the whole time and injured soldiers were taken off on stretchers.

"Oh no!" Captain Thompson groaned. "They made a mistake again. I asked for an expert on aircraft air-conditioning, so what did they send me? An optician." I told him, "Captain, don't worry. I'll get my hands on a few instructional manuals and I'll repair the air-conditioning systems for you too." A pilot there named Breyer who flew to Palestine as part of his assignment brought me some books, and within a few days I could fix anything that was in need of repair. The captain was pleased, and I was also satisfied. Ultimately they needed someone to repair optical sights, as well as air conditioners, which were not a

Adolescence, Bahrain, and the Palmach

common product then, and a technician for the diesel-powered generator used to supply electricity. So I had no shortage of work once I demonstrated that I was able to learn just about anything.

But my seven months there serving as a civilian were tough. The weather was hot and humid; we slept in straw huts and suffered from poor hygiene and nutrition; many soldiers became ill with tropical diseases. I was as strict as possible about cleanliness.

During my free time I studied engineering at a British institute, watched the young locals retrieving pearl oysters from the depths of the sea, and explored the city, which was not yet a center for oil drilling. I found most of the Jews from Palestine there to be unpleasant and dishonest, so I became friends with two British soldiers, and dived—sometimes successfully—for pearl oysters.

There I came to know the Georgy family, who were from Basra in Iraq, who warmly welcomed me into their home. The parents wanted me to help their daughter emigrate to Palestine and asked me to take her as my wife in a fictitious marriage. One evening, when I arrived at their home, I was shocked to discover that riots had erupted in the neighborhood. The Georgy home was locked, and the entire family had disappeared without a trace. It was close to the end of my period of service there, just as the news began to trickle in about the Holocaust. The combination of the dark news from Europe and the ominous fate of the Georgy family filled me with helpless anger. I was not yet eighteen years old, and I suddenly discovered what it really meant to be Jewish. Here too, as in Europe, Jews were being persecuted.

I returned to Palestine with many gifts: expensive German books for Father, a lot of classical music records for Mother, and a field hockey stick for Doris, who was starting to learn the game.

THE HABIT OF LABOR

At that time the Gut Company in Nahalat was looking for a lathe operator. The company was constructing bridges on the Tigris and Euphrates Rivers in Iraq and building sewage systems in Tel Aviv. I was hired, even though my training was in a different field. I worked for about six months at Gut as the company's sole lathe operator, making parts for bridges.

Meanwhile, I strengthened my friendship with Miriam. She had a boyfriend, Natan, who would write her love notes; he was worried about the deepening relationship between Miriam and me and recruited Ruth to inquire about the intentions of that "wild man" who was courting her. When Ruth asked me about my intentions, I told her, "Listen, I do not intend to give up on her under any circumstances!"

There were other concerns as well. The shocking news about the Holocaust, knowing that some of my cousins were murdered there, the memory of the Georgy family in Bahrain, the intensifying struggle against the British, and the long conversations until dawn about ways to fight occupied my friends and me. Around this time Miriam's sister Ruth joined the Lehi Group (also known as the Stern Gang) after its founder, Avraham Stern), a fact that she kept secret for a long time. Lehi was more extreme than the three other paramilitary groups that existed in the early 1940s in Palestine—the Haganah, the Palmach, and Etzel (also known as the Irgun)—and was considered by many, including the British, to be a terrorist organization. I was not an ideological Zionist, but I had to find a way to participate.

My friends were already engaged in practical action. I had long arguments with members of two rival paramilitary groups, the leftist Palmach and the rightist Etzel. Both sides tried to persuade me to join them, but the truth is that I found it very difficult to see the differences between the two. Once, when I went with Miriam to a movie at the Ophir Theater, some guys

Adolescence, Bahrain, and the Palmach

standing near the ticket booth decided to provoke me: "Coward! Slacker!" The atmosphere heated up, and it was only because of Miriam that we did not come to blows. But I would not allow them to force me to identify with one side or another; I wanted to decide on my own.

In the end, the decision was easy. At the beginning of 1945 I joined the Palmach and not the Etzel because my friend Aryeh Geva joined the Palmach, and I was sent to Kibbutz Givat Brenner for a nine-month basic training course with weapons. At first, they did not exactly know what to do with me. Oded Arazi, from Kfar Yehoshua, was the platoon commander. Most of the soldiers in the platoon, including young women, came from moshavim and kibbutzim. They were a more homogeneous group than our group, the city folks.

I immediately liked Oded. I came from a world of new immigrants, a technical world. And here was someone different, someone rooted and sure of his identity. I felt that he was better, truer, and more basic: a thinking young man, hardworking, decisive, and straightforward, with leadership ability, courage, and composure who engaged in something real—agriculture—and left everything behind to mobilize for the national mission. Only there, in Givat Brenner, with Oded and others, did I discover the new "proto-Israeli," who was the answer to the stereotype of the *galuti* (Diasporic) Jew. I had always been searching for meaning for myself, and a sense of belonging, and there, in the tents of the Palmach, I found it. My friendship with Oded continued until his death in 1997.

At Givat Brenner I worked in the kibbutz metal workshop to make water sprinklers and drippers. It was not that I looked down at farming; on the contrary. But by then I had already realized that my future was tied to industrialization. The development of our weapons industry was a very critical issue then so that we would not be dependent on foreign entities. I felt that my greatest contribution would be to help produce a barrel for the Sten submachine gun that would make it as accurate as the British Thompson submachine gun, or Tommy gun.

The training at the kibbutz was both simple and quite sophisticated. The fitness I had developed through years of swimming and sports activity helped me greatly, but even more important was the mental training, the way that they prepared us for survival—to adapt to harsh conditions, to respond to unforeseen challenges with innovative solutions, to keep our eyes on the goal, and to keep our secrets. I was satisfied because I knew it was where I needed to be. There was a feeling that the commanders—Oded and his squad leaders—had complete faith in what they were doing. I was also caught up in this feeling, and it gave me a sense of fulfillment. For the first time in my life, I *belonged*. My skills were essential in the most natural way, in the most crucial place and time.

There were also lighter moments. There was never enough sugar for the coffee, so I invented something. We inserted a long, thin, flexible tube into the sack of sugar on the top shelf of the storehouse, providing the desired flow. The kibbutz storehouse manager never figured out how the sugar had disappeared from the sack.

Since I had brought with me a hand-cranked record player, a device that was quite uncommon at the time, our tent became a gathering spot. Everyone in the Atom Platoon came again and again to listen to my few 78-rpm records. But here, too, a few problems arose for me as a new immigrant. Some kibbutzniks were arrogant toward the city dwellers in the platoon, and the *yekkes* in particular provoked disparaging remarks. Though my original name, Stefan, was shortened to Stef in the

Adolescence, Bahrain, and the Palmach

Palmach, my German accent remained—as did my pride. And I never refrained from responding to a haughty remark by a sabra kibbutznik, and always defended the honor of the city dwellers and German immigrants.

I had to keep fighting for my rights, including when they began to select soldiers for operational missions; I did not want to be among those left behind. So, after we were considered too green to take part in the Night of the Bridges operation (in June 1946, when the Palmach and other Jewish fighting groups blew up eleven bridges), I insisted on participating in the second bombing of the British radar facility at the beach near Herzliya. (The British quickly rebuilt the entire radar facility that was destroyed in the first bombing, and again threatened to use it to detect ships carrying illegal immigrants.) I was afraid the Palmach would not include me because I was not "one of the gang." I went to the platoon commander's tent and told Oded, "Either I'm in, or I'm out of here!" And Oded, said to me, "What are you talking about? Of course you're participating."

The mission went like this: A Palmachnik would pretend to be a plumber and get a job installing a new water and sewage system at the British radar facility. Every day he would plant a small amount of explosives in the sewage pipes. So they forged an identity card for me with the name Schwartz and I passed as a plumber. I managed to get hired for work in the radar complex, but a few days later the operation was called off because someone turned on the sewage system prematurely, and all of the explosives placed in it were swept out to sea.

The issue of assigning soldiers to missions arose again after nine months of basic training, when Oded had to select two of his soldiers for the Palmach's pilot course. He chose Nahum Biran from Afikim and me, and we set out for Kibbutz Na'an on foot, carrying our suitcases; there we underwent and joined

THE HABIT OF LABOR

the group of flight cadets. I am grateful to Oded for the pilot's course; he was the first one to have faith in me. He was also the first to drum into my head that Zionism is not lofty words about what needs to be done; Zionism is *doing* what needs to be done.

The yearlong course was the Palmach's second pilots' class, disguised as a civilian course of the Aviron airline company. It also included a gliding course. The training flights took place at a civilian airfield in Ramle, on the Polish RWD-8 aircraft from the 1930s. Each pilot had to log twelve hours of flying with an instructor before he could solo. During one of these flights, the head instructor Ernst Rappaport supervised me as I flew over the curve in the railroad tracks between Ramle and Jerusalem. Apparently I flew much lower than was permissible, leaving him speechless with panic. As part of the course, we also went on an exhausting trek in the scorching Judean Desert to identify prospective sites for landing strips. I really enjoyed the lessons, the drills, and the flights and the wonderful feeling of infinity, hovering in seventh heaven.

At the Nusbaum Café in Tel Aviv, I met with many friends. Some of them remained my friends for years, like Ra'anana (Eliyahu Sela) and others. I also met Aharonchik (Aharon Donagi), a Palmachnik who was recruited for the technical unit, which later served as the foundation for the Science Corps (HEMED), and engaged in sabotage. Donagi spoke with me about delay mechanisms for explosives that would enable sappers to escape injury, and put me in contact with his colleagues who were developing weapons for the Haganah. I was asked to help them. Aharonchik brought me a diagram for a small rocket and, in the evenings, I would go to the large welding workshop at Na'an and try to create rocket parts from scraps of metal. This was a fascinating mission: the attempt to produce artillery and rocket weaponry.

I successfully completed the pilot's course in mid-1946 and received my pilot's license from the mandatory Palestine

Adolescence, Bahrain, and the Palmach

government in January 1947. There were about a dozen graduates of the pilot's course at Na'an; some were later killed in Israel's War of Independence. Once the clandestine course ended, it was not possible to maintain regular training and scheduled flights or to accumulate flight hours. Over the years, I occasionally returned to the helm of a plane but, despite my love of flying, I never did it regularly.

After the course ended I took a demolitions course and assisted the Palmach's top demolitions expert, Haim Singer, the commander of Company G (which also included the pilots of the Palmach) in planting magnetic mines to blow up British warships.

The British did not wait long to respond. They rounded up a great number of us, and I was caught on horseback while doing guard duty at the gates of Na'an kibbutz. It was June 29, 1946, a day that came to be known as Black Saturday by the Jews and Operation Agatha by the British. They arrested most of the leadership of prestate Israel, including all of the graduates of the course at Na'an. Yitzhak Sadeh, the Palmach's commander (and, incidentally, the uncle of philosopher Isaiah Berlin), who spent that weekend in Na'an, managed to elude arrest. We were all taken to the army base at Latrun and later to the base in Gaza at Rafah.

The three or four months of detention were one of the most meaningful periods of my life. Behind barbed wire, I came to recognize the nobility of my compatriots—hundreds of members of kibbutzim and moshavim, of the Palmach and Haganah, and immigration activists, who all cared deeply, engaged in serious thought, and were driven by a sense of responsibility. There was a wonderful feeling of camaraderie and belonging, and I knew that we would not relent in our quest to establish a state. We learned a lot, sang, exercised, and played brain games and ball games to keep in shape. I think that in Rafah, after Givat

THE HABIT OF LABOR

Brenner and Na'an, I became a true Israeli, part of a community united in togetherness and a reliance on one other.

In September 1946 I was released from the detention camp, and I awaited my next assignment. I was in reserve status because a British prohibition made it impossible to continue flight activity. I was ordered by the Palmach headquarters not to stay with my parents for security reasons, and I took a room in the house of the Ney family, opposite my parents' home.

I was not particularly worried about the future; I knew I would do what was necessary. I was almost twenty-one years old; I knew English and had gained experience; I had been in Bahrain and had taken a pilot's course; I had a profession and knowledge in other fields. I was not unemployed for long; Yisrael Sakhorov, who was then the deputy director of the first incarnation of Israel Military Industries, waited for me in a secret location and brought me to the Nahalat Yitzhak neighborhood in Tel Aviv to a facility called S that was housed next to my father's former flour mill. Opposite the facility was also a dairy barn operated by Miriam's uncle, so I knew the area well.

There was a workshop in the facility with about twenty people, an excellent group that assembled machines for manufacturing Stens, the Palmach's submachine guns, and machines for making bullets. They put me at a lathe and asked me to make molds for Sten bullets. So I started to work in the clandestine weapons industry of the Israeli state in the making. My coworkers included Yossi Harel, who also served as an illustrious captain of illegal immigration ships, and Avner Shmueli, one of the most superb craftsmen I have ever known. All of us worked on the weapons that would soon be required.

The day of reckoning was near; the state was within reach. I wanted to do something more important—to fly or to join the Palyam, to sail to Europe and bring back illegal immi-

Adolescence, Bahrain, and the Palmach

grants. The day of the UN General Assembly vote arrived, November 29, 1947, and the partition declaration was followed first by celebrations and then by war. Discharged Palmach veterans, including all my friends, were summoned to arms again. When I also hurried to report to duty, my Palmach commander told me, "There's a problem with you. The military industry does not want to release you. It's essential to continue to produce Stens and to improve the Johnston machine guns." So I missed an opportunity to join my fellow pilots, who departed for Czechoslovakia to train on fighter aircraft and bring them back to the nascent state.

This made me very angry. I went to Yosef Slavin, a tough man who was in charge of the underground weapons industry, and I told him, "We don't have a lot of pilots. They went to great efforts to clandestinely train the few who know how to fly. Each one of them is very important now—and I'm one of them. So, I have to go." He was furious. "Over my dead body," he thundered. "And if necessary, I'll go all the way to David Ben-Gurion!" A few days later, he told me, "A directive was sent to everyone concerned, informing them that they would not receive you in other units under any circumstances." I did not give up. I tried during the following weeks to persuade him, until he declared, "Listen, young man. Stop bothering me with your airplanes. It's *luftgesheft* [a Yiddish word meaning "flighty," lacking in substance]. The most important thing now is for you to produce more weapons." I got angry and said to him, "If that's how it is, I'm not staying here. You can start looking for me!" And I left.

I went to the airbase at Sde Dov, joining my friends from the course who already served there as pilots. The first volunteers were already arriving, Jewish pilots from Britain, the United States, Rhodesia, and South Africa. And since I had fewer flight hours than everyone, I was a copilot in light planes. We flew over

THE HABIT OF LABOR

the besieged and isolated Gush Etzion bloc and dropped packages of food and weapons on its four communities: Kfar Etzion, Revadim, Ein Zurim, and Mesuot Yitzhak. But I was not used much because there were more pilots than there were aircraft.

One day, about a month after arriving at this unit, I flew with Yigal Allon, who wanted to conduct an aerial survey of potential sites for the Palmach's nascent Yiftach Brigade. "Why are you being wasted in the air force?" Allon asked. "You have technical experience and know-how in weapons and explosives. Come, help me establish the brigade as a technical officer in the Palmach." He knew that Miriam was serving in Yiftach, which of course contributed to my desire to transfer there. I was asked to assume responsibility for operating all of the protomilitary workshops in the Tel Aviv region several months before the British left the country. I worked on developing weapons, and the Palmach sent me to everyone who planned to do something out of the ordinary. Allon sent me to the Negev, to Bir Asluj, to assist Nahum Sarig in enhancing the range of the PIAT, which was then our antitank weapon.

Miriam and I met up in the Galilee, which would become our home a few years later. Allon asked me to assist the area's kibbutzim in setting up infrastructure for the independent manufacture, assembly, and repair of weaponry so that the Galilee would not be dependent on sources in the center of the country. This was a lesson drawn from the siege on the Deganya kibbutzim and from the trauma that developed in its wake, regarding the possible cutoff of communities and regions.

Allon listed the missions for me: to produce weapons and to equip the brigade; to assist Dan Lanner at Malkiya in assembling a twenty-millimeter cannon and several Browning machine guns; and to develop a smaller and more portable Davidka mortar that could be carried on the back. "And besides this," Yigal said, "you'll initiate things in your field, according to your best judgment." So began my connection with the Galilee, which continues to this very day.

Donagi introduced to me to the HEMED group working on the research-theoretical side of weaponry. It was a group of physicists headed by Jenka Ratner, who was involved in weapons development in the British Army during World War II. At the time there were very few professional lathe operators in the country capable of producing the rocket and launcher parts the unit planned. Ratner was pleased with my precision, and I became a member of his team.

The Yiftach Brigade had just been formed; one company and several platoons of Palmach members were deployed in the kibbutzim in the area. I also worked at Tel Hai for three months. Miriam and I were there together until she was sent to a course in Tel Aviv. I would travel from Tel Hai, as needed, to Malkiya or to Kfar Giladi, to prepare our armored vehicles or to work on creating the Parosh ("flea"), a sort of small Davidka, easy to transport and operate in the field, which Ratner devised and we fabricated at the welding workshop at Kfar Giladi.

The Davidka, which weighed about 200 kilograms (440 pounds), was too heavy to use in the field. It launched a shell, with thunderous noise, to a distance of about two hundred meters (656 feet). The Parosh weighed less than 100 kilograms (220 pounds) and could be disassembled into three parts and easily moved.

We obtained the cannons' parts from discarded planes found in British Army warehouses—axles, pipes, and shock absorbers. Often the funds for our meager budget did not arrive from the center of the country. I would then travel between the north and the center to get the money. The guys joked that I never took no for an answer, and that if they kicked me out the door I would return through the window.

THE HABIT OF LABOR

We conducted tests at the quarry and in the fields of Kfar Giladi. I brought Miriam to the first test firing of the Parosh. The frightening sound it created was its principal attribute. There were some early deviations from the target; when the rocket finally found its mark, there was great joy.

The Parosh was urgently dispatched to help lift the siege on the Deganya kibbutzim in the Jordan Valley. It succeeded, and several copies were produced and transferred from one front to another to serve the fighters as needed. Several of these weapons remain today in the Haganah Museum and the Hashomer Museum at Kfar Giladi.

I returned to the center of the country with the Yiftach Brigade, which set up headquarters at Sarafand (Zerifin). I continued to work with the HEMED group where everyone was busy planning weapons. Donagi, I, and others would connect our theories with the reality of the time, build models of weapons and test them. I became a first lieutenant and had the title of technical officer. I formed a support platoon of about thirty good people.

Ratner's group was working to develop the M2 at the time, an enhanced anti-armor PIAT launcher with a range of four hundred meters (1,312 feet). This was a significant improvement over the original range of eighty meters (263 feet), which was dangerous to operate in. Prior to the PIAT, they used antitank weapons with a hollow charge. We knew that even the developed M2 would be a limited weapon, with some risks, designed as a stopgap measure until weapons arrived from overseas. And indeed, in the meantime this weapon gave our fighters a sense of security, so that they could stand with something in their hands when facing the enemy's armored vehicles.

The unit was independent, open to ideas, and quick to decide. We needed to solve difficult problems under time constraints and quickly reach the stage of product implementation. We would go into the field, study the needs of the fighters, and then come to HEMED and the military industry with an idea, sit with Ratner and the other designers, set forth the possible solutions, create prototypes, take the models into the field, and test and revise.

We conducted the real tests of the M2 on the battlefields of the road to Jerusalem after the opening of the alternative route we had created known as the Burma Road, and also in battles in the Negev at Bir Asluj. Members of the platoon were also sent with the M2, one squad after another, to Hirbet Jala, Beit Hanoun, and Kadesh Naftali—to all of the fronts where the Palmach fought as well as to other units that requested it. There was no time to instruct the soldiers on the use of the weapon; we operated the weapon ourselves, and the M2 proved itself successful wherever it was deployed.

I would come to these places to see what needed to be improved, but they would also summon me for other missions. For example, I was called to Jerusalem when they were not sure how to blow up part of the wall to gain access to the Jewish Quarter. I tried to find a solution for the problem, but the action was never carried out. I was also called to the Negev to develop a device to help clear minefields. Later we also organized at Sarafand the first, two-week course for operators of antitank weapons. I did not really know much about tanks, so Sadeh took me to Ramle, where his men explained to me in two days everything one needed to know for designing an effective antitank weapon. With this knowledge I was able to confidently deliver the opening lecture to forty participants in the first course.

In blood, fire, and smoke, the war came to a close in 1948. Many friends did not return from it. Others came back injured and maimed. We tried to recuperate and prepare ourselves for the new mission, the building of an independent state. David Ben-Gurion's decision to disband the Palmach was a fateful mistake; he squandered a terrific pool of human resources to ensure his political rule. The Palmach had many who had exhibited innovative thinking, courage, and great leadership, and this pool of talent should have been integrated into the new country's main army, the Israel Defense Forces.

I went to Yigal Allon's apartment in Tel Aviv, on 10 Adam Hacohen Street, and I said to him, "The guys don't know exactly what to do now. Let's decide that the Palmach will attack—in a civilian framework—a city like Beersheva and start to fill it with industries that will provide jobs for its residents." Just as Allon had assigned me to develop weapons during wartime, I hoped that he would now instruct me to develop a glorious Palmach project in Beersheva during peacetime. But this did not happen. Apparently I no longer spoke his language. Perhaps he was tired. He spoke about wanting to return to the kibbutz, to Ginossar. I told him, "This will be the biggest mistake of your life, to run home instead of preserving the Palmach framework for socioeconomic goals."

Allon sent me to Kibbutz Hameuhad to check out the potential for my idea. But after repeatedly getting the runaround, I realized that the whole idea would fizzle out between offices. Bureaucracy had already begun to conquer the public institutions in Israel. I returned as a civilian to work at the HEMED workshop called Institute 3.

My industrial worldview was already developed. We had won the war and brought reasonable security to the people, and now we needed to concentrate on building a state. A state can stand on its feet only with a strong economic foundation, with industry and agriculture, so that people have jobs. I opposed the prevailing idea of turning Israel into a country of tourism, a nation of waiters, chambermaids, and tour guides dependent on tips. Already I believed strongly in the possibilities that industry could offer.

My relationship with Yigal Allon continued for many years. During the days of the Palmach, I viewed him as a sort of demigod. He was a model Israeli: a sabra, commander, and friend, sincere and genuine. Perhaps he was also a father figure for me, because he was my commander and eight years older. His authority also derived from friendship, from someone who says something like "I'm relying on you." I still have some notes he wrote for me, with various instructions. For example: "Allow the bearer of this note to pass with his entire vehicle, and don't ask questions." I knew him during both his highs and lows.

As a national leader Allon was too gentle. He did not engage in intrigue. He understood the state and its essence better than any of his contemporaries, but he was late to the fray, citing personal and family reasons as an excuse—and perhaps he was already exhausted by what the political commissars did to him, undermining him and pushing Ben-Gurion to dismantle the Palmach. As minister of education Allon actually boosted the power of the academic institutions and the Council for Higher Education and its Planning and Budgeting Committee, which relegated vocational education to the sidelines. In my office there is a portrait of him. In a few delicate lines, the artist Aryeh Navon managed to capture the complex character of the commander, the leader, the man of vision, and the friend.

CHAPTER 3

INDEPENDENCE

My persistent courting of Miriam paid off. We became a couple during our military service in the Galilee; she was there with her friends from Balfour High School. Miriam was very special and beautiful; she was serious but also had a good sense of humor. Her parents were not particularly pleased with the boyfriend she chose, but they were about to get divorced, and were busy with those matters, and so did not interfere.

In the fall of 1948 we went to register for marriage at the rabbinate. The rabbis told us we needed two witnesses, so we went outside and looked for two guys wearing "sock hats" (knitted hats worn in the Palmach) whom we could trust. We found two Palmachniks we had never met before, and they agreed to help. They testified that they knew Miriam and me for years and that everything was perfectly okay. "What are the names of the witnesses?" the rabbi asked me, and I was dumbstruck.

On December 16, 1948, we were married in the Ihud Shivat Zion synagogue, not far from my parents' home, in the presence of our parents, other family members, and friends. Miriam was nineteen, and I was twenty-two. We rented an apartment in Holon. When Irit, our first child, was born, we moved in temporarily with my cousin Erich in Haifa. As a demobilized officer with the rank of first lieutenant, I was offered an abandoned Arab home—but I was against this. We did not have money. Rachel Kagan, who was a member of the Knesset then, sold me plot of land in Nahariya for a price that was about the cost of a car. But my cash reserves were so low that she agreed to let me pay it in five installments.

I met a man named Greenberg who wanted to produce small prefab sheds. On our lot we built the first model, a small shed, six meters by four meters (about 19-1/2 feet by 13 feet), at the end of Herzl Street in the southern part of Nahariya.

But before moving into the shed I had to travel to Belgium for a few months on behalf of HEMED, and Miriam did not want to remain alone with the baby in Nahariya. She was part of the group that founded Yiron in the Galilee, and she asked that we join this young kibbutz. Though I was skeptical about the idea of the ideological socioeconomic collective, I was willing to try.

The first year at Yiron was a difficult one. There was no running water, and we heated water for showers in a kettle over an open fire. With no paved pathways, the ground was muddy and rocky. Periodically one of the members would bring a large can of halvah from Lebanon, and we ate bread and halva at the kibbutz, sometimes for a full month. The bread came regularly from the city on the roof of the bus; it was drenched in the winter and parched in the summer.

I managed the workshop of Institute 3 (the forerunner of Rafael, Israel's major defense industry) that HEMED established at Kurdani, near Acre, where, with the help of an expert and equipment from the United States, we produced bazookas for the army. I rode to work every morning on my BSA 500 motorcycle, and every evening I returned to the family at the kibbutz.

There I proposed getting involved in kibbutz industrialization. I spoke about a joint regional factory for metal process-

Independence

ing. The general meeting of the kibbutz rejected the proposal; they preferred agriculture. It was clear to me that my future would not be at the kibbutz. Miriam, on the other hand, was not so sure, but we both knew that this uncertainty could not continue for very long.

I worked both at HEMED and Israel Military Industries, and my managers at the two places wanted me to continue developing weapons and ammunition. I was not enamored of this work and also felt that Israel's priorities had changed following the war; with diminishing desire I continued to work for about another two years in the field. Then my boss, the chief scientist Professor Bergman, suggested that I go to the Fabrique Nationale in Belgium to learn manufacturing.

It was not an organized study trip. I became familiar with the new production material, a mixture of metal powder that reached a peak level of rigidity. I learned what I needed to know—how to drill into the steel barrel—and returned to Israel. The information I acquired helped improve efficiency at Institute 3 and Israel Military Industries, which saved valuable time and enhanced the level of professional precision in production.

It was my first encounter with processing hard metal, the raw material that several years later ushered in my life as an industrialist. And incidentally, though I am no longer involved in that field, I still remember how to manufacture large barrels. It is very important to constantly learn; every visit to another factory, every review of an industrial initiative, every experience provides me with more knowledge.

After the Palmach was dismantled, I realized to my dismay that many people I had believed in were wasting their talents. Some of them returned to the kibbutz; some traveled for three years to America for so-called advanced training; some became bureaucrats, officials, or politicians; and some could not find their calling and wandered about, crestfallen.

While I was still in Belgium, Miriam also decided that the kibbutz was not the place where she wanted to raise a family even though she was happy there, working, dancing, and singing. She and her friends were a very close-knit group; after many of them were killed in the battle for Nebi Yusha the others remained especially close. She wrote to me,

> There's no way we can live on the kibbutz (by the way, it's already quite clear that we won't live there) because we'll never accept the authority of society. With us, the family—you, me, and the children—will always come first, before any other thing. And it's not that way on the kibbutz, where there is authority and everyone decides for you.

The connection with Yiron continued even after we left. And then Miriam presented me with a condition: We would not run around from place to place, from one rental apartment to the next. We needed a home, a permanent place in which to raise the family and to work. I had no intention of returning to Tel Aviv, and not only because I had no financial possibilities. I knew from the war period that the real heart of the Land of Israel is in the Negev or Galilee. Ben-Gurion believed the future of the country lay in the Negev. He and I could agree on this: our future was in the outlying areas, not in the crowded and congested center around Tel Aviv. In both the Negev and the Galilee there was ample land, fresh air, and possibilities for expanding one's horizons. We chose the Galilee.

Every morning, for a year and a half, I would set out on my motorcycle for work at Kurdani. During that period, inspectors for the "minister of austerity," Dov Yosef, would stop vehicles at every intersection and search the passengers' belongings to check whether they were smuggling rationed eggs or chicken. I wrote a letter to Dov Yosef:

> Honorable Minister,
> Oded, a friend of mine from Kfar Yehoshua, tells me that with 350 more people it would be possible to raise all of the poultry and provide all of the meat and egg consumption for the residents of the state. But every time I pass on my motor scooter from the valley to Haifa, your inspectors stop me, in different places, and check whether I am smuggling chickens or eggs. So maybe you can explain to me what the logic is? After all, the same 350 people could raise chickens and collect enough eggs to meet the needs of the State of Israel.

I did not receive a response. I imagine that, like the British king in his day, Dr. Yosef was also completely engrossed in national matters of greater import.

I was then working at drilling barrels for the recoilless cannons, but my enthusiasm faded quickly. I thought that things were not being done right, that the bureaucracy was growing, accompanied by a growing waste of resources. It seemed that original thinking and independent initiative were not appreciated. And if I had once believed that I would find a productive corner for myself, it now became clear that my managers—political commissars who had replaced the professionals—did not know what to do with me. There was one engineer who delayed my proposals at Israel Military Industries, blocked creative thinking, and stifled motivation. At Institute 3 there was another person who would suppress any attempt at original thinking.

I was apparently too big for Institute 3 and too small for Israel Military Industries. I was different, a Palmach veteran, independent, and eager to fulfill my ideas. After the dismantling of the Palmach, they gave its veterans a feeling that they should also fall apart. Then they tried to make me a sort of assistant to someone important, a general adviser of sorts for the rapid processing of metal. "Don't make me an assistant," I said; "let me *make* something." But since I always got along better with the professionals than with the *machers* (big shots), I received no response. Had I been allowed to continue at Israel Military Industries in my own way, I would have been content to continue working there to this very day as a practical engineer—but this did not happen.

Eitan, our second child, was born in 1951. I was taking care of Irit in the shack when Herbert, my Aunt Kaeta's husband, entered and proclaimed, "Mazel tov, you have a son!" I told him, "Stay and look after Irit," and hurried to the hospital. I found Miriam in good spirits there; the delivery had gone well, and I brought her and Eitan home the next day.

"I want to start my own industry," I told Miriam. I wanted to stay close to home to help her and to enjoy the children; and that is what led me to manufacture a small product at home that no one was yet producing in Israel.

It was a tough decision to give up a steady job that provided a secure salary and high status and return to manual labor at a machine, all as a first step toward realizing a dream that appeared far-fetched at the time. But I had to try.

As I had no initial capital to start a factory, and since raw materials were expensive, I had to choose a product I could manufacture and sell by myself at low cost, a product that still had no other manufacturers in Israel. After much deliberation I decided to produce cutting tools. A cutting tool is made of hard metal, and it has a lot of applications for metal cutting, lathing, and milling, primarily with iron and steel, in all industries, from

Independence

automobile manufacturing, shipbuilding, and the aircraft industry to the arms industry.

Miriam understood my decision, but I was also mulling over an offer from private investors. A precision mechanics factory, Bulova, was being established in Tel Aviv and the founder, an American named Kraus, invited me to serve as the head foreman. "I need to be home now," I said to Miriam. "And that's also a good reason to be self-employed. So, I'll turn down the offer and start to work here."

And thus ISCAR was born. This small initiative to make precision cutting tools succeeded beyond my expectations. Decades later it was to become second in its field in the world and then to become the only offshore investment of American investor Warren Buffett. Today his investment firm, Berkshire Hathaway, owns it and some ancillary firms that I established.

But no one can see the future, and the prospects from those early days looked uncertain. One day, I was sitting on a bus next to a Palmach veteran.

"What are you doing these days, Stef?" she asked.

"I'm going to start an industry!" I responded.

"What?" she exclaimed, bursting into such laughter that all of the passengers turned their heads toward us. My response sounded to her like a wonderful joke.

When I looked for a product to manufacture, I wanted to go into an area that I knew and loved—metalworking. Throughout my life I have collected professional literature on metals and metalworking. Therefore, I focused on tools for turning operations that are mounted on a lathe. This was a relatively small field of manufacturing, which did not require a large investment, and, indeed, I had no money to spare.

Kibbutz Hanita allowed me to work on its machines at night, for a fee, when the equipment was idle. As raw material I

THE HABIT OF LABOR

used hard metal, which I had learned to appreciate during my stay in Belgium. This type of raw material—*widia*—was almost unknown in Israel, even though weapons industries abroad were using it to manufacture parts that required great durability. It seemed to be the metal of the future.

ISCAR began operating on the kitchen porch of my home at 129 Herzl Street in January 1952 with a small, inexpensive machine that consisted entirely of a motor turning a grinding wheel. I purchased imported hard metal and a steel rod in Tel Aviv. I brazed a tooth from the hard metal onto the rod and sharpened it, and then went over to my neighbor to paint the product. It was the first cutting tool I produced with my own hands. I looked for a name for our factory and wanted at first to call it Eitan, after our son. But Miriam asked, "And if, heaven forbid, you go bankrupt, will Eitan always symbolize for us a reminder of this failure?" So, the name chosen from the first day of my independent work was ISCAR, a combination of the words *Israel* and *carbide*, the hard material made of carbon and heavy metals that is used to make tools that cut metal. This was the hardest material that we then knew how to produce; only diamonds were harder.

And who would buy my products? In 1952, one had to gauge the potential market through actual experience. Therefore, I would produce tools and set off to look for customers in the area. In the entire country at that time there were only a few hundred lathe shops—that is, potential buyers.

I soon realized that I had invested time, money, and goodwill to manufacture the wrong kind of tool. I had produced a large-size tool, but the customers all wanted the smaller model. Thus I was left with no money and a huge inventory (for those days)—fifty cutting tools—for which there was no demand. The threat posed by the unsold inventory has stayed with me as a warning sign. You can exhaust your entire potential profit in

Independence

stock that has no buyers. Here was a first lesson in entrepreneurship that I learned in the early days of my self-employment.

The failure in choosing the right type of product and the lack of prospective customers for cutting tools at that time, compounded with the refusal of the country's largest potential buyer, Israel Military Industries, to try my tools resulted in the most difficult financial period of our lives. We did not even have money to pay for groceries. The banks—Leumi and Hapoalim—would not agree to lend me money; a small factory appeared risky to them. Miriam asked cautiously whether perhaps I should look for a job as a salaried worker. But I insisted and persevered. At twenty-six years old I felt that I was already very mature and experienced. I had lowered my standard of living so that I could be independent, but I was not worried. I knew that I could always go back to supporting my family by working as a salaried expert lathe operator. And we still were not in the worst situation. I had not fallen into debt that I was unable to repay, and I was not entangled in any commitments.

I started to make smaller models of tools. I would sharpen and paint them, with the help of our good neighbors, and set out with my samples, a sort of traveling salesman. I would receive orders and return home to Nahariya to work on them. I also repaired tools to supplement my income a bit. Later, I rented an unused German lathe at Kibbutz Yiron and moved it to the workshop of a welder in Nahariya, and there too I worked on preparing my tools. Later, when the porch at home became too crowded, I bought a tin shack from the Jewish Agency, and I placed it near the porch. We made do with two small rooms as a living space.

I found four or five regular customers who until then had used an imported cutting tool and were pleased by the local production. The situation improved a bit. I manufactured and sold,

THE HABIT OF LABOR

and Miriam helped me with the bookkeeping and correspondence. Six months later I found some discarded machine parts in the warehouse of the Solel Boneh Company at Kurdani. I bought them for next to nothing, added other parts, and assembled from everything a milling machine that enabled me to do metalwork in my workshop instead of renting a lathe by the hour.

After nearly two years I received a large order from the Mekorot Water Company to produce coronas, hollow bits for drilling into basalt and for test drillings, which were required to fit the drills used to dig tunnels for the National Water Carrier of Israel. I earned my first big money—and I decided that now I would buy my first good grinding machine.

Miriam, for whom the needs of the home and family were no less important, understood the importance of this step and consented. She always stood by my side, despite hesitations and fears. I rode to Tel Aviv and purchased a sophisticated, fifteen-year-old Jones and Shipman grinding machine that was standing idle in the Katav fountain pen factory; I brought it home, with great pride, to my factory. By then I already recognized the vital need to renew, to keep up to date, and not to get stuck in a routine—that is, to continually search for the next tool and the next objective. The Jones and Shipman machine joined another grinding machine I had built myself using an old engine. I recently rediscovered this old grinding machine, stored in the scraps warehouse at ISCAR. I asked for it to be cleaned and placed in the factory as a museum exhibit. It demonstrates how you can start production even when your pockets are empty.

My main work then was to repair drilling tools for the Ilabun Tunnel of the National Water Carrier and for oil exploration drillings. Additional orders came in. I closed in the porch of the house where I worked with screens to keep out the flies in

Independence

the summer, and I added a wooden barrier to block the mice that scurried in from the adjacent field. During that period, a fifteen-year-old came to me looking for work who had immigrated from Turkey with his family a few years earlier. This teenager was Yossi Pano, who worked at ISCAR until his retirement; it was he who developed the revolutionary Self-Grip parting off system, which led to our big international breakthrough in the 1970s.

Yossi's father maintained the train tracks for Israel Railways. Yossi told me later that due to the family's difficult financial situation he did not want to come to the high school in Nahariya in patched trousers and without money for class trips. He quit school and sought work in a factory for precision mechanics. He told me that he could only work for a year at ISCAR because he wanted, in parallel, to complete ninth grade at evening high school and later—he already had everything planned—he would continue to the pilot's course at the air force's technical high school. But Yossi's time at ISCAR stretched on and on. The atmosphere in our work environment was very positive, despite the hot summers' dust and flies (which managed to penetrate the screening) and the cold winters' mud and rain. I taught Yossi and Ephraim Smooha, another teenager who came to the workshop, applying an educational principle I learned in the Palmach: take action when necessary and act in an unconventional way when there is no alternative. Just as I learned in the Palmach to be a soldier, I could also learn and teach how to be a worker in industry. "If I had gone in those days to a vocational high school," Yossi told me, "this would have helped but also hindered me, because my thinking would have become rigid. The fact that I did not know solutions in advance led me to search for alternatives."

When I would travel to sell products, Yossi would have to find answers on his own to questions that arose. In this way, he says, he taught himself to perform the most complex operations on our only lathe to manufacture products that would normally require the use of tools that we lacked. He was forced to improvise a lot when I was absent, and he says that he would imagine himself asking me questions and thinking how I would answer them, and would then act upon the imagined responses.

Ephraim and Yossi would prepare the mounts for the tools in the steel elements and weld the blades to them, and they would sharpen old tools. In those days, they still sharpened cutting tools until almost nothing remained to sharpen.

When I was not traveling I would work at the grinding machine or the sharpening wheel and show Yossi and Ephraim the work. But the true instruction and real education were in the mutual understanding that there is, in fact, no teacher and that you need to solve problems using your own resourcefulness.

That is how we worked. My own family was barely making ends meet; every morning Miriam would bring us each a cup of milk. The old record player was set up, and we enjoyed music while working. At the time, it was hard to detect in Yossi the attributes that would later make him such an important inventor in ISCAR, but he was worked hard and was eager to learn. And this continued until the time came for Yossi's military service in the Golani infantry brigade. He would come to us during his furloughs, and without wasting much time would find a corner for his work. It was a foregone conclusion that he would return to us after he finished his stint in the army.

In the small yard, our daughter Irit loved to climb the big margosa tree. Miriam, who was afraid that the toddler would fall from the tree, warned her several times, and one day, while I was in Tel Aviv, she told her, "Irit, if you climb up the tree again, I won't take you down!" Irit did not heed her warning,

Independence

and one day had to stay on a branch until my return from Tel Aviv that evening.

During our free time, we would travel to Kfar Yehoshua to visit Oded and his wife Tirza, and I would often tell Oded that his *moshav* (a type of cooperative agricultural community) could contribute much more if it engaged in industry within a rural framework. We would host our friends Aryeh and Ruth on their vacations from the kibbutz. Here too, there would often be stormy disagreements; I argued that agriculture no longer played a central role in the national economy and had fully exploited its potential. At one time, everyone was proud to be a farmer because Jews in the Diaspora were never farmers. The kibbutzniks and the moshavniks accorded great respect to the joint concept of agriculture and army; they had turned it into a value. Why not do the same thing now for industry? After all, the future belonged to industry. Aryeh, who had devoted his life to agriculture, not only as a livelihood but also as an ideal, held an opposite view, of course. Our loud arguments would continue until the women rushed in to intervene: "Stop, you'll wake up the children!"

We operated the first five years—including three difficult years—without any monetary reserves and with a firm decision to avoid entering debt. These years were a test of persistence. I already knew everything I needed to know, and I was mature, with responsibility for my family, employees, and customers. But I did not have enough capital to apply the knowledge and experience I had accumulated.

Our parents did not object to the path we chose, but they could only offer us modest support. Father was wary of investing the little he had in a tentative venture. He sent me, without great enthusiasm, small sums from time to time, while continually warning me to stay out of debt. Miriam's divorced parents, who

THE HABIT OF LABOR

were busy with their own problems, helped even less. Once, in a time of severe financial distress, during ISCAR's second or third year, I sent a proposal to both fathers. They would together invest the three thousand Israeli pounds I needed to purchase a lathe, and each of them would own a 30 percent share of "the factory." They did not accept my proposal, and we were forced to continue on our own. I think the employees were unaware of our troubles, even though there were days when I had difficulty providing them with steady work. But I am confident that I gave them a sense of basic security.

This was a period of austerity: the economic situation was difficult throughout Israel, and there was a lack of security about the future and a lack of available money. Bureaucracy flourished. Everything required a license, including the purchase of hard metal from overseas. There was always some official standing in the way, blocking the road to production. One such official, who was in charge of the import of raw materials at the Haifa branch of the Ministry of Trade and Industry, and whom I faced every two weeks after standing in line, would ask me the same question: "Why do you need this hard metal?" The fourth time I lost patience and pulled out a small blade of hard metal, cut a slit across the sheet of glass covering his desk, tapped along the slit until the glass cracked into two—and I told him: "You see? *That* is hard metal!" The stunned man promptly issued the permit I had requested.

There was no private market in Israel in those days. You could not even dream of an export industry. To do business abroad you needed to have a permit and pay about a hundred dollars for the plane ticket. Everyone was busy with the absorption of more than one million new immigrants, and who had time to think about an export industry? Perhaps because I had already seen the world—I was born in Germany, had worked in

Independence

Bahrain, and had acquired know-how in Belgium—I was convinced that as a nation we needed to produce for ourselves the things that were vital for our existence: in wartime, our own weapons and aircraft; in peacetime, products whose sales abroad would provide a stable basis for our lives here. But in the Israel of the early 1950s, no support was offered for new factories. The importance of industry was not recognized, and the free market perspective, with each person trying to succeed on his own, was nonexistent because the local economic reality did not allow conditions of freedom of action and competition.

The banks, for example, were unwilling to give loans for capital investment. They specialized in loans for importers or for the corner kiosk, and the new concept of industry—not to speak of export industry—was entirely foreign to them. It was also difficult to convince friends and relatives on this subject. I remember showing an acquaintance several of my cutting tools and told him, "You see these? One day I'll be selling them in Switzerland." He admitted years later that he harbored some doubts about my sanity.

Most of the established industry in Israel had developed during the War of Independence. The moment the war ended, the period of the state in the making began, and the defense industry brought a livelihood to those employed in it. The others produced for the local market—textiles, food, and furniture. Agriculture flourished then because it received proper attention, and research institutes conducted studies in it. Local industries for auxiliary products such as sprinklers and pipes were established at the kibbutzim.

But now we were already four or five years after the war, a young and vigorous state. An entrepreneur like me should have been able to enter a bank and request a loan, but this was not happening. Applications for bank loans were rejected again and again.

THE HABIT OF LABOR

I desperately needed financing to purchase raw materials from abroad. I went to the Bank Leumi branch in Haifa and requested a loan of three thousand Israeli pounds. "We'll come by to check," they told me. And indeed, one day a fancy car arrived on our street and several bank officials emerged, dressed in suits and ties. They looked at the workshop, the workers, the machines, and the cutting tools with a very serious expression—and then drove away. Later, they sent a negative reply to my application, together with a bill for the visit they made to the factory. I sent the bill back to them, unpaid, with a note saying, more or less, "You've gotta be kidding!"

I scraped together small loans from here and there. These financing obstacles were the main reason I had wasted so much time during difficult years. The decision to be self-employed put me to the test: Would I able to start from scratch as a private entrepreneur after having already served successfully as an officer? The first five years proved to me that it was difficult, but not impossible.

The problems and the difficult decisions came home with me at night. Miriam was a partner in everything: every decision, every idea, every step—we weighed and assessed everything together. During the initial years, as part of our year-end summary, I would write down on a pad of paper our objectives for the next three years. And she would save this document so that we could later check how close we came to these goals.

As the years went by, the volume of orders increased, driving higher production; additional employees were hired to boost output. The shack I built in the yard proved to be only a temporary solution; after five years, there were already fifteen production workers, including Elias Araf from Me'ilia (ISCAR's first Arab employee, who worked with us for more than forty years, from 1959 to 2001). We moved part of the factory to a larger workshop, farther up Herzl Street, renting a small space in the welding shop of

Independence

a neighbor, Andreas Mayer. We placed the two milling machines there, as well as the two grinding machines and the small lathe from the shack, and added another large lathe, as well as another milling machine and another grinding machine. Outside, we set up a small station for painting the products. Due to the need for additional electric lines, I rented a place in the welding shop of our neighbor, Fuchs, and also put the old German lathe there.

We produced cutting and milling tools and quarry drills. Eli Zarur was the man of all seasons in the area of administration at ISCAR: stock keeper, salesman, cashier, and even telephone operator on occasion. Every day Eli would search my pockets to pull out the checks given to me by customers so that they would not inadvertently wind up in the laundry. The factory operated simultaneously in our home, in Andreas's workshop and in Fuch's welding shop, and I ran around a lot, by foot or on a bicycle, among the three workplaces.

At last we began to see some success, and I attribute part of that success to my love of my product. I would also gladly instruct our customers in its proper use to show its efficiency; in future years, all of our marketing personnel would know how to demonstrate the product's capabilities to customers. But we needed to decide on our next steps because the goal was to continuously grow. Even today, this goal guides ISCAR's hundreds of sales and marketing personnel. "Now we are *importers*," I would say back then to the workers. "We're purchasing our raw materials from overseas suppliers, but the day will come when we will be *exporters* and sell them our products."

The decision to produce the hard metal ourselves was almost a revolutionary decision for those days, and it transformed ISCAR from a workshop into a bona fide factory. The process involved compacting metal powders into tablets the size of aspirin pills. Afterward, as in ceramic glazing, the tablets are

THE HABIT OF LABOR

heated in a sintering furnace, which transforms powders into objects by employing very high temperatures: 800–1,500 degrees Celsius (1,472–2,732 degrees Fahrenheit). By this process, it is possible to produce metal alloys of varying degrees of hardness.

Hard metal is a basic product in my field, and our complete dependence on imports was our most fundamental limitation. Having to import the raw material from abroad entailed exhausting and infuriating government bureaucracy, with each delivery subject to an import license.

Bureaucracy is not a divine decree. It is a mechanism driven by many professionals—lawyers, executives, officials, and accountants—who control budgets and make a living from them, and amass great power based on their ability to decide who will receive budget allocations and who will not. There are always some who systematically hinder the process. And if a private entrepreneur manages to succeed without their help he becomes, in effect, their enemy. This is because the source of their power is their prerogative *not* to help. The moment they say yes and issue an approval, they lose their power.

When we decided to produce hard metal, we started to learn about the production process, to procure machines, to find a suitable place, and to build a new factory that would work in parallel with the factory for tools. Everything would be at one site, so I would not have to run around Nahariya to the various places where ISCAR was operating. I needed two furnaces and a compactor, and these were not available in Israel. All this required capital that I did not have.

For the first time I was forced to look for a partner, but one was close at hand: Belu Dohan, the owner of the local butcher shop. Following the period of austerity, meat businesses flourished in Israel; and when Dohan heard that I needed money, he proposed investing a certain amount in exchange for 50 per-

Independence

cent of the shares without a controlling interest. He had his own economic theories, but this did not bother me as long as he promised not to interfere in the actual operation of the business. I issued ISCAR shares for the first time and sold them to him—and thus I acquired a partner.

This partnership continued for four or five years and ended with us parting on good terms. He was alarmed by my racing forward, fearing that I was growing too rapidly, and I did not really understand his economic thinking. He sold his shares at a 300 percent profit to the Tibor Rosenbaum investment firm and to another investor, Yehezkel Dagan, who was connected with Bank Leumi. Dohan may have later regretted this decision when the value of ISCAR grew almost immeasurably.

Now that I had a partner and some capital, I could acquire the know-how and special equipment for producing hard metal. There were about thirty manufacturers of hard metal in the world at the time. In 1956 I traveled, first of all, to Europe. In Austria, I met with officials at a company named Plansee. Then I visited Wickman in Britain. Both of these manufacturers refused to cooperate because they were afraid of competition.

I found what I was seeking only when I came to the United States, at Adamas Carbide Corporation in New Jersey, from which I had previously purchased sheets of hard metal. One of Adamas's early investors was the silent movie star Gloria Swanson. The company agreed to teach me how to produce hard metal because they knew that they would profit from the supply of metal powder for its production. Ed Dreyer of Adamas helped me to get my first customers overseas; this was the beginning of my exporting. We signed a ten-year agreement, and they assisted me in acquiring the furnaces, compactors, and the rest of the machinery required to establish the factory.

My parents were worried about this transaction, no

doubt fearing that I would lose the thousands of dollars that I had to pay to secure the partnership. Recently I found a letter from my Uncle Richard (a successful businessman who had brought his family from Kippenheim to New York). Dated October 19, 1956—the Friday before the week I was to begin my official affiliation with Adamas—this letter seeks to reassure my parents on three counts. First, Uncle Richard underscores his trust in me. Second, he states that "der Jung weiss, was er will" (the boy knows what he wants). For emphasis, he writes this twice. And third, he mentions that the people at Adamas respect and like me, so much so that they have even allowed me to use their name. This he also writes two times. Apparently, he knew my parents well enough to know that they required some convincing.

Later I bought a tape recorder, a device that was still almost unknown in Israel at this time. I sat and recorded the detailed explanations of the Jewish owner of the business, Ed Drayer, and of Jerry Shire, a Jew who fled Germany during the war and who had developed the special method of production. Jerry was the technical manager of Adamas, and he helped me a great deal. Years later he became the technical adviser of ISCAR America and helped to teach my son Eitan about technical issues.

In 1956, in the middle of my training, the Sinai War erupted, and I returned home on the first plane I was able to catch, with others who were leaving America and rushing back to save the homeland. When we arrived, however, everything was already over.

On the seashore in northern Nahariya, near the Isasbest asbestos factory, stood two abandoned tobacco warehouses, large buildings with an area of seven hundred square meters (7,534 square feet), connected to electricity and water, with a big yard. In 1957, we rented one of the buildings and renovated it while setting up our factory.

Independence

We set up two departments of ISCAR in a single building; one produced the hard metal and the second produced the cutting tools. To manage the metal department I appointed Moshe Gleichman, then a new immigrant from Poland. Today his children and grandchildren work at ISCAR.

In our first attempt to produce the hard metal alloy, the sheets emerged with bubbles, but after that we achieved better results. At first it was difficult to sell our hard metal; during the first two years of its production, the Ministry of Defense refused to do business with us. Believing that it was impossible to produce top-quality hard metal in Israel, the ministry preferred to procure the hard metal it needed abroad—and at a steep price. Again, the government drove us crazy with quality testing and made my life difficult with trivial problems. Decisions of the ministry could boost or hinder the advancement of many factories. We did not understand why it would want to buy something overseas when it could buy locally from us at a lower price. The defense establishment's refusal to purchase my product was one of the worst insults of my life. But our product was excellent, and eventually the Ministry of Defense became the leading buyer in Israel.

Perhaps that initial refusal was ultimately for the best, because it forced us to search for external markets. The choice we faced was either to transition to manufacturing other products, such as engine parts for cars, or to stick with what we knew: to produce hard metal and cutting tools, and then try to export them abroad. I knew that ISCAR would be judged by the quality of its products in competition with the world's other producers, but the local market was becoming too narrow for our expanding production.

At the end of 1958 we reached the conclusion that production for export was not only an objective, but a raison d'être.

THE HABIT OF LABOR

A state like Israel has to be able to do business with the world. This simple truth became our first commandment: achieve a position of advantage in the markets—that is, develop outstanding products for which there is demand. From the outset, ISCAR developed innovative products that met the needs of the buyers throughout the world, and it continues to do so today. Exports are at the center of ISCAR's activity.

I wanted to go abroad and search for export markets. We knew nothing then about export methods, the demands of the global market, market surveys, advertising, and so on. Nonetheless, and despite the fact that our products offered no unique or qualitative advantage at the time, I decided to take a big step forward. I did homework; through reading the general and professional press, I learned about the competitors and the customers in the global market and about their requirements, and I memorized the rules of brokering, pricing, and licensing.

During this period we published our first catalog: "ISCAR, Factory for Hard Metal, Tel: 183, Nahariya, Israel." I also still have the first article written about us, in the German-language Israeli newspaper *Yedioth Hadashot*: "25 Employees at ISCAR," the article reported. "Modern equipment, a production agreement with an important American company—Adamas—1.25 million Israeli pounds invested in the factory's infrastructure." I am not sure how they arrived at this sum.

Equipped with the catalog and a newspaper clipping, I set out on a business trip to Europe in late 1958. I landed in Athens to arrange an entry visa to Yugoslavia, where several meetings were scheduled with potential sales agents. The meetings were set up for me by Israeli neighbors who had come from Yugoslavia. I spent two days in Athens waiting for the visa and I thought, Why not visit the commercial district, where they also buy and sell lathes, cutting and quarrying tools? On one narrow

Independence

street I found four shops that sold lathe tools. I entered one of them and told the owner, Panos Dendrinos, that I was from Israel and had samples of the tools that we produced. He became ISCAR's first overseas customer and also our first overseas agent, and he served in this position for about thirty years.

I continued on to Yugoslavia and there, too, I found an agent within two days: Mr. Rice from the Yugo Commerce Company in Zagreb, who was a relative of acquaintances from Nahariya. Later I returned to Yugoslavia and remained with him and his employees for several weeks to help them open our sales branch. We found customers there, including the country's biggest automobile factory. Rice continued as ISCAR's agent in Yugoslavia until the state broke diplomatic relations with Israel in 1967. After I finished my meetings there, I traveled to Basel, Switzerland—by train, to save money. The money I had was enough to travel as far as the Swiss border, and there, too, I found someone who agreed to sell our products: Raul Molina, who managed the Mecanis Company. I only requested that he place in the show window a sign saying: "ISCAR, Israel-Basel." He remained our Swiss agent until his death.

I returned to Israel with production orders totaling about five thousand dollars, and we started to work day and night to deliver the orders on time. We also began to devote attention to aspects of the business that were new to us and whose great importance we came to appreciate: export licenses, packaging, shipping, and printing quality catalogs and labels. After the initial three European markets, our overseas sales expanded to include the United States. Via the Adamas Company I sent samples of tiny lathe tools that I could produce less expensively at ISCAR. I received a large order for five thousand cutting tools for the Babcock and Wilcox Company at a relatively low price, two dollars per unit, but this relationship did not continue.

THE HABIT OF LABOR

I also wanted to expand our markets in the United States, and in 1960 I asked Ed Dreyer to organize an event for me with people involved in selling such products who were not competitors with Adamas. He introduced me to a few people who referred me to others. In this way, I reached a number of buyers, most of them Jews, whose primary interest was to find a less expensive supplier; and if while doing this they would also be helping Israel's economy a bit—well, all the better, they said. Of course, if you are not good enough, such sentiments do not come into play a second time. I returned with orders totaling between $20,000 and $30,000. It was a start.

But it was only a start. ISCAR was not yet capable, of course, of becoming a major player for lathe tools in the United States. The American and global market belonged primarily to giants like the Swedish company Sandvik and the American companies Kennametal and Carboloy. But we started to make a profit and, needless to say, the income was reinvested in the business.

There were already thirty employees working in our metal factory. There was no training program, as is customary today. The initial workers, who had already acquired experience, were promoted from privates to squad commanders and took the new employees under their wings.

Yossi Pano, our first quality-control person, set up this department in a rather unexpected fashion. One day he suggested to me that it would be wise if someone would check the expensive steel rods that he was turning to make sure they were in good shape before they were sent on to other processes; finding any defects early on would save time and money. I assigned him to set up a table immediately with measuring tools and to do just that. Yossi later told me that his position as a control supervisor was very important for his later contributions to ISCAR. This position required solving prob-

Independence

lems in all the production processes, and it honed his analytic skills.

In this way a new division was born at ISCAR that started from scratch because we had no one to guide us in this field. Yossi prepared various measuring instruments, randomly pulled products from the production line, examined welded tools, found many defective ones, and sent them back for repair. It turned out that about 70 percent of our output was of good quality—but we wanted to reach 99 percent.

Since I am a cautious person by nature, I tried to avoid accepting funding from the chief scientist of the Ministry of Trade and Industry. The ministry pursued what I considered to be a flawed industrial policy: it would offer funding to manufacturers for product research and development, but not for the manufacturing and marketing of these same products. This is still true today, and as a result, many companies engage in development—for example, the various branches of high technology. But the government funding has not been available for other essential functions, such as the production, marketing, or sales of such development. Israeli industry thus focuses more on research and development and less on production, but this research does not generate the jobs we need so badly.

ISCAR also never ventured into the stock market. Never a gambler by nature, I have always preferred to invest in making a good product. In Israel, and in most of the world, the stock market has become a gambling arena, with the help of the media, which focuses great attention on rising and falling share prices and the value of money. The stock market has created a class of speculators who prefer not to engage in productive work but instead to buy and sell securities. This has enabled such people to become wealthy and has turned the gamble of the stock market into part of our system of values. In this way it moves us away from the values of production, work, and independence.

The stock market is an essential institution for mobilizing capital and making productive investments that contribute to national independence, or in promoting professionalism and the joy of creating. But by itself it cannot develop factories or educate workers; it has no long-term thinking at all. As we know, money that comes easily also goes easily, and the stock market has poured huge sums of money into the pockets of gamblers.

The global collapse of stock markets and high-tech companies in 2008 clearly demonstrated the huge danger in the manipulation of money that generates money. It is true that industry is also affected by such major economic storms, but if it is managed wisely it will weather these storms. Perhaps it will be forced to develop at a slower pace and more modestly in light of the difficult circumstances, but it will survive.

As ISCAR did not play the accepted finance game in the semi-nationalized Israeli economy, we had to be more cautious and always profitable. My basic approach was to avoid spending more than we could afford and to refrain from growing beyond realistic projections—that is, to eat less in the present so as to eat better in the future.

I have always believed that one should rely on independent financing and be extremely cautious about taking on debt. Thus, the decision to expand, to raise capital and mobilize large partners, was revolutionary for me. But the desire to push forward was very great, and a strong partner who would bear some of the responsibility and enable ISCAR to develop was essential. Sasha Goldberg, the president of Technion, the Israel Institute of Technology, introduced me in 1961 to his nephew, Dan Tolkovsky, a mechanical engineer and a former commander of the Israeli Air Force. Dan was then the deputy of Augusto Levy, the CEO of Israel Discount Bank's investment company.

Independence

After visiting the factory Tolkovsky assessed the company's technological and professional foundation and our chances for the future.

At that time I was embarking on my first foreign venture—establishing a factory in the Netherlands. Tolkovsky introduced me to Levy, a charming and unique man who was about seventy years old when he founded Discount Investments. The three of us sat and talked, and Tolkovsky later told me that after I left Levy said, "I'm troubled. I like that man too much."

In the middle of the night, the new partnership between ISCAR and Discount Investments was forged, with my friend who was ISCAR's attorney at the time, a wise man named Otto Levy, summarizing the official terms of the deal. Discount purchased the share of the previous partners for $150,000 and became a fifty-fifty partner in ISCAR.

This was the beginning of a long, fruitful and friendly partnership. Discount did not hinder me in moving forward at my own pace and in my own style. The important decisions were discussed in a forum of the four directors: Miriam, Augusto Levy, Dan Tolkovsky, and me. Dan Tolkovsky and Shlomo Lahat, and later Yaakov Eshel as the bank's representative, were fair partners all along the way. Miriam, as always, was a loyal partner in every move. She was more critical than I was, and she was blessed with intuition, perceptiveness, and wisdom. Her opinions of the workers and her recommendations were very important to me, and she was very proud of ISCAR and its successes.

At the same time, I felt that we were not making progress in Israel. Even before Discount became our partner, I had decided to look abroad, and I had proposed to Ed Dreyer—the American from Adamas who sold me the know-how on producing hard metal and purchased the products we made from it—

that we build a factory together in Europe. I wanted to prove, first of all to myself, that we were as good as any other people in industry, and to see whether an Israeli factory located in Europe, close to the markets, could achieve better success in selling its products. Why Europe? Because I came from there, am familiar with the European mentality, speak German and English, and I felt that I had to break the European resistance to importing foreign products. I thought of reproducing the ISCAR model there: a factory for cutting tools and an adjacent factory for hard metal. With the cash flow from Discount and the explicit encouragement of Augusto and Dan—who, like me, recognized the vital necessity of developing export industries—this plan became a reality. This was the second major step that exposed us to industrial work in the international marketplace.

Pinhas Sapir was then the minister of finance, and I needed his approval to invest currency overseas, an activity that was almost unknown in Israel at the time. "I don't know exactly what you want to do there, but if you believe in it, I'll approve it," Sapir mumbled as he signed. He had healthy instincts, and he understood the importance of establishing Israeli factories abroad. I said to him, "It's not enough to fly to Brussels and register for the Common Market. We also have to sell them Israeli products—and we'll only be able to do this if we're there."

I knew Sapir well. He was the only one, except for the forgotten Zeev Sharf, who worked to encourage exports and develop industry. Sapir was a positive man, creative and likable, a powerful personality who moved things quickly. As the minister of trade and industry he had tried to help industry, but as minister of finance he was too bound to the tired norms of the time.

In 1967, when I was appointed as one of the two curators of *Isratech*, the first exhibition of Israeli technological exports, held at the Tel Aviv Hilton, I spoke a lot with Sapir. He still held to conservative principles regarding economic planning and exports. His priorities, like those of his successors, were correct for that particular period: security, settling the country, employment, and raising money. Thus, ultimately also with Sapir, industry and vocational education also fell between the cracks of the development towns that were built to house the new immigrants and the education system and security.

Sapir was late in recognizing that industry could become autonomous and not rely on government allocations. He put me on the board of the Company for Financing Industry, which aimed to generate more jobs and promote more export products. The program operated for ten years and was quite successful in stimulating industrialization.

My assessment at the time was that the largest potential market was in West Germany, but I was still averse to involvement in that country. I searched for a suitable place in Alsace, in the Netherlands, or in Switzerland. We ultimately chose the Netherlands, close to the West German border. Yehezkel Dagan, the partner who had acquired Dohan's share, was wary of embarking on this adventure and sold it to Discount. I had part of the money, and Discount and the American partner provided the rest of the financing, each according to his share of the project (50 percent from the Americans and 25 percent each from Discount Investments and me). The government of the Netherlands sold us land at a discounted price in the town of Weert, about thirty kilometers south of Eindhoven, where the manufacturing centers of the global giants Philips and DAF are located. Later, when we chose the Tefen region in the Galilee to develop, I had in mind this precedent from the Netherlands that demonstrated that it is possible to succeed in a distant place, removed from the center of industry.

THE HABIT OF LABOR

In Weert we established Duracarb (*dura* means "hard" in Latin; *carbide* is a basic element in hard metal), our first overseas factory, which manufactured products like those made at ISCAR Nahariya. At first, in February 1962, Duracarb operated with six local workers in a small rented building (next to a noisy pig slaughterhouse). In June 1962 we moved to a modern facility.

My family and I were in the Netherlands for a year and a half, and I was engrossed in my work, as usual. I prepared a cautious estimate of projected sales: $500,000, approximately the same as our sales volume at ISCAR Nahariya. In parallel to the small-scale work at the rented facility, we built a structure in the town of Weert, purchased equipment, and hired about fifty employees. Yossi Pano and Shlomo Gertler, whom I had brought with me to the Netherlands, taught the new staff how to make cutting tools from hard metal. We looked for potential customers, studied new technologies, and produced standard cutting tools and special-order tools. In the Netherlands the bureaucracy was not the natural enemy of the entrepreneur; the officials there did their utmost to assist and not to hinder.

Efficient and profitable, Duracarb sold its products to Belgium, England, and West Germany. However, we were a small company and the Dutch label did not boost sales more than the Israeli label, so we still did not have a substantial impact on the market. But the Netherlands provided invaluable lessons about the global market; it also demonstrated that the know-how we had developed in Israel was an international asset.

Later, when Israeli prime minister Levi Eshkol traveled to Brussels for talks with ministers of the European Common Market, I suggested to Sapir that he mention that Israel already had a factory in the Netherlands, which was a step toward a new export policy. But this subject was not brought up in these talks;

they apparently feared that this achievement might damage the image of Israel as a needy state. The invitation I sent to Eshkol, foreign minister Abba Eban, and other officials responsible for Israel's economic and foreign relations policies to visit the Israeli factory in the Netherlands and witness an initial and tangible Israeli success in Europe went unanswered.

From 1962 to 1964, I worked in the Netherlands, making frequent trips to Israel and other countries. In the Netherlands we first encountered the method of attaching the carbide tip to its steel base with a screw rather than via brazing, and ISCAR also adopted this method. After six years we sold the factory in the Netherlands to our American partners because I was very busy establishing a new factory for jet engine blades, and because I do not believe in management by remote control. In addition, as an entrepreneur, I lost some interest after I had succeeded in proving that Israeli manufacturing could be advanced abroad.

I returned to Israel knowing that we could develop the company only if we trained a reserve of professional workers. In contrast to Israel, in Europe there is usually a permanent connection between the factory and the educational system. In fact, part of the curriculum in technical high schools and universities is even planned to conform to the current needs of industry. In addition, of course, on-site training takes place in the factory, with the skilled workers teaching those who are newly hired. During my first days as a manufacturer I was also constantly training my first workers. Perhaps deep inside of me, in the teenager who was once expelled from school and sent out to work because he did not get along with his teachers, lies the soul of a teacher and mentor.

We made another effort to expand our overseas markets, and we located our first agents in Britain and Italy. The results were mediocre. The real breakthrough occurred only when we decided to start a marketing effort and local branches ourselves.

We started out small given the limited means at our disposal. It was difficult to build our network of branches, and we erred many times in choosing the first managers. There were several places—Belgium, Britain, and France—where we purchased the agency from our agents; in other places, such as Italy and Spain, the agents became partners, and this proved successful.

And then I turned my sights across the ocean, to the enormous market of the United States. The Midwest and its car manufacturing was the biggest market for our tools—and the biggest challenge. Cleveland seemed to be the best choice. On one of his trips to Israel, I had met Cleveland entrepreneur and philanthropist Max Ratner, who was a partner in Electro-Chemical Industries in Israel and who did a lot to encourage the growth of Israel's economy. He had immigrated to the United States with his family as a teenager from Poland. He and his brothers founded the firm Forest City Materials, which supplied building materials to contractors. Today, under the name Forest City Enterprises, it has grown into a leading real estate concern. Max agreed to help me explore whether a marketing branch could be established in Cleveland and also assisted me in finding the first location there for it.

I've always had a positive feeling about America. I spent a lot of time on Euclid Avenue in Cleveland. In the 1960s, TRW was one of the main suppliers of jet engine blades for Pratt and Whitney. We contacted TRW and became partners in 1969, a collaboration that lasted until 1995. Then, when TRW decided to move into a more electronic line and left the turbine blades business, I bought my shares back from them.

CHAPTER 4

A VISION FOR EDUCATION

Education has been an abiding interest all my life, even though —or perhaps because—I am a school dropout. Although I was bored by the standard classroom style of education—the learning process itself has always been exciting to me. So has teaching. There is nothing more gratifying than to teach someone a new skill that enables him to create something. I have always gotten great pleasure from instructing not only my workers but also my customers.

Advanced technical education underlies the success of export industries. These industries are vital to any country's economic future, but especially so in the case of a young country like Israel. A manufacturing sector composed of skilled workers and entrepreneurs is what will ensure the economic vitality of Israel's future.

But the overriding importance of industry for Israel is not simply economic. Its significance lies also in its ability to heal the Jewish psyche, to undo the centuries of persecution in which Jews were forced into unseemly positions such as moneylending. By gaining skills to produce and export top-quality products, we can become proud of our work and become a nation like any other.

A. D. Gordon—the early Zionist pioneer who promoted

manual labor as a national value—knew this, as did many other early founders of the State of Israel. Influenced by the writings of Leo Tolstoy in his homeland of Russia, Gordon immigrated at the age of forty-eight to Israel; this not-so-young man toiled as a hired agricultural worker by day and wrote down his philosophical treatises at night. He valued manual labor, whether it meant tilling the soil or working on a lathe. He believed that through hard physical work the Jews could find redemption from the centuries of discrimination they had suffered in foreign lands as minorities. "If national revival could be achieved by direct physical labor, then Gordon was determined that he would personally put his shoulder to the task."[7] He saw the challenge thus: "Tearing us from our roots, from our natural soil, from the Land of Israel, and the subjugation and persecution in the exile, which first of all distanced us from all nature, from all natural life, from productive work, turned us into a parasitic people. . . . We must correct all this and to a great extent create all this anew."[8] Manual work would be the antidote to exile.

In the early decades of this country, we had a robust technical education system, but it has been allowed to rust like so many of the schools' machines. Fifty years ago, half of Israel's students learned in technical schools. Today only 10 percent follow this course of study. As a result, Israeli industry does not have enough skilled workers.

Perhaps a bit of history is in order here. In 1928, European émigrés at Technion established Bosmat as a vocational school. Most of these founding professors were of German origin, and they brought with them that country's prized tradition

---

[7] Rabbi Herbert H. Rose, *The Life and Thought of A. D. Gordon, Pioneer Philosopher and Prophet of Modern Israel* (New York: Block, 1964), p. 40.

[8] A. D. Gordon, *The Nation and Work*, S.H. Bergman and L. Shohat (editors), (Haifa, the Haifa Workers Council, the Zionist Library), p. 263.

of industry and manufacturing. They felt that it would not suffice to educate engineers; one must also train the technicians and the Meisters (master craftspeople). So these professors taught not only at the university but also in the vocational schools, such as Bosmat, Yad Singalovski in Tel Aviv and Brandeis in Jerusalem.

In the early 1970s our educational system started its decline, losing sight of its true purposes. The superb Bosmat School also deteriorated. Technion and other universities began to focus on excellence only in academic subjects and did not give any academic credit for vocational training.

By the end of the 1970s our educational system had fallen to a dismal position, and the heritage of A. D. Gordon was relegated to a dusty corner. The demand increased for university graduates, attorneys, and stockbrokers—those who make their living from problems and not from problem solving. The result is evident each year when the country bestows its highest honor, the Israel Prize: most of the recipients are professors. I am one of the few industrialists to have received this honor, although I can think of many others who deserve it.

By 2004 the dismantling of this once proud system was complete. That year Technion announced that it would end its registration for Bosmat. And in August 2007 the seventy-nine-year-old school closed, after training thousands of graduates for industry, including my son Eitan. When Bosmat shut its doors, the need for skilled workers became more acute and the dependence on highly trained workers from abroad intensified.

There are several reasons for this regrettable decline. First, vocational schools were replaced by an inferior version of secondary schools in which the training component was eliminated completely and the number of technology hours was reduced. Second, in the comprehensive schools, the practical track was considered suitable only for the less intelligent student. Third was the parents' attitude (encouraged also by the Ministry of Education) that manual labor, manufacturing, and production are inferior goals and that students should strive instead for white collar professions.

Until the 1970s the educational system employed a method of tracking that did not take into consideration the talents or desires of youth or the needs of the country. It was mainly immigrant children from other parts of the Middle East (who were unfairly presumed to be unsuited for academic education) who were placed into vocational schools. Industry began to hold the stigma of a dirty and noisy workplace, low pay, and inferior social status. With the indirect support of the universities and the Ministry of Education, our graduates aspired to go into fields that promised the highest salaries, and, if possible, to do this overseas: a perpetuation of the Jewish exile.

Reduced budgets resulted in aging and poorly maintained equipment in the schools, and the quality of teachers in the vocational schools also declined. None of this, of course, went unnoticed by the students. As one vocational track student in the 1960s described the situation, "We were the cellar students, invisible to the upper floors of the system."

My late commander and friend, Yigal Allon, in his role as minister of education and culture, encouraged independent budgeting for academic institutions. The universities abused this legislation in an anti-industry direction. Allon's decision gave them a monopoly on the future of education in Israel; his successors were unable to change anything.

When it became clear that the government was not going to rectify the situation, I took matters into my own hands. In the early 1960s, my Palmach friend Yisrael Goralnik worked with troubled teenagers on behalf of the Ministry of Labor. Before he became the ministry's director-general, he and I searched the villages of the Galilee for teenagers who could be trained for industry. Together we founded the Zur-Nahariyah Vocational School in the plot between ISCAR and our neighboring firm, the Isasbest Company. This joint initiative of the two companies was active from 1964 to 1985.

When we approached David Eisenstadt, another Palmach friend, to serve as the school's principal, he was embarrassed; he saw himself as merely a simple worker who was willing to teach metalworking. But we finally persuaded this excellent craftsman to take the position for one year, and he remained in the post for nineteen years, serving as an outstanding educator, with common sense, warmth, and charm.

Zur-Nahariya's three-year program, which focused on practical learning, taught more than twenty pupils in each grade; half the time was spent in the classroom, and the other half in factories. It did not award matriculation certificates but gave its graduates professional skills, as well as entrepreneurial, management, and manufacturing training. Its advantage was its ability to secure jobs for the students in factories in the Galilee.

The school produced impressive results. Today many of its graduates hold management positions at ISCAR and at other large companies. Others run successful businesses of their own, providing jobs that sustain many families. They have defied the low expectations others had for them and instead became the backbone of western Galilee's development. Many years ago, my son Eitan also failed to complete his academic high school studies and transferred to a vocational school. He and I, each in our own way, have demonstrated that academic degrees are not what make a true entrepreneur. Rather, the key is in the love of work, experience, and initiative.

Zur-Nahariya provided a special educational experience.

THE HABIT OF LABOR

It followed the high standards of the industrial schools in Europe, especially those in Germany, which train their students not for jobs but instead for careers in highly respected firms such as Mercedes Benz. Like its European counterparts, the school also promised its graduates employment in industry once they finished. We offered an intimate learning atmosphere that turned the educational enterprise into a kind of extended family. Treated with respect, these students gained both motivation and a sense of self-worth.

Just before I entered the Knesset, we established Maof, a different type of school. I offered my old house in Nahariya as its setting. It opened with fifteen students on June 29, 1979, under the auspices of Technion's School for Practical Engineers and with recognition from the Ministry of Trade and Industry. Here we sought to train Meisters for midlevel management positions, and each student received a scholarship. During the final three months of study, the students toured several European countries, working in factories, attending trade fairs, and establishing connections that might prove helpful in their future work.

My interest in education has proved to be ongoing, resulting in a variety of new initiatives. In 1988, I worked with Israeli Defense Forces (IDF) chief of staff Rafael ("Raful") Eitan to create a course to expose soldiers to industry. Over the course of five years, the Zionism and Industry Initiative taught more than twenty-five thousand students. The Tefen Industrial Park was full of young soldiers who became acquainted with the Galilee, its industries, and the concept of entrepreneurship. But I also wanted to create a more in-depth program to train new entrepreneurs who would create their own export industries and thereby bolster Israel's financial future. So in 1992 we established the College for Entrepreneurship at Tefen Industrial Park, which I hoped would become the University of Tefen. It operated for three years under the guidance of Dr. Dan Sharon and produced about seventy graduates.

Another initiative was one that was nicknamed the Generals Project. This was a technical workshop for the plastics industry that we held at the Tefen Industrial Park. We chose young people, most of whom had completed command tracks in the IDF field units. Our approach was unconventional: we first put the students to work so that they could acquire skills, and then they started studying; we found that the more they acquired skills initially, the greater their understanding was of the subsequent theoretical studies. After completing the course, they found work in plastics factories.

Creating an industrial university was another dream of mine, and it started to take shape in 1994. I remember the remark of one student, "I lack the knowledge of an engineer and his tools. We know how to produce the part, but not how to plan it." He was right. I felt that we should harness all of our energies to build a much more ambitious program—one that would provide training for a range of key positions in industry and would help to foster entrepreneurial talents.

With the help of professor Abraham Ginsburg, who taught mathematics and computer science at Technion and also served as president of the Open University, we patterned the program after similar initiatives in Germany and Switzerland. We also collaborated with professor Manfred Hess and his institution in Stuttgart, the Berufsakademie. We brought many good professors from there, as well as professors from Technion. We made sure to plan the program so that it would meet the criteria of the Ministry of Trade and Industry's Institute for Technological and Scientific Training. In this way our students would receive an Israeli practical engineer degree.

The four-year program was rigid and without electives.

THE HABIT OF LABOR

Of the three hundred applicants, we selected thirty. We employed a pedagogical approach known as reinforced instruction. Instead of classroom lectures, the students received the materials, studied on their own, and then met once a week with a professor to review the material. The curriculum combined mechanical engineering studies with practical experience in a factory and also gave the tools for entrepreneurship. Our concept was innovative: a "live" university.

This was a substantial investment—about $1.5 million for one year of study for thirty students. The first students were housed in the hilltop community of Lavon, which is just a fifteen-minute drive from Tefen. They received room and board, and they traveled to Germany to attend a trade show and to tour factories and research institutes. The overwhelming majority of the graduates found their future in industry, and not necessarily at ISCAR or our other factories. Each graduate was free to choose his or her place of work.

But the university establishment was opposed to the program. In the fall of 1995, the Council for Higher Education refused to recognize our institution as a college. As a result, we could not offer degrees to our graduates.

Professor Ginsburg agreed with me. Addressing the Council for Higher Education, he noted, "Stef argued that he needed industrial engineers trained in the German style, training that requires the engineer to have practical experience at the machines, compared to Technion, which trains its students in a way that is almost purely theoretical. We easily proved Stef's theory: An engineering graduate of Technion required a year, approximately, to become fully involved in the work of the factory. On the other hand, there was almost no incubation process for a Zur graduate. A week of general orientation at the new place of work—and he already was fully involved in the work."

A Vision for Education

Ultimately the academic red tape forced me to shut down Zur-Nahariya, and we transferred the last class of students to the ORT Braude College in Karmiel. In the end, eighty students in four classes graduated from Zur-Nahariya. They received a practical engineering degree from the Berufsakademie in Germany as well as an interdisciplinary bachelor's degree from the Open University.

My ongoing concern for technical education extends to all sectors of our society. There are two large groups that are underrepresented in the workforce: the Arab sector, which comprises 20 percent of our population, and the ultra-Orthodox Jewish community (known as the Haredim), which is now about 10 percent of Israel's total population of 8,081,000 as of September 2013. A few months before he left his post as governor of the Bank of Israel, my friend Stanley Fischer spoke emphatically about the need to incorporate our Haredi and Arab citizens into the workforce. Both of them support their families primarily on one income; 80 percent of Arab women do not have salaried work, while 60 percent of Haredi men opt to study Torah rather than work. And these groups are increasing in number. Since 1980, Israel's Haredi population has more than doubled, from 4 to 10 percent, and the Arab sector has increased from 16 to 20 percent of the population. One need not be an economist to realize that such unemployment figures bode poorly for our economic situation in the decades to come.

This is one of the reasons that drove me more than a decade ago to establish the Arab-Jewish Course for Industrial Entrepreneurship and Management. It operated from 2001 to 2007 under the driving spirit of my friend Seev Hirsch, professor emeritus at Tel Aviv University. The university's Lahav Managerial Training Program devised the academic part of the program, and the Arab-Jewish Center for Economic Development was also a partner.

The program, which trained two hundred participants during its six years of operation, had three main goals: to develop the professional skills of potential entrepreneurs in Israel's Arab and Jewish sectors, to foster new export industries, and to encourage Arab-Jewish cooperation. A follow-up program provided additional guidance to those who started a venture.

The participants worked and lived together at the same hotel. Much of the program took place during the Second Intifada—a time of intensified fear of the other on both sides. The students' proximity to one another enabled them to form important channels of understanding and trust. Some groups were so closely knit that they were reluctant to separate at the end of the course and planned group trips to keep the relationships alive.

The course has had several real success stories. One of our former students is Ran Wellington, CEO and cofounder of Intucell, a firm that develops, produces, and markets systems that optimize the provision of mobile communications. The company was sold to Cisco for $475 million, and Cisco has said that it intends to incorporate Intucell into its research and development center in Netanya. It pleases me to know that the jobs will remain here in Israel.

We are also proud of one of our alumnae, Mass Watad, founder and CEO of Maas Watad Clinics, which teaches healthy food and eating habits. It operates about thirty women's clubs in Arab villages in the center of the country and in the Galilee, and she has plans to expand to Jordan.

And then it became clear that I had to turn my sights to our ultra religious sector, the Haredim. With concern for this community, several years ago I started an initiative with Israel Prize laureate Rabbi Dovid Grossman. This training program in

A Vision for Education

metalworking is now being advanced by the vocational school system, ORT.

Education includes the broadening of viewpoints and capabilities as well as individual and social values that help the student to succeed. Here we challenge the conventional and mistaken view that mobility is provided via a matriculation certificate. Mobility after matriculation depends on the development of skills. A vocation is no less an instrument of mobility than academics, and in some cases it is even better.

In selecting our staff we look first at their human qualities and then at their degrees. While Dan Sharon and David Rosenfeld both hold doctorate degrees, some of our highly capable educators and administrators do not. David Eisenstadt, whose only specialty was his skill on the lathe, became a superb principal for us for many years. Dan Prat, who leads our Shalem Premilitary Preparatory Program, is a Reform rabbi. Anat Dagan, the managing director for our high school education network, studied education but spent years working in the field of personnel for Karmiel. Avi Ziegler, our high school's principal, was for many years a commander in the Israeli Navy and an electronic engineer before he turned his sights to education. Mookie Zamberg, the principal of the Zur Yam (navy school), was previously a policeman in Karmiel. These people have all become highly professional not necessarily because of a degree but because of their passion for the learning process, their ability to connect with the students, and their talent for innovation.

Our thinking is also somewhat unconventional with regard to the physical plant for education. The core of good education rests with its teachers, not with its facilities. This led me to believe that my former house in Nahariya would be a good setting for a school. It led me to think that a former army facility, composed of a number of small prefabricated houses, would lend itself to a rigorous high school program. In both cases the students' achievements proved me right. I like testing programs before putting a good deal of funds into building a structure to house them.

Now that the programs have proved to be successful, we are planning new facilities to house them. At Lavon, on the site of the rudimentary former army facility that housed my technical high school, architects Ulrik Plesner and his daughter Maya have designed an extensive educational campus and a bridge that will link it to the industrial park across the street.

The site, a dramatic promontory overlooking Karmiel and Deir al-Assad, will be home to six of our eight current educational initiatives: our new mold-making course, with its factory; the high school; the vocational teacher training program; the Zur Lavon Training Center; the School for Meisters; and the Shalem Premilitary Preparatory Program. Our schools operate in collaboration with what is now called the Ministry of Industry, Trade and Labor. The previous education minister, Shay Piron, also understood the critical situation facing vocational education and worked to assist us in redressing it. We look forward to continuing these efforts with whatever person is heading that ministry after the next election.

Two of these programs—the high school and the Shalem program—provide a second chance for those who are considered poor students to prove themselves. In these young students I see a mirror image of myself seven decades ago after my expulsion from school. I am keenly aware of how the right type of mentoring can convince a discouraged youth that he or she has the ability to succeed.

The immediate aim of all our educational initiatives is to educate a new generation of skilled workers and entrepreneurs for meaningful work. The broader objective is to advance the

A Vision for Education

economic and social stability of this country by creating industries that will employ the various sectors of Israeli society—Jews, Muslims, Druze, and Christians—in working toward a common goal: the global market.

In a small country like Israel, the threads of society are closely woven. Old ties are reestablished on a regular basis, and someone you worked with decades ago is likely to find his way to you again with a new idea. But what was less expected was the strong partnership that developed between me and my boyhood region of Baden-Württemberg with regard to education. Amid today's global economic crisis, the world looks to this region of Germany to learn its success in maintaining a strong economy and low unemployment.

Its secret lies in an uninterrupted commitment to technical education, one that is grounded in what is termed the dual education system. This type of learning combines theoretical classroom education with apprenticeships in the workplace. It is what Bosmat, Zur-Nahariya, and many other technical schools here in Israel encouraged before their decline. It is the main ingredient behind Germany and Switzerland's excellent reputation with regard to the products they produce. It provides students with the know-how they need to be successful—and pride in what they do. Those countries educate their students to find the right jobs. Germany offers its students more than 350 apprenticeship trades in the dual system, and 60 percent of students there partake of these courses. It carries no stigma; in fact, many university students will study in the dual system because it affords them an entry point to good jobs in industry after they complete their degrees. It also offers technical students a chance to pursue academic careers if they so choose. And it is this lively model I looked to in my attempts to resuscitate Israel's moribund technical education system.

Here's how this collaboration came to be. While in Stuttgart at a trade show a few years ago, I met my friend Berthold Leibinger, who headed the world-renowned firm Trumpf for many years before passing the reins on to his children.

Leibinger put me in touch with Baden-Württemberg's minister-president, Guenther Oettinger, who was about to make an official visit to Israel. After seeing Tefen and Zur Lavon, Oettinger agreed to a partnership to advance vocational teacher training in Israel. The Ministry of Industry, Trade and Labor also joined this venture. Oettinger's successors—Stefan Mappus and the current minister-president, Winfried Kretschmann—both made a commitment to continue on this same course. I applaud the hard work that both sides have put forth. Two of our German counterparts, Elisabeth Moser and Hartmut Mattes, deserve special thanks for the many hours they have devoted—both here in Israel and in Germany—to ensure its success.

It was difficult to find students for the initial class, because those who have experience in professional industrial work are very much in demand in industry. Of about a hundred potential candidates, we chose seven who were ready for professional upgrading. All professional metalworkers, they started the program in the fall of 2010, and all have successfully been awarded the title of Meister by the professional association, the Handwerkskammer, Region Stuttgart. They include both secular and religious individuals from our Jewish, Muslim, and Christian communities. The program, which provides partial stipends for the students, runs for two years and includes a visit of several weeks in Germany to factories and technical schools. We are conducting the training for teaching in cooperation with the Kerschensteinerschule in Stuttgart, which is guiding us and providing the auspices for granting the certifications until a suitable Israeli system is established. The training as a Meister includes

A Vision for Education

not only advanced training in operating metalworking machines but also training in production processes and management, as well as furthering an ability to teach. At the graduation ceremony that we held for this group in Nazareth on June 28, 2013, minister-president Winfried Kretschmann presented me with quite a surprise: an honorary Meister degree, the first of its kind ever awarded by the Handwerkskammer Stuttgart.

A problem still remains with certifying teachers in this field in Israel and in receiving official Israeli recognition from the institutions. The existing law recognizes teachers for technological subjects only when they have academic degrees; there is no requirement for practical expertise in the field. There is a difference between teaching *about* and teaching *how*. We insist on the practical and technical skill of the teachers in training, as is the case in Germany. Still in its initial stages is a legislative effort to change the law regarding the certification of vocational teachers.

We also have another joint program with the government of Baden-Württemberg and the Handwerkskammer. The School for Meisters is integrated with several other programs: one to train professional manufacturing mold makers, and one to train vocational teachers in metalworking.

In the future, other fields of industry will be added to the program, such as the plastics industry. Establishing the Meister course of study, the examinations, and the degree is of extreme importance—more than it would appear at first glance. It redresses the problems of Jewish history in that it finally confers honor on the acquisition of manual skills—something that has been largely omitted as a professional path for Jews for centuries. In addition, the actual training itself is significant, but so too is its ability to create a parallel path to the academic track, one that will have the same status For some decades, ambitious young people have not had a choice in determining their professions; academics reigned supreme, and those who did not go to the university had few options. Our educational programs are actively engaged in changing this status quo.

We operate several programs off-site because they are run jointly with the military and located on their bases. Several years ago, the commander of the Israeli Navy requested our assistance in establishing a vocational school to train its conscripts in the construction, repair, and maintenance work required for the navy's systems. The Zur Yam opened in September 2008 at the navy's training base at the Port of Haifa. The Ministry of Defense and the Ministry of Industry, Trade and Labor are partners in the project, which is now training about a hundred students.

The Israeli Army became interested in our technical programs as well. To accommodate their needs, we founded Zur Barak in 2009. In collaboration with ORT, it now trains about 160 students at the Ordnance Corps' Immanuel base in southern Israel near Kiryat Malachi and operates another school in Arad. Many of these students are those that the army would not have accepted without this training. This is a chance to prove themselves. As with all of our educational programs, the students spend one or two days a week engaged in practical work in industry.

To ensure the financial viability of our education programs, we are operating mini-factories within the Zur network—even in our high school. Real work on real products raises the quality of vocational education, and both students and teachers profit from creating real products for real customers. It provides a strong incentive and important feedback that pushes the quality of education even higher. We have also learned that our educational framework must include ways to develop the students' general skills as managers and tutors. Thus, our curriculum now trains the students to learn all stages of work—from design and planning to manufacturing, testing, and the delivery of projects. This new approach will strengthen the knowledge of our graduates, allowing them to succeed even faster in their chosen careers.

Our graduates will be the best ambassadors for the idea of personal, economic, and national independence. They will find common ground with their neighbors here in Israel as well as with those throughout the world who share their skills. Our program will be a model whose success will lead to a system of ten to twenty institutions for vocational studies in the future.

All of these initiatives derive from the concern that many of our young people will travel overseas and will not come back to Israel to build the state. Most who return will opt for academic studies without considering how their decision relates to the state's future needs. I believe strongly that in an emerging nation such as Israel the individual has a special responsibility to the nation. This may sound strange to readers in the West, where individual freedom reigns supreme, but for many years the collective spirit was necessary here in Israel to create a state. In many regards it still is. A small country like Israel must have a distribution of jobs that relates to the current societal needs. My generation saw the building of this country as its primary purpose. Physicians, musicians, and other professionals were willing to put their equipment to the side and work in the fields during the day to create a homeland here. We were rewarded with a strong sense of community and, for the first time in two thousand years, the feeling that we truly had a home. This was a major achievement, and we were keenly aware of its significance. Some of that philosophy must still hold true with the younger generation if we are to advance as a nation. Their reward in doing so will be the elimination of the alienation they feel when living abroad and the gratification of lending their talents to strengthen this country for generations to come.

CHAPTER 5

BRANCHING OUT TO TURBINE BLADES

In 1967 the Israeli Metals Committee, which I chaired with colonel Yerachmiel Katz, organized *Isratech*, the first international exhibition on metal and its products on behalf of the Ministry of Trade and Industry and the Manufacturers' Association. We invited visitors from around the world, with the aim of boosting awareness about the industry. Israelis began to realize that industry is not only textiles and food but also sophisticated products based on specialized knowledge, advanced technology, and the professionalism of workers and managers. For the first time they began to speak about the possibility of exporting—and not only defense exports.

It was then that I first met Avraham Asheri. He was serving at the Ministry of Trade and Industry. He later represented the Investments Authority in the United States, and held positions in the private market and at Israel Discount Bank. Asheri was to become a dedicated partner in fulfilling the dream of industrial parks.

But then the Six-Day War broke out.

We quickly converted the factory in Nahariya into a unit of Rafael, Israel's armaments industry. The few ISCAR personnel who were not called up for the war worked for a month at the factory producing parts for heavy bombs for the air force. This war and others did not prevent us from continuing the contractual supply of our products to customers, however, and we met all of our obligations.

During ISCAR's first fifteen years we received various proposals for expanding our areas of production into, for example, spare parts for automobiles or electronic products. I turned down all of these offers. I believe in specialization of a field in which you have expertise, and I did not want to thin out our knowledge and experience by expanding our product line. But soon something happened that forced a changed of outlook.

In June 1967 French president Charles de Gaulle imposed an embargo on arms sales to Israel, and a shipment of fifty Mirage aircraft for our air force was canceled. Several months earlier I had received a message from the minister of defense and from the air force: It was essential to build a factory in Israel to produce blades for jet aircraft engines so that if an embargo were imposed we would not have to ground fighter aircraft with damaged engines. In jet aircraft engines, the aluminum blade in the compressor wears out relatively rapidly, generally after five hundred to one thousand flight hours. In each engine there are about five hundred such blades, so an ongoing supply of spare parts is required.

Why did they contact me? I am an industrialist who specializes in metalworking—and a former pilot. I was concerned that Israel Aircraft Industries would not welcome a newcomer in this field, but Dan Tolkovsky reassured me that the company already had a full workload and would not be able to take over another field.

Blades—slices of metal that transform the energy of the jet engines to circular motion—must withstand very high heat and wear. If just one of the hundreds of blades in the engine

Branching Out to Turbine Blades

suffers early wear, the aircraft could be in jeopardy. They are expensive components: today the price of an individual blade ranges between tens and hundreds of dollars, depending on the blade's location in the engine. The subject was foreign to me—both the processing of the metal and the nature of the product—but at that time this was a critical national security issue.

I went to the Bedek repair shop at the airport to learn about jet engines. This project would require learning, building, and operating five unfamiliar technologies, five different factories in one framework: a forging factory; a factory for processing complex forms; a factory for coating the blades with hard materials; a division for quality control, metallurgical control, and coating control; and a product design division. It was particularly difficult to learn this subject because only a few factories in the world specialized in manufacturing blades.

I still have many pages on which I scribbled my thoughts: to ask for specifications on cooling materials, to check forms and sizes of work tables, to ascertain control methods, and to ask questions regarding maintenance, shipping, water arrangements, electricity, and pricing.

In the first stage, Tolkovsky and I flew to France to the Snecma factory, which still had a contract with our air force to supply engines and blades for Mirage aircraft. I went from division to division, from machine to machine, and became acquainted with the production process for the blades.

In negotiations with the French at Snecma on the sale of rights and know-how, I presented a condition: "I want to eventually export without competing with the French." Dan feared that this condition would jeopardize the signing of an agreement, but the French did not object, since they considered the prospect of Israeli competition to be ridiculous. About a month later, I re-

THE HABIT OF LABOR

turned to France with the architect Moshe Zarhi,[9] whom I had met back in our days at HEMED, so that he could plan the new building in Nahariya. I received the blueprints and hurried back to Israel.

Immediately afterward, De Gaulle's embargo was also imposed on Snecma and on the knowledge agreements—a serious blow—and the gates were closed to us in France. The air force no longer received Mirage fighter aircraft from the French and turned to planes from the United States. We were forced to roam the world, to factories in Belgium, Britain, Sweden, and the United States, to learn how to make them. Not every factory was keen on collaborating, but eventually, with the advice of professional friends from these countries and several who did this surreptitiously from closed-off France, I learned in one place what I had to know about forging, in another place some basic facts about coating, in a third place something about control, and so on.

We assembled a management team, which we called ISCAR Blades, and later Blades Technology, or Blades for short. We rented a building from Israel Discount Bank in Nahariya as our temporary headquarters, and we started to go around the world, ordering equipment and machines and conducting training courses for the team. With the help of supportive Americans who were involved in these fields, we started to plan production. The new factory was standing within a year. We received an advance payment from the Ministry of Defense, and at the beginning of 1969 the first blade emerged from the factory's machines. This was accomplished in record time, and was possible because bureaucratic procedures were expedited and red tape was cut.

---

[9] My dear friend Moshe Zarhi died in February 2015.

Branching Out to Turbine Blades

I wore four different hats at the factory: I was a private industrialist and was also a representative of the partnership with the Ministry of Defense, the Ministry of Finance, and the Ministry of Trade and Industry. I would consult by telephone with the partners and then make important decisions on my own within a day or two. Otherwise it is not likely that we could have succeeded so quickly.

We delivered the finished products to the air force, and soon, after meeting the local demand, we began to look for overseas markets too. Ironically, our first overseas customer for the blades was none other than Snecma of France. When the Israeli Air Force transitioned to American Skyhawks and we needed to adapt the blades' technical requirements to their Pratt and Whitney engines, we established contacts with this giant corporation, one of the largest in the world in its field. I was already familiar with Pratt and Whitney from my involvement in the Beit Shemesh Engines factory. The company checked the quality of our output and approved it. In fact, I still have a letter from the president of Pratt and Whitney, Robert J. Carlson, dated April 1, 1982. In it he remarks how ISCAR's "Nahariya facility looks orderly and neat—a veritable oasis."

We were competitive from the outset. We enjoyed the fruitful collaboration of the Ministry of Defense and the air force, and we learned how to enhance the quality of the products. A procurement manager at an aircraft manufacturer or airline wants a reliable supplier that makes a quality product at a competitive price, on schedule. That's all.

Unlike the global market for hard metals, with thousands of agents and buyers purchasing the output, here the market of buyers is limited to several giant corporations. Nearly every country with the wherewithal seeks to develop a capacity for self-production of blades. This case clearly demonstrated that it was possible to transform a deficiency in the local market into a catalyst for production and an advantage in exporting.

In 1969, we established a partnership between TRW, one of the world's few manufacturers of blades. This partnership lasted until 1995, when TRW decided to discontinue this area of production. We bought their shares and, in the same year entered into a fifty-fifty partnership with Pratt and Whitney, which was Blades' largest regular customer by far. Pratt and Whitney received our know-how, experience, quality, and focus on a single product. We, in exchange, moved closer to the American and world markets.

In 1972, ISCAR Blades and I were awarded the Kaplan Prize for "initiative and dynamism in establishing a factory for manufacturing blades for aircraft engines, copy production and use of new and special technologies." This was the second time that I was awarded this prize. I invested ten years of my life in Blades, from its first day until I was elected to the Knesset. My son Eitan assumed the reins of management in 1995; twelve years later, the company was able to show a tenfold increase in revenues.

In 1995, Blades and Pratt and Whitney began joint production of compressors and gas turbine engines for the space and aviation industries. In 1997 China, Israel, and the United States signed an agreement to build a joint Blades factory in Xian, in western China near the site of the amazing terracotta soldiers. Eitan continued the trend of recruiting international partners that I had started with TRW and Pratt and Whitney and in 1999, after two years of discussions, also brought in Rolls-Royce as a partner.

Today Blades is a highly successful and solid company, led by a management group that was educated and grew at the factory. Our American partners, Pratt and Whitney, value it highly as well—so much so that they purchased our half of the firm in the summer of 2014. Their representative, Beth Schwarz, was an active force in ensuring its success. She traveled to Israel from her home in Connecticut every few months—so frequently, in fact, that she almost seemed like one of our permanent staff.

Blades has branches in Tefen and Nahariya in Israel; in Columbus, Georgia, in the United States; and in Xian, China. It employs about two thousand people in the Galilee and throughout the globe, and its products are found in aircraft all over the world.

While there is stability in this market, the production requirements are constantly advancing. Aircraft that are more sophisticated require stronger and enhanced engines whose parts must withstand very high temperatures. The trend is toward more power and less weight, and the technologies are developing with the demands. And, of course, a basic condition in our contemporary reality is fuel efficiency.

As Blades was taking its first steps, the mother factory, ISCAR, continued to improve its range of exports. In 1968, its sales rose 80 percent, and it had more than two hundred employees working in the factory. In 1969 we opened a showroom and service office in Tel Aviv. In 1971, we opened ISCAR Metals in Clifton, New Jersey, to market our products in the United States. Nine years later, we laid the cornerstone for ISCAR's new facility in Hackettstown, New Jersey.

The Wertheimer IMC Group, which includes the cutting tool producers ISCAR, TaeguTec, Ingersoll, and Tungaloy (which began as a subsidiary of the Japanese company Toshiba), are all now are part of Warren Buffett's corporation Berkshire Hathaway.

CHAPTER 6

HOME

The children were growing up and becoming more independent. Miriam and I always encouraged them to assume responsibility for themselves.

ISCAR was a sort of older sibling, a regular member of the family in the children's lives. The problems and the news would come up at the dinner table—and Miriam made the meal times a sacred institution, no less than her afternoon nap. All four children spent a lot of time at the factory and knew the workers and the machines. I would bring visitors and friends from Israel and abroad for home-cooked meals and explain everything to the children.

With the children I was more lenient and less stubborn and strict than Miriam. Most of the burden fell upon her, a woman of principles for whom life seemed simple and clear, including the solutions to problems she encountered. While I believed more in loosening the reins, in allowing freedom of action and self-responsibility, Miriam placed the emphasis on supervision and guidance. While I was stricter on issues of precision and order, Miriam did not relent on the issue of ambition.

My success as someone who had not completed his formal education was an exception that was not to be emulated by the children. They had to study and excel. Both of us wanted them to be well prepared for encounters with the wider world.

Soon after our return from the Netherlands, Irit asked me to take her on a tour of ISCAR. She wanted to understand everything as a grownup, to be involved. We walked through the various departments, and I explained every detail to her. At the end I said to her, "Now prepare a summary of the things you learned here today." I still have the detailed report she prepared.

Eitan was well behaved until age fourteen, and then he began to assert his independence. Together with friends, he purchased and repaired an old lawn mower and began to earn his pocket money from work after school. However, at the Weizmann Elementary School in Nahariya, his affairs were a bit more trying: disciplinary issues and a lack of desire to study. He was not a diligent and disciplined pupil, and this was a source of tension with Miriam. In an interview with the Israeli publication *Globes* on November 11, 1994, Eitan recalled some details of his childhood:

> We lived in a shack. Even when there was something—everything went into the business. As a child, at 6:30 in the morning I went to bring bread and milk from the grocery store. I was envious of many children. At home, Mother was very dominant. She strongly shaped the family. Set high standards and raised us with rigid Spartan concepts: "Get to work and stop your nonsense. Don't complain, just do it!" It was a demanding education in which much was expected of you. So, from the age of six I delivered flowers, set up seats for the movies, and worked during vacations. There was no such concept of "not working." Because of the need and because of the atmosphere. Every summer, I worked at Degania Bet to imbibe the values of work and not to become a loafer. Did I have a tough childhood? I had my childhood. That's what I know. I lost an eye, I had

polio. I'm not complaining. I started in a way that gave me ambition for many years.[10]

I understood Eitan well; after all, at his age I, too, was a rebellious youth. I knew that he was adept with his hands and had a good head on his shoulders. He visited the factory, learned to work at the machines, was involved with the workers, and was an alert participant in conversations about ISCAR at the factory and at home. Ruti also, while studying at the Bezalel Academy of Arts and Design, had to prepare some type of exhibit from metal—and without any problem operated the lathe and made the exhibit with her own hands.

Before he was fifteen years old, I sent Eitan, on his own, to the factory of a friend in Switzerland for a few days to learn a new method of grinding there. When he returned, he pulled out a well-organized notebook in which he had written and sketched everything.

Eitan started at the regional agricultural high school, but soon decided that everything bored him and would often play hooky. In the evening he would disappear, returning home in the wee hours of the night—he had a room with a separate entrance on the lower floor—and sometimes he would not return at all. Much later he revealed to me that he would sometimes sleep at a friend's house and occasionally even in a yard or stairwell. He would wake up at dawn, read the newspaper, and go to school.

Miriam got along with him less and less. I think she did not trust him. He was too frivolous in her view, and she complained that she could no longer communicate with him. I repeatedly said that I was not worried; I was always sure that he was a bright youngster who would eventually find his way on his own.

---

[10] Avital Inbar (interviewer), "Eitan is also a Wertheimer," in the magazine *Globes*, November 11, 1994.

THE HABIT OF LABOR

At the end of his second year in high school, after the Six-Day War, Eitan brought home such a depressing report card that I shared Miriam's anger over his wasting time. Eitan then announced that he would like to transfer to the Bosmat vocational school attached to Technion in Haifa, where some of his friends were studying. We expected him to fail the entrance exam because of his low grades, but he surprised everyone and did very well.

At Bosmat, Eitan became a good student, except in one or two subjects, because—so he claimed—the teachers were boring in those classes. He excelled in manual lathe work. When he completed his studies, with good grades, we thought it would be best for him to continue at Technion. Eitan went to hear a few lectures but left disappointed; "I don't understand what they are talking about there," he said.

For his military service it was obvious that Eitan would be in the Ordnance Corps and become involved in technical work on tanks and in development for routine security purposes, spending a lot of time with the forces in the field. Here, too, my son's path was reminiscent of my own decades earlier. Prior to his release from the army, he discovered a mountain hideaway and prepared it as a "place of refuge" where he planned to spend several months after his release—painting, hiking, and contemplating in seclusion.

But reality intruded. Three days after his release, the Yom Kippur War broke out, and he left his hideout in Mount Carmel. He headed to the Golan Heights without any call-up order. He became an operations sergeant in the field, requisitioning jeeps and equipment with his friends to prepare the unit for action—and between Saturday and Sunday, he was already overloaded with arming, repairing, refurbishing, and solving technical problems. He discovered that he could work for days on end without sleep.

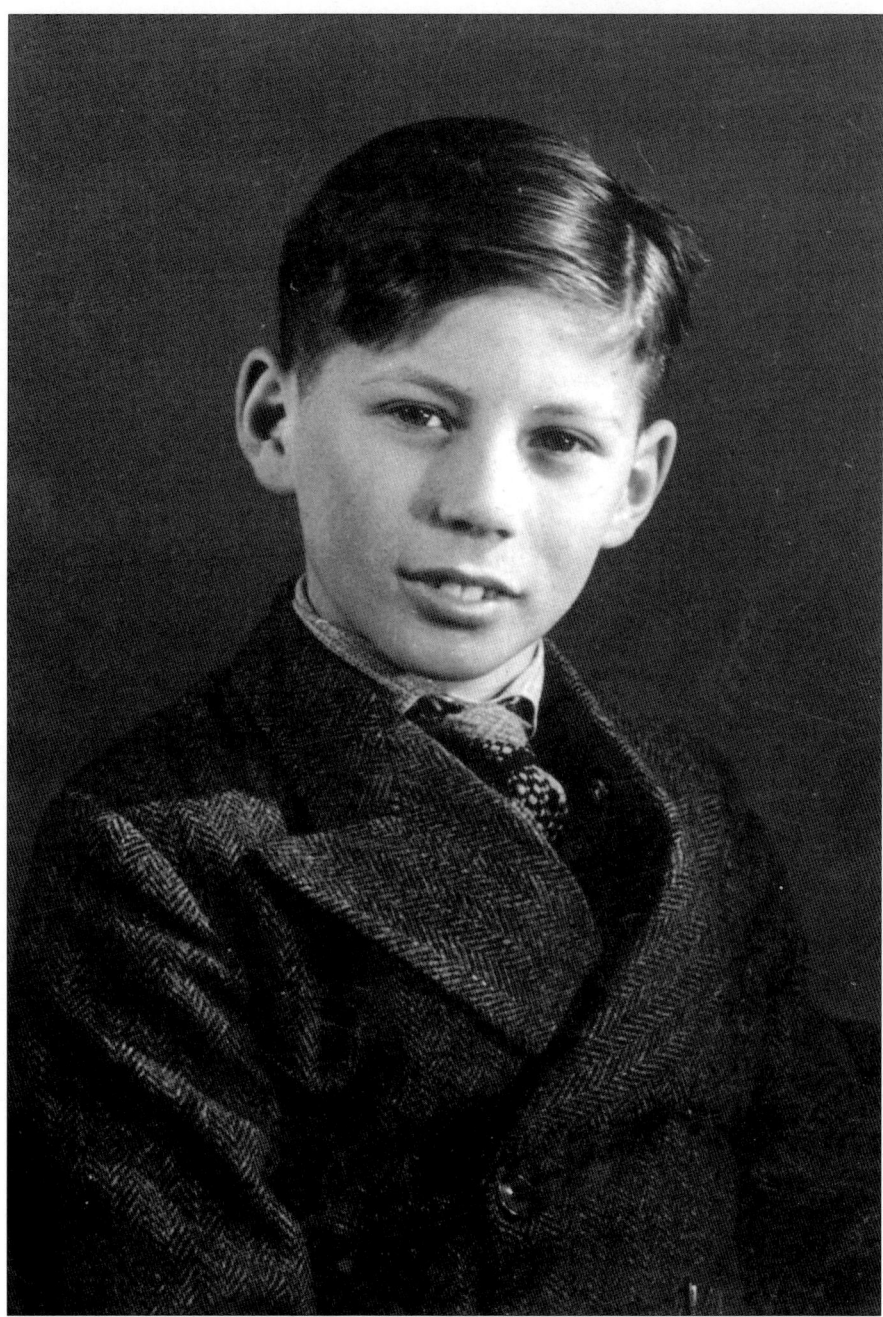

Stef at about 8

Unless noted otherwise, all photos are from the ISCAR archives
or Stef Wertheimer's personal collection.

Above: Eugen as a soldier

Right: Kippenheim Synagogue

Below: The house with the many windows is the former Wertheimer home in Kippenheim

Above: The new immigrants

Left: Stef, at age 16, now dressed like the locals

Cohen Optica (Credit: Schuftan family)

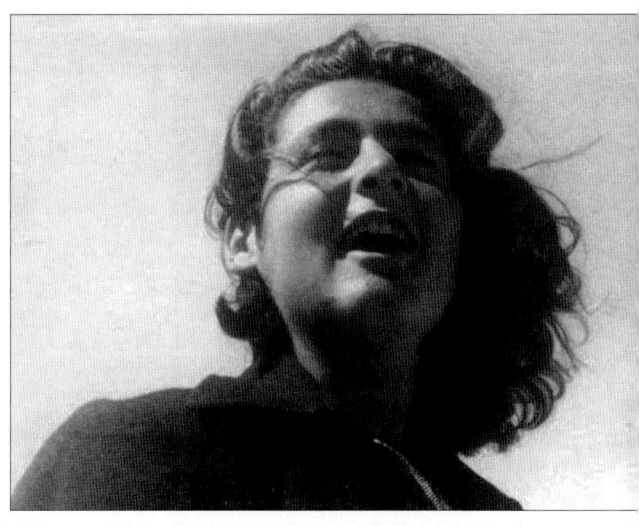

Miriam at about 16

Palmach tents at Kibbutz Givat Brenner

ISCAR at the start

The early vocational school at Zur Nahariyah (Courtesy of Mula Haramati)

Yossi Pano (right) and Stef

Stef with Iftak on his shoulders, Miriam, Irit, Eitan, and Ruthie

Stef receives the Kaplan Prize from Yigal Alon, 1962

Stef and Eitan with ISCAR's professional representatives in Europe

Stef with Pratt & Whitney officials in a turbine engine
(Courtesy of Blades Technology)

Industree logo

With Prime Minister Menachem Begin (center)

Stef receiving his nation's highest honor, the Israel Prize, from Prime Minister Yitzhak Shamir, 1991 (Credit: Israeli Ministry of Education)

Yitzhak Rabin visits ISCAR

Stef, President Yitzhak Navon, and Yigal Yadin at the cornerstone ceremony at Kfar Vradim

Palmach friends visiting ISCAR to celebrate Stef's Israel Prize

From left: Dr. Abdul Malik al-Jabar, Dr. Saadi al-Krunz, and Stef

From left: Vice Prime Minister Ehud Olmert, Turkey's Minister of State Ali Babacan, former U.S. Senator George J. Mitchell, Dr. Bilal Bashir from Jordan, Stef, and former U.S. Congressman Robert Livingston, January 2004, at a conference at ISCAR

Above: Prime Minister Recep Tayyip Erdogan (left) and Stef at GOSB Industrial Park in Turkey

Lynn Holstein, Stef, and Shawki Khatib at the Nazareth Industrial Park

Left: German President Joachim Gauck and Stef at the ceremony at which Stef received Germany's highest honor

Below: With Warren Buffett, 2006 (Credit: Tefen Open Museum)

The ever-expanding Wertheimer family

Aerial view of the Nazareth Industrial Park

Danny Goldman

Jacob Harpaz, Haim Cohen

Home

Eitan performed this additional service for seven months, and was released in April 1974. He did not join the family business. "I didn't want to be regarded as 'the son of,'" he said later. He traveled around in an old car in Europe and the United States, getting away from it all and avoiding decisions.

Then Eitan decided that he would work for himself—perhaps to prove himself. I did not stop him. He rented a facility in Shlomi and started to repair machines and sharpen tools for nearby factories. When he succeeded, he bought a small and failing factory in Karmiel, rehabilitated it, and sold it at a profit—and continued to do this, buying businesses, restoring them to the production cycle, and moving onward.

Eitan has been active in initiatives to advance our society. For many years he has served as chairman of Atidim, a program for promoting talented youth of limited means from the periphery. Thus far, the program has helped to prepare more than fifteen thousand individuals—Jews, Muslims, Druze, and Christians—for academic studies that lead to practical work. He is also engaged in encouraging industrialization in northern Israel, developing southern Israel, and rebuilding the Rambam Hospital in Haifa.

Like me, Eitan has no diplomas; he is only a high school graduate who took several courses at Harvard Business School, but his enormous achievements speak for him.

Ruti was a well-behaved child and good pupil, but she also complained that she was bored in her classes at school. She participated in courses for gifted children at Technion. In the army she served as an operations sergeant in the Northern Command, as part of the Israeli Defense Forces' experiment in placing women in this position, and she received a letter of commendation for her resourcefulness in managing an event that saved lives. Throughout the years she has demonstrated independent and original thinking. She studied industrial design at the Bezalel Academy, specializing in sculpting with glass. This path led her to study with renowned glass artists in the Czech Republic, Italy, and the United States, and glass work is still today a source of pleasure for her.

While pursuing her own activities, Ruti kept involved in what was happening at ISCAR. From a very young age she traveled to exhibitions and visited the company's branches abroad. Already in 1984, she suggested the idea of computerizing the decision-making process related to adapting ISCAR products for our customers. This process, which is taken for granted today, required us to incorporate the knowledge of our experienced workers into a computerized system to improve the sales process. For many years Ruti was a member of the board of directors of the IMC Group. As part of her independent path, she chose to continue to combine industry and family. In the framework of her family office, she founded a company named 7 Industries to invest in excellent industrial companies that are family owned.

Yiftach is my beloved youngest child. He was born an alert baby who filled the house with laughter and joy. Only later did Miriam and I begin to realize that Yiftach was struggling with various difficulties. The active and beautiful boy had trouble with the demands of the education system. We often witnessed his great frustration when he failed to perform various tasks. Years later we began to attribute Yiftach's difficulties to his complicated birth, which apparently affected the supply of oxygen to his brain.

Miriam and I did all we could to help him. He spent some time at an anthroposophist village in Switzerland, a place that accepted a wide range of people and focused on their capabilities instead of their difficulties. We missed Yiftach and would visit him there often.

Home

Later, Yiftach moved to a residential village called Kfar Tikva. Holding the belief that every person should feel useful, I helped to start a small industry there for plastic packaging, including packaging for tools produced at ISCAR. Some of the residents of the village were regularly employed in the factory, and thus could feel that they were supporting themselves.

After Miriam's death from cancer in 1989, it was important that Yiftach and I would live close to each other. Therefore, together with Yael Shilo, the daughter of my Palmach friend Eli Lamberger, I joined in establishing Kishurit, a rehabilitative village located near Lavon. Yael and I were a couple for several years and then married, but the marriage did not last very long and we divorced. At Kishurit I started a factory for wooden toys, which was well run by members of the village. Yiftach also worked there on his lathes with great pleasure, as a scion of a family of industry.

Yiftach has a love of mankind and a joy of life. He is a perfect gentleman, sensitive to those around him and sometimes, like me, he can be impatient. We both share a love for music, and one of the most moving times I have experienced was listening to a song he composed in memory of his mother. When he sang the song, "Where Are You, Mom?" at the memorial service for Miriam, there was not a dry eye among us.

I cannot finish this part about Yiftach without noting how much I admire his strength and his ability to contend with a reality of life that is not simple at all. Still, I sometimes ask myself whether he realizes how much I love him and worry about him. I know that I am also important to him, and I still feel thrilled every time I hear Yiftach, who was a heavy smoker, explain that he quit smoking "so that Father would be proud of me."

And what became of my parents? Father died in 1961.

He was able to witness only the beginning of my success. Mother, who outlived him by six years, was able to see my former commander, Yigal Allon, award me the Kaplan Prize in 1962.

Today I share my life with Lynn Holstein, whom I met in the summer of 1996. She had come to Kfar Vradim to visit the family of Noam Greenberg, who was dating her daughter Alizah. They came to see Tefen, and Lynn, who had earned a graduate degree from Harvard University and then later became an administrator at Harvard's Graduate School of Design, was impressed by the industrial park's architecture, the landscape architecture, and the urban planning elements—all fields that are taught at the design school. In a burst of enthusiasm, she said that she'd like to meet the person who was behind it all.

The next morning Avner Greenberg called me. I invited Lynn to come to my office, where she suggested that I consider supporting a study that would bring some bright young Harvard students in these three fields to assess the new park I was building at the time in nearby Lavon. In the spring of 1997, she returned with professor Carl Steinitz, and we agreed to proceed with this on-site study (which is called a studio at Harvard).

They returned soon thereafter with fourteen students, and did a presentation on their findings, which were also included in a subsequent publication titled "Alternative Futures in the Western Galilee, Israel." Among their findings were some recommendations that we are now or will soon be implementing, such as the construction of a bridge to link the two parts of Lavon that are now separated by the existing road, the establishment of a major educational complex at Lavon, and a conservation strategy to preserve the beautiful landscape.

I was, in fact, so pleased with the results of this studio that I invited them to return to investigate our plans to build twin parks: one in Gaza at al-Shoka (near Rafiah) and one just across the border in Kerem Shalom. It sounds like ancient history now, but the mandate for these Harvard students was to design the parks so that they could work closely together when the border was opened—which, at the time, seemed like a good possibility.

In 2000, when Lynn made aliyah (formal immigration to Israel), I offered her a job working with me. I had always been impressed by the Marshall Plan that revived Europe after World War II. It was Lynn's idea to take this concept to Washington, DC, and she directed my New Marshall Plan initiative for several years. As will be explored in more detail in chapter 15, we went repeatedly to America's capital to meet with policy makers on Capitol Hill and in the US government. The immediate aim was to create an industrial park in Aqaba with a Jordanian who had agreed to be my partner. The longer-term goal was to establish between twenty-five and fifty industrial parks in the Middle East to do precisely what Ireland, Japan, and South Korea had done—namely, to move a region from conflict to peace via meaningful jobs and a higher standard of living.

CHAPTER 7

PUBLIC SERVICE

On the morning of Yom Kippur in 1973, we convened the managers and met with those older individuals who would not be called up for service but would instead do their service in the factories. It was clear that we would serve as a branch of Israel Military Industries and HEMED. We began to produce shells and various metal accessories the Israeli Defense Forces (IDF) needed in the war. In addition, we became a central mechanics shop for the IDF in the north. Soldiers came to us with war-damaged vehicles and weapons, which we would then repair. Although few workers remained in the factories, those who were not mobilized managed to assist the army while also fulfilling our ongoing orders.

Swamped with work and worried about the situation, I went from the factories to the funerals of fallen soldiers. The border was closed, and the sense of security of the local residents needed to be strengthened. To encourage the people, the director of the hospital in Nahariya, professor Sasha Shaul, and I organized sing-along evenings. But these evenings did not prevent gloomy thoughts about everything that had happened to us since the Six-Day War, and how Israel had become, in just six years, a state managed by military people whose thinking was security oriented and for whom the occupied territories were a central part of this security outlook. The overconfidence of these army officers led them to believe—falsely, in my mind—that the goals of peacemaking and industrialization could be put on the back burner. To me, establishing normal relations with our former enemies through a fair peace process and advancing our country through exports was the way to a secure future. Perhaps we had no other alternative in our situation, but it seemed that we were losing time.

In this context I was already concerned with the development of the Galilee, where I had chosen to live, to raise my family, and to make a living. This strip of land shared by Jews and Arabs seemed a place where we could start to join hands and work together for the welfare of both peoples. Then the idea arose of planning a community there and transforming the mainly agricultural region into a large and joint industrial and educational cultural center with factories, parks, and residential neighborhoods, something that would fill in the bare landscape of the Galilee along the border.

For years I tried my best to persuade policy makers to adopt this idea. In 1974, Yigal Allon, then the minister of labor, arranged a meeting for me with Yitzhak Rabin, who had become prime minister after Golda Meir resigned. Although Rabin listened to my plans for stimulating growth in the Galilee via export industries, it appeared that his priorities were elsewhere.

A meeting with Haim Bar-Lev, then the minister of trade and industry, led to similar results. I came to him with a proposal for a "global" solution: small factories in these peripheral towns, which would succeed where giant factories had failed and entangled the state. These small factories would solve problems of society, employment, and education in the neglected towns. I think Bar-Lev saw me as a fantasizer.

And thus, in light of the difficulty in persuading the de-

Public Service

cision makers, the people from the financial world and the media, my inclination to enter politics—to try to personally change what needed to be changed—grew stronger.

The beginning was modest, at the local level, in my city of Nahariya. The tranquil *yekke*, somewhat phlegmatic town, with the flavor of the 1940s and 1950s, had changed beyond recognition. Thousands of new immigrants had expanded its boundaries and turned it into a vibrant local center for tourism. Yet there were many annoying aspects: the litter, the poor municipal management, the disconnection from the center of the country, the construction along the coastline that had destroyed its natural charm. And ISCAR was almost the only factory in the north, outside of Muller's textile factory and Isasbest.

The choice was to leave Nahariya or to fight for the city. In conversations with friends and workers, there was a consensus that we had to do something for the Galilee. This led to the idea of replacing the city's management and changing its administration.

I agreed to run for mayor. Miriam did not oppose the decision, but she was not very enthusiastic. I was not enamored of the field of politics. I entered the election race as a complete novice, with supporters who wanted to change the party system and to fight against bureaucracy, inefficiency, corruption, and nepotism.

We embarked on a campaign under the slogan "A Clean Municipality in a Clean City." Everything was new for us: the advertisements, the speeches, the parlor meetings, and the attempts to persuade. Ultimately, despite our inexperience, my running mates and I achieved results that were not bad at all: nearly 35 percent of the votes and five of twelve seats on the city council. This was almost the same as the winning Mapai candidate received. We remained in the opposition.

For two years I participated in the city council meetings every week, and the faction and I did good work. With a city planner I prepared a plan for enhancing the city's appearance, which would have transformed Nahariya into a first-rate tourist and industrial site. But due to my work in the factories and frequent travel abroad, I was absent from several meetings. My political rivals found it convenient to exploit a clause in the bylaws stipulating that occasional absences can result in expulsion from the council. And indeed, they managed to expel me, even though I represented nearly 35 percent of the residents of Nahariya and despite the fact that I was actually present for most of the meetings and chaired several active committees.

The Shinui movement was one of the many protest movements that arose in the wake of the Yom Kippur War. It all began on March 5, 1974, at a closed meeting at Tel Aviv University. About a hundred people participated, all of us wishing to initiate change in Israel. We listened to a lecture by the sociologist Yonatan Shapira, who presented eight principles for managing a healthy state and society. What he said about limiting the government's involvement in the economy, changing the election system, a territorial compromise, and other subjects was definitely attuned to my way of thinking. At the end of his lecture, Professor Shapira called for establishing a new political movement that would bring down the old regime and instill a new set of values.

I found myself acting with others to initiate a new ideological movement that would change everything: a centrist party as a strong political entity between the left and the right.

Three weeks later, on March 26, we convened our founding convention at the B'nai B'rith building in Tel Aviv. The auditorium was packed with industrialists, businessmen, professors, economists, attorneys, artists, architects, writers, and journalists.

Public Service

Members had already begun to register for the movement, which after some deliberation was named Shinui ("change" in Hebrew).

The ensuing period was full of trips, meetings, conferences, and the coordination of opinions. There were negotiations with the Citizen's Rights Movement (Ratz), led by Shulamit Aloni, about uniting (which did not happen) and meetings with people who had left Mapai, from the right and from the left. About thirty branches were established throughout the country. The media reported extensively about our new, energetic movement, and we sensed the hopes that the public pinned on us.

I was swamped with work at the factory and with the movement. Miriam, Eitan, or Ruti would occasionally accompany me to parlor gatherings, but none of them liked the new field I had entered. Miriam worried that I would be hurt in the brutal reality of politics, but she understood why I jumped into these murky waters. Ruti said she did not like the political hacks, the *machers*, and the influence peddling that came with politics.

I focused on the need to settle and industrialize the north and the idea of industry as an economic alternative. I thought that Shinui should show that it was different from all of the other parties. Our coalition truly looked fresh, optimistic, and different from the old political leadership. Although the party's founders came mostly from academia, I felt that there were also too many attorneys, which elicited the moniker Ali Baba and the Forty Lawyers. We instituted a rapid rotation in our ranks so that our supporters would get to know all of those speaking on their behalf. Thus, I also served as chairman of the movement for a period of time.

In time, Shinui expanded. We thought, in line with the security-oriented thinking at the time, that if we recruited a general or two to our ranks, our chances of success would improve. But we did not want the new party to become an abode for retired generals. When the time came to choose a like-minded leader, we selected professor Yigal Yadin, a native-born Israeli, the second chief of staff of the IDF, and a respected scholar and archaeologist of international renown. For many years Yadin had stayed away from politics, as if waiting for the right moment to be called upon to serve Israel.

Yadin stirred great excitement among people who were looking for an authoritative figure, wise and decisive, as a response to the crisis of leadership during that period. This was the time following the resignation of Meir's government and the only modest success of the Rabin government.

Amnon Rubinstein, a professor of law who was one of the founding members of Shinui, had shaky relations with Yadin. He had written a scathing article about the conclusions of the Agranat Commission of Inquiry that sought to investigate how Israel could have been so unprepared when Egypt led its surprise attack in the Yom Kippur War of 1973. (Yadin was a member of this commission.)

I worked to conciliate Yadin, Meir Amit, Meir Zorea, and Rubinstein. On October 30, 1976, an agreement was signed between Yadin's group and Shinui to found the Democratic Movement for Change (Dash). Yadin brought his friends with him—former security personnel like Yochai Ben-Nun, my friend Dan Tolkovsky, several former top police officials, and a few scientists. Later, many others joined us—from the protest movements, the Oded group (a party of social aspirations), those wishing to change the elections system, people from the Mapai Party and the Histadrut labor federation, and others. I was one of many, yet I still did not completely feel that I really belonged.

Thus, under the new name of Dash, we became active with Yadin as our leader. And though many of the problems among its components were not resolved, Yadin announced the

Public Service

new political movement and presented its objectives, upon which all of us agreed.

Then events befell us. First, in December 1976, the Rabin government faced a serious crisis when three new American F-15 aircraft were received in Israel in a state ceremony after the onset of the Jewish Sabbath. The religious parties raised a ruckus, initiated a no-confidence vote, and Rabin dismissed the government ministers from the National Religious Party. The elections were moved up by six months, to May 17, 1977. Then, in April, Rabin withdrew his candidacy for prime minister following the exposure of his wife Leah's personal bank account in Washington, DC, from the days when he served as Israel's ambassador there. (In those days it was illegal for Israelis to hold foreign bank accounts.)

During this period the internal contradictions within Dash began to surface, including personal rivalries and opposing interests. Each step was accompanied by endless fighting: the appointment of Zorea as the director-general of Dash, the factional composition of the movement's executive body, and the elections for the secretariat and various committees. I was appointed chairman of the party's economics committee and placed as a candidate on the Knesset slate. I had already proposed that we submit two new and important socioeconomic laws when we entered the Knesset: the Budget Restraint Law, which would define the ratio between the size of the budget and gross domestic product (GDP) and would gradually result in a sound budget that would not exceed 50 percent of GDP; and the Law to Regulate Manpower, which would encourage the transition from service jobs to manufacturing, a law that also sought to freeze wages in the public sector. I also added a proposal to prohibit strikes in this sector because they are a type of monopoly. These proposals remained on paper only; they are part of a fair number of personal failures I have accumulated in my lifetime.

The very complicated election system we decided upon in Dash, innocently and out of a desire to zealously maintain democratic rules, led to unexpected results. Marginal groups won large representation, well beyond their relative strength. A list of candidates was chosen for the Knesset, and I was elected to the sixth slot. But already the nascent party was starting to undergo a rapid process of deterioration. Mutual recriminations were exchanged, every clause in the party platform was only adopted after fierce arguments, each faction pulled in its own direction, and Yadin—the leader who quickly lost the support of his close colleagues—did not succeed in imposing order among its factions.

The principles that Yadin had declared as the party's "red lines" slipped away as we retreated from our fundamental demands, one after another. Yadin did not know how to draw the correct conclusions from our platform. He was not a shallow personality, lacking strength or principles, as his rivals—both within and outside Dash—tried to portray him. Yet he was not the national leader of great stature that we had hoped he would be. In the negotiations Dash conducted with the Likud Party after the Knesset elections, Yadin did not achieve a thing. The disappointment in him was undoubtedly one of the factors behind the rapid demise of the movement.

But during the weeks prior to the elections, with the broad public support, the cumulative failures of the previous regime, and the great excitement over a new and hope-inspiring ideological movement that had sprouted in less than four years from its twenty or so founders into a party with massive support, we ignored the problems and potential obstacles and arrived at the elections of 1977, the "upheaval" elections.

Public Service

Unlike many others, I did not regard the political turnabout that brought the Likud Party and Menachem Begin to power as an earthquake. I thought that the old regime had reached the end of its path after about thirty years of leadership. Even though friends such as Allon, Rabin, and Bar-Lev were among its ranks, they did not understand the great need to repair the fundamental problems in Israel's economy and society. This alignment was also opposed to general ideas of privatization and of business success on the part of individuals—anything that it viewed as the seeds of local capitalism.

In the general elections, Dash received 202,515 votes, turning the new party into the third largest political force, hoping for substantial change in the national leadership and its objectives. But the elections also brought great disappointment to many of us. The shock within Labor's alignment, which was ousted from power after so many consecutive years, was enormous. The fifteen seats Dash won in the Knesset, an unprecedented achievement for a completely new movement, were not enough to generate the great change we sought. We became just another political party in which the ugly contradictions—political, ideological, and personal—quickly came to the fore.

Protracted negotiations began with the Likud Party on joining Begin's government. Begin was a good politician and cunningly manipulated our negotiating team, which was led by Yadin. First of all, Begin showed us that he could form a narrow coalition without us but that he was interested in bolstering it with our help. I thought it was possible to exploit the achievement of fifteen seats in negotiations with him so as to moderate the government and move it toward the center. But what was once obvious—that we would only join a government that agreed to our ironclad principles—became a panicked dash to jump onto the government bandwagon, hoping that Begin would be kind enough to pull us aboard. Dash, which was already split between Yadin's and Rubinstein's groups, with its other factions at loggerheads, lost all its bargaining power.

Eventually we entered the government, with Yadin as deputy prime minister, Shmuel Tamir as minister of justice, Meir Amit as minister of transportation, and Yisrael Katz as minister of labor and welfare. I was one of the fifteen representatives Dash sent to the Knesset. I would have taken the position of minister of trade and industry, but it was not offered to us, and I was not interested in any other position. We entered the Knesset, but we did not wield any meaningful influence. Yadin was an honest man with good intentions, but he was weak and held an essentially unimportant post.

During my initial days as a member of the Knesset, when I was still naive and hopeful, I trusted that if I went from the Galilee to Jerusalem three days a week to talk with the other elected officials I would surely succeed in infecting them with my faith in the future of export industries. This was my *idée fixe*, one that could change the future of the state.

But I soon was in for a rude awakening. I did not learn the diplomatic language of the Knesset, a language that avoids clear definitions. I was not proficient in its rules, in its dos and don'ts. I did not become acclimated to the bargaining and compromising. Besides, I was not a brilliant orator, I did not stir the curiosity of the journalists roaming the Knesset because industry and community development in the Galilee are not sensational subjects, and my conversations with ministers did not generate a significant change.

I did not know then the power of the allocation—the power vested in those in charge of allocating the honors, jobs, and budgets. The Israeli people elect 120 people to the Knesset. Generally speaking, one-third is elected with the aim of calming

Public Service

the people's existential security fears; these are former military officers. A second third is comprised of foreign policy experts. The remainder are *machers*—party hacks and officials. You will not find industrialists there. The nation's election results should better reflect the trends of its future—and the future is in industry and production.

Thus, I was in the Knesset, but a part of me was again an outsider. Naturally I had a closer look at how the system operates—how everyone uses it, from the most junior officials to the decision makers. The system is epitomized by what an air force procurement officer once told me: "I'm going to say no to you so many times, until you start to realize that I exist."

I felt then that the system was one of allocation in which the money entering the state's treasury from the United States or from the taxpayers becomes the power base of the government and its ministers. This is the negative power of the allocators, those who hold the funds and budgets: to say no. It is the power to abuse the applicant, to hinder his initiatives. It is the power of every minister, and first and foremost, the power of the chief allocator, the minister of finance. Most of them were lawyers, those who live from problems and not from solutions. One time, frustrated after running into yet another bureaucratic obstacle, I decided to announce a special bonus to be awarded for each day of work that an official stayed home and did not hinder or obstruct.

There is an enormous difference between economics and finance. Economics is the production of goods that make money. In Israel, this distinction was blurred long ago because we do not have enough respect for production. When the money is not created here through work and via exports but arrives as a grant or loan from outside, all that is needed is an efficient system for its allocation. This approach distorts everything.

THE HABIT OF LABOR

On my eightieth birthday, a book was published that collected a number of memories of others about me. Here is an interesting excerpt from the piece that former member of the Knesset Arie Lova Eliav wrote for that book:

> In the mid-1960s, when I was a deputy minister in charge of the industrialization of development zones, I chose Nahariya. . . . I'll never forget the visit to ISCAR. I had come to offer Stef a government grant or loan for his factory. . . .
>
> Much to my surprise, Stef answered delicately but firmly: "No, thank you. I don't need and don't want any government grant or loan. I'm building the factory by myself. All you can help me with is to make sure the government bureaucracy won't bother me."
>
> This response was utterly uncommon because "everyone," every factory owner in the development zones, was very eager to get government aid. At that time, I already knew how special Stef was, a person who wanted to develop an industrial sector using his skills, initiative, and proverbial élan.[11]

As a member of the Knesset I would get involved in debates with the power brokers in the upper echelons. I would explain that Israel's economic independence was really just around the corner, and that if we worked correctly, we could reach a surplus of tens of billions in one decade, as in Taiwan. But they would shrug disparagingly: "Oh, what do you understand about the reciprocal relationships in the economy, Stef?" I actually did understand. I understood that politics, not the economy, was what drove the ministers and their minions.

---

[11] Ruthi Ofek (editor), *Stef Wertheimer: Memories between the Lines*, (Tefen, The Open Museum, 2006), p. 4.

Public Service

I felt that if Israel were a strong exporting nation it could function efficiently with a government of only five ministries. First would be a Ministry of Defense, which would focus solely on security and would not expand its purview to the fields of industry, employment, economics, and social welfare, as is the case in Israel today. Second would be a Ministry of Export Economy; the minister for exports, second in importance only to the defense minister, would coordinate all of the state's economic initiatives, including the means of production and local (nonexport) industries, all with one main objective: developing industry for export. In such an economic ministry, the Ministry of Finance would become a treasurer's office serving all of the economic activity. Instead of a minister of finance who acts as an allocator, there would be a strong minister of export who would assign funds for essential investment in export industry. Third would be a Ministry of Foreign Affairs to deal with Israel's foreign relations and also assist in expanding its export markets in the world. Fourth would be a Ministry of the Interior to provide all of the essential services—police, law, health, and the like—with minimal interference in private life. Finally, there would be a Ministry of Education, Academia, and Labor, which would focus much more on vocational education, would guide workers to new jobs created by the expanding export industries, and would handle all of the cultural activity, including the encouragement of artistic work.

I was convinced that we should eliminate the redundancies imposed by the multiplicity of state authorities whose leadership was obliged to pay its supporters in jobs and budgets. In a slimmer government, we could do without the Ministry of Housing, which derives its power from its ability to block independent civil companies from building rental apartments; the Ministry of Transportation, which should be a purely professional body, devoted to transportation and road safety; the Ministry of Social Welfare, which would be unnecessary because my proposed Ministry of Education, Academia, and Labor would create profitable places of employment for everyone; and the Ministry of Health, whose work would be taken over by the Ministry of the Interior. The affairs of agriculture, the police, justice, immigrant absorption, tourism, science, development, communication, environmental protection and religion would be managed within the efficient frameworks of the five government ministries.

Today this is still a dream that is very far from realization. In the foreseeable future, the politicians will continue to present broad and inefficient governments that are primarily intended to generate power for themselves: governments with more than thirty ministers, with and without defined responsibilities. This is because the system, which protects itself, will remain hostile toward true creativity, which, in fact, is the healthy opposite of the system.

The more I realized I was unable to change things, the more I began to feel that each additional day at the Knesset was a waste of time. My patience wore thin for the plenum sessions and committee meetings, the endless speeches and words, the things people said in the corridors and the completely opposite things they said in the Knesset plenum; the empty promises, the political horse trading, and the hypocrisy. I did not know how to create a lobby for my ideas and forge effective alliances, and I was clueless about promoting myself in the media.

I asked the government to prepare a five-year plan that would create more jobs and increase GDP. I organized a special session of the Knesset Economics Committee to discuss the importance of increasing industrial exports. I fought against issuing government bonds to the public, arguing that these bonds con-

Public Service

tributed to the onerous inflation of 100 percent at the time. The Israeli Muslim sect known as the Druze serve in the Israeli Army, and I advocated developing sources of livelihood in the Druze villages for these individuals once they are discharged from service. I encouraged the government and the Histadrut labor federation to jointly create a social contract that would prevent strikes. "Because one thing we cannot permit ourselves," I said, "is wasting a single day of work that does not advance the building of the state."

I called upon the minister of industry, trade and tourism to encourage the transition of workers from the public sector to the manufacturing sector by creating favorable corporate tax rates, as in Switzerland.

In the Knesset session of March 23, 1979, which was devoted to the peace treaty between Israel and Egypt, I congratulated the government on the peace talks and said,

> We need to revise the order of the challenges, from almost exclusively security challenges to both civilian and security challenges. The challenges we need to pose for ourselves now are to reach a Western standard of living that will attract new immigrants and enable us to reach six million Jews by the year 2000. In order to sign peace treaties with the other Arab states . . . we must recognize the fact that some of the reasons for the conflict between us and our neighbors were always land and water. Therefore, we must conclude that the key to the growth of the Jewish society and the absorption of three million Jews is only by creating sources of industrial employment; some of the factories can be situated on the borders, with doors to both sides, constituting a natural bridge between us and our neighbors. Only the posing of scientific and industrial challenges, together with the establishment of new urban cen-

THE HABIT OF LABOR

ters offering clear quality of life, will mark the transition of the Land of Israel from a fortified and conflicted region to a prosperous, cultural, pleasant and industrious region.

I tried to mobilize support among Knesset members for the idea of industrial exports as a key to the state's stability and to excite them with the idea of entrepreneurship, adding, "Give me 1,000 entrepreneurs and the Israeli economy will change completely. One thousand smart entrepreneurs will start 1,000 small enterprises in every corner of the country. And if they follow the right path, choose correct products, become familiar with the markets and their demands, export their products wisely and grow from year to year—we will reach economic independence."[12]

But none of the ministers, including members of my own party, understood my idée fixe. There was a preoccupation with security concerns and efforts to bring inflation under control. I felt that I was perceived at the Knesset as an eccentric or nudnik. The media also only ran after the members of Knesset who ran after them—and who would be interested in proposals that seemed so naïve and unrealistic? I lost the hope of changing something after the first six months of my term. I saw that I was not advancing any of the issues I had set as objectives. I realized that I was a failure as a member of the Knesset.

I also saw how Dash, the *wunderkind* of Israeli politics, which entered the Knesset with high expectations to change Israel from within, was worn down by unrelenting internal disputes and the steamroller that was the Knesset. The poison of allocation—the distribution of means, positions of power, and jobs—also seeped into its ranks.

---

[12] Government meeting No. 206 announcing the peace agreement between Israel and Egypt, March 3, 1979, p. 117.

Public Service

Our new political movement would prove to be very short-lived. Ten months after Dash joined the government, strong pressures developed within the party to leave the ruling coalition. The party's ranks of members had already dwindled, but Yadin, Tamir, and Katz refused to quit the government; Amit hesitated. He became the deciding factor within Dash. The rift widened until it became irreparable, and in August 1978 an agreement was signed to dismantle Dash and divide its assets. From the fragmented party three factions remained, but they, too, were destined to crumble. Some of their members returned to their mother parties; others established one-man factions, and several quit the Knesset completely.

In my years in the Knesset, not a single serious discussion was held on bringing émigrés back from abroad, on the state's educational objectives, or on ways to absorb new immigrants. Most of the debate centered around defense and religion, and on the allocation of budgets and grants. I felt more and more unproductive. No one consulted with me any longer on issues on which I was considered knowledgeable.

Here and there I found common cause with some Knesset members, not necessarily from our faction—members such as Yitzhak Berman, who later became the speaker of the Knesset. He and I tried to facilitate the sale of government factories to the public and to amend tax laws during a period of rampant inflation.

I spoke occasionally with prime minister Menachem Begin, and he came once or twice to visit me in the north. Begin was a perfect Polish gentleman, a man of pleasant conduct and conversation. My impression was that he did not trust anyone except himself. In the matters that I raised before him—industrial parks, for example—he had neither understanding nor interest. He focused solely on the territorial issue: how to expand the borders of the State of Israel. He did not grasp the compelling need to strengthen Israeli society and its economic independence. His successor, Yitzhak Shamir, was no more open to this subject.

There were several other people with whom I found a common language—Avraham Katz-Oz, Moshe Arens, and the late Moshe Dayan, who showed great interest in my ideas about industry and offered his assistance.

My friendship with Allon lasted throughout his lifetime. As a leader he disappointed me; over the years he became a very political person and overly cautious. He never came to the Tefen area and to Kfar Vradim to see them flourishing, even though he was a son of the Galilee and always said that it was very dear to his heart.

In a last-ditch effort to make an impact, I tried to establish the Council for Productive Zionism. I hoped we would be able to constitute a lobby for developing export industries and embark on the third stage of fulfilling Zionism—industry. (The first stage was settling the land through agriculture and construction; the second stage was defending it.) The president of Israel at the time, Yitzhak Navon, agreed to head the council. At our meetings, I came to know creative figures such as Naomi Shemer, Amos Kenan, and Moti Kirshenbaum. We rented an office in Tel Aviv and appointed a director for the council, but the final result was negligible, and the group soon disbanded. I decided, finally, that the time had come for me to resign from the Knesset.

I left the Knesset in February 1981, two months prior to the end of my term, because I wanted to yield my seat to colonel Stella Levy. Apparently no one in the Knesset or in Dash was sorry to see me leave—and, for that matter, neither was I. Precious time had mostly gone to waste; I had flirted with politics

Public Service

for more than a decade. Journalists asked what led to this crazy decision. After all, when had a member of the Knesset decided to resign of his own accord, to leave behind the honors and the focus of media interest?

On February 18, 1981, I delivered my farewell speech at the Knesset podium with a motion titled "Accelerated Industrialization as a Key to Our Zionist Existence." Looking back now after thirty years, there is still validity in the things I said then, and the actions I subsequently took to advance my ideas: "In this state, there are too many people who look after the unfortunate and therefore the unfortunate people do not enter the circle of production, do not regain their dignity and instead become a burden. This is the system I found here in the Knesset."

About a month after my resignation, artist and journalist Amos Kenan published a series of articles in *Yedioth Ahronoth*— and it could be said that his eloquent and persuasive language did more to promote my ideas than my years of frenetic political activity. The articles made waves. Here are samples from two of the many he wrote:

> Switzerland is a green land. But Swiss industry is what ensures that Switzerland will remain green. Serene people live there under red-tiled roofs and hear the cowbells in the meadow, but industry ensures that the red roofs will remain. If not for it, the Swiss would not be able to even eat the cheese they produce.
>
> This week I was in Switzerland.
>
> Switzerland is situated north of Nahariya, almost at the border with Lebanon. And it has the funny name "the industrial zone of Nahariya." But here lies Israel's future, the future of Zionism and, to a considerable extent, the future of the Jewish people.

THE HABIT OF LABOR

Opposite the seashore, which is very blue today, there is a giant lawn. On the lawn is a class of pupils and a teacher. Around them are small buildings, clothed in greenery. And this is not a village and this is not a kibbutz, and it is also not a college campus. This is, all in all, a factory. All in all, an industrial enterprise. Situated here are all of the production facilities of ISCAR, founded by Stef Wertheimer, and they are bringing to Israel this year $50 million.

In the most natural way, Stage C of Zionism should have grown out of Stage B. The defense effort should have established industry. Defense should have created the ideological infrastructure, the motivation and the ethos of the industry of Israel—as a continuation of the defense of Israel and as a continuation of Jewish settlement, and as the crowning achievement of this great enterprise of returning to Zion and of creating a free people, living on its land.

Who knows where to look for the failure and the disconnection? Did the defense establishment fossilize from the social perspective? Did it remain locked into an outlook ("conception") from bygone days and thus fail to take the necessary steps to jump forward? Was it simply a case here of wear and tear, and the ideological ammunition ran out? Is the paradox that says in order to be stronger and more independent we must be more dependent on the United States the ultimate source of this disconnection? Is the great military power we built, and which is entirely propped up by the "free world," the obstacle on which we stumbled?[13]

---

[13] Amos Kenan, "Industry Is Beautiful," *Yedioth Ahronoth*, March 27, 1981.

Public Service

Two real achievements, at least, I took with me from the Knesset: first, the right to act as a trustee for the establishment of Kfar Vradim, a new and different type of industrial community; and second, official approval for establishing ten industrial parks to house new export factories and provide an initial boost for creative entrepreneurship.

The idea of industrial parks had been in my mind even earlier, but it began to move toward implementation when I was asked to chair a committee aimed at assisting failing factories. We reached clear conclusions: what was important was not to rehabilitate failing factories but to rapidly promote initiatives for small export manufacturing enterprises seeking to expand. We devised a basic framework of several small export businesses under a single roof. The committee's report recommended establishing ten such industrial parks throughout the country. (My six industrial parks in Israel seem to have inspired the construction of another three that are now fully operational, near Rosh Pina, at Bar Lev, and near Sahknin. So the goal has almost been reached, and I hope the work will continue.)

The finance minister and the minister of industry and labor adopted the report in 1980. They appointed me to chair the public committee to coordinate the formation of the parks, select the entrepreneurs, instruct them, organize the services they required, and supervise their operation.

But the story of Israel's first industrial park starts earlier, in the story of Kfar Vradim, which is the continuation of the story of the Tefen region—and, in fact, the story of the struggle to settle and industrialize the Galilee with our Druze and Arab neighbors.

CHAPTER 8

FOUNDING A VILLAGE

Tefen's beautiful hill of green pines overlooking the town of Ma'alot was in 1979 a realization of a worldview.

This worldview was Zionist from the outset, addressing the independence of the Jewish people in their land. The dream of settling and industrializing the Galilee and the Negev is the third stage of Zionism, after the agricultural and construction stage and the defense stage. To best develop these peripheral areas, there is a need to find sources of employment for all their residents—Jews, Arabs, Bedouins, Druze, and the Circassians, a group of about four thousand Sunni Muslims whose men, like the Druze, serve in the Israeli Army.

I have, to date, built six industrial parks in the peripheral areas of Israel. Five of them are in the Galilee, ranging from the northernmost Tel Hai Industrial Park on the Lebanese border near Kiryat Shmona to the Dalton, Tefen, and Lavon Industrial Parks in the Lower Galilee, to the Nazareth Industrial Park in the Western Galilee, to the south is Omer Industrial Park in the Negev near Beersheva. To strengthen our ties with Turkey, I also built a park in Gebze with Turkish partners in 2005.

The story of the industrial park initiative began in Tefen, a region at the edge of Israel about ten kilometers from the

Lebanese border between Ma'alot and Karmiel. It is about a two-hour drive from the center of the country.

Today, from the hilltop of Kfar Vradim, it is possible to see the green campuses of the industrial park filled with sculptures and the complex of ISCAR and other factories. Not far from there, to the southeast, on a small and green hill overlooking Karmiel and Deir al-Assad is Lavon, a community that has been renewed and is now flourishing with a successful industrial park and a good education center. Nearby are other communities: Kishurit (a rehabilitative community for the disabled), Har Halutz, Lapidot, Tuval, Pelech, and the Druze villages of Yanuh-Jat and Kisra-Samia. Next to the communities are olive groves and rocky hills, arid in the summer and blooming and alive with colors in the spring.

The Tefen Initiative began with a persistent sense that we must not allow the Galilee to remain desolate and neglected. The Yom Kippur War further intensified this feeling. What would have happened if the war had reached the Galilee? How would its sparse and dispersed community have withstood the dangers?

After the war I told Haim Bar-Lev, who was then minister of trade and industry, that we needed to do something in the Galilee to populate it. We tried to jointly formulate an initial plan and possible locations. I told him, "Haim, you're thinking like a grasshopper, hopping from one security area to another. I, on the other hand, think like an ink stain that slowly expands. I think about an area that will provide the current and future residents—Jews and non-Jews—a suitable standard of living, steady employment, and security."

When I suggested to Bar-Lev the construction of a continuous line of sophisticated industrial enterprises that would start near Kabri, he was enthusiastic. But it quickly became apparent that the local kibbutz members did not like the idea, and the leaders of Ma'alot were opposed. Bar-Lev was evidently pressured by the Labor party, and he caved in. However, I did not give up.

There were also more prosaic reasons for fighting for the idea. Nahariya's leaders thought about industry in distorted terms. For twenty years they dumped Nahariya's garbage opposite my ISCAR factories. We needed to think about another place, one cleaner and more beautiful, quieter, smarter, and more productive. Thus, we relocated ISCAR's operations to Tefen, adjacent to Kfar Vradim.

I started work on the idea of a planned village, a living model of the future Israel. I drew the inspiration from Tapiola in Finland, a city of people from various income levels, many of whom are employed in local factories. Many artists came to this city to live and create there, and the University of Finland also opened a branch there. The city is built in uniform construction and receives uniform utility services.

I believed many families would be interested in sharing this dream, and I hoped that the government would implement the idea. However, because there was no progress, I decided to independently establish a model community for the government authorities to adopt.

The idea of Kfar Vradim preceded the idea of the industrial park, though I always knew that a new town must have its own sources of employment. We chose a hill adjacent to Ma'alot for the future community, but then strong opposition started to mount. I never imagined the tribulations an Israeli would need to overcome to build a community in a remote area of the Galilee. I had no idea that those coming to live in this new community—taxpaying citizens, who fulfill all of their civic duties—would have to fight for their rights. This is a community whose residents sought to build it with their own money, without being dependent on state entities. Yet every possible mine was planted in our path during the seven years that passed until Kfar Vradim stood securely on its land.

The strong opposition was completely unexpected. There were those who claimed I wished to garner publicity for myself and for Dash. Others declared that we were exploiting the state, the neighboring immigrant community of Ma'alot, and the Druze villages Me'iliya, Yanuh-Jat, and Kisra-Samia. Some saw the idea as a megalomanic, arrogant, or racist campaign.

A few friends suggested the beautiful Tefen region as a place to implement my idea. I asked Arik Sharon, then the minister of agriculture, to allocate land for this project. Sharon, unlike others, helped to expedite the process. On his directive, the Israel Lands Administration rezoned a bit of land. The truth is that any other entrepreneur could have received similar land if he had committed to investing hundreds of millions of shekels in building infrastructure for hundreds of the initial homes in the new community without a profit motive and had agreed to wait ten or twenty years until beginning to receive a return on his investment.

In 1979 we signed a contract with the Israel Lands Administration to develop 7,250 dunams (1,792 acres). We also exchanged lands with the local Druze. We received final approval in early 1981 for an area of about 5,500 dunams (1,359 acres).

About a year earlier we had placed a newspaper ad inviting people to contact us if they were interested in living a quality life in the Galilee, in nature, far from the hubbub of the cities. The ad showed a bicycle rider, with a rainbow in the background, and this image still appears at the entrance of Kfar Vradim.

Our idea struck a chord: an initial meeting at the Penguin

Founding a Village

Café in Nahariya drew hundreds, most of them young families. In August 1980 we invited them for a tour of the spacious Tefen area, a twenty-minute drive from Nahariya. I was amazed to see how the entire hill was covered with a large crowd of people excited by the idea.

In September of that year, the Israeli government's Settlement Committee and the Jewish Agency approved the establishment of the community, but the mayor of neighboring Ma'alot, Shlomo Bochbut, began a vocal campaign against the plan because he wanted Kfar Vradim to be integrated into the jurisdiction of his city. If this were not the case, he warned that an independent Kfar Vradim would transform Ma'alot into the source of a cheap labor force for the new city, which would be devoid of welfare cases.

I argued that this was slander, because I always had been involved in helping disadvantaged individuals become productive people, and all who wished to improve their situation and become productive members of society would certainly be warmly accepted in Kfar Vradim. It was inconceivable to me that the desire to settle the Galilee could be contingent on the approval of Ma'alot's leadership.

In response, Ma'alot renounced its membership in the Association for the Development of the Western Galilee. Bochbut also later threatened to initiate legal action against Kfar Vradim if the government did not withdraw its support for the new village.

Thus I found myself in a confrontation that purportedly entailed exploitation versus deprivation; wealth and progress versus poverty, backwardness, and ethnic disparity; and Ashkenazim versus Mizrahim (Jews from Europe or Eastern Europe versus Jews from Spain or the Middle East). These definitions, which portrayed the founders of the village, its residents, and

THE HABIT OF LABOR

me as bad guys and exploiters, were ugly and contrary to everything I believed in. We did not wage a war of words, however. We tried to lower the flames, to explain that everyone—including Ma'alot-Tarshiha, the planned Kfar Vradim, the Arab neighbors, the Galilee, and the people of Israel—would ultimately benefit.

I hoped that the dispute would be solved via compromise. I noted at the time that the idea was not to build another development town in the Galilee but instead to create something new. The city would indeed enjoy the status of a development town to encourage investment in industrialization, but the difference would be that each new resident would need to bring an original "dowry": an ability to contribute to the region, whether in industry, educational services, or another field. I also said that what Jews were lacking, among other things, were roots in the soil of the homeland.

We came to realize that each of the potential residents had a plan for a "dream home" in mind. Clearly it was impossible to satisfy Israeli individualism with planning architectural uniformity as in Finland, but we decided to maintain a common aesthetic discipline and collective responsibility to unify the community.

Shmulik Eyal began to coordinate the project and consulted with James Rouse, the well-known American city planner who had designed a new city, Columbia, between Baltimore and Washington, DC. The concept was a "capitalist kibbutz"—homes in an open landscape, situated close together (also due to financial constraints, since the costly infrastructure work was at our expense), and gathered around a shared center for security (the border is nearby) and for creating a sense of community. The planning foresaw three stages of development until reaching a population of ten thousand people. We also understood that modern telecommunications could turn any distant community into a central point; thus, each house in the village would be connected via underground cables to computer terminals and cable television. On April 9, 1981, we laid the cornerstone for Kfar Vradim; Israel's president Yitzhak Navon delivered words of welcome at the ceremony.

The relations with Ma'alot-Tarshiha were improving. I felt that many jobs would be created for local residents when ISCAR moved its factories to Tefen, and this indeed occurred. We also built two small factories in Ma'alot, each of them employing about ten workers: ISCAR Saws, producing saws and rotaries for woodworking, and ISCAR Coatings.

Mayor Bochbut succeeded in shaking Ma'alot free from the accepted Israeli image of development towns. He became convinced that the solution for such towns was not the perpetuation of government assistance funds to silence complaints and preserve dependence on the political parties. As an active mayor, he started to encourage private initiative and investments in export industries in Ma'alot, lowered municipal taxes, and helped each new enterprise to get started. Today the unemployment rate in Ma'alot is low, and the city is self-confident, advanced, and beautiful, with well-groomed neighborhoods of single-family homes and its own active industrial zone. A number of Ma'alot residents today hold key positions in ISCAR and in other enterprises in the area. Kfar Vradim raised the value of Ma'alot, and vice versa. The city's relations with the neighboring non-Jewish population are fair and good. In this way, all of us benefited from this proximity, which started out on the wrong foot.

On Friday, April 28, 2006, I was honored by Bochbut at a ceremony held at the Ma'alot Music Conservatory. This award was given "in recognition and appreciation for [my] work in the field of industry and in promoting the development of the Galilee, and the city of Ma'alot in particular." During the course of my life, I have received many prizes, awards, and citations. But this award, I think, is a milestone in the complex relations that prevailed for many years between Ma'alot-Tarshiha and Tefen, the industrial park and ISCAR—and between Bochbut and me. In December 2013, Mayor Bochbut presented me with another, similar award.

The lessons derived from the way this long-term disagreement was resolved are relevant for the basic issues that Israeli society faces. Kfar Vradim shows that it is possible to do things independently, despite obstacles and narrow-mindedness. Just as it is possible to reproduce one successful industrial park many times in all parts of the country—and emerging export enterprises in each park—with almost no government assistance, it is also possible to establish many other communities like Kfar Vradim throughout the country.

However, I cannot complete the story of the creation of Kfar Vradim without talking about the bitter pills some of the government authorities have forced upon the village's leadership, its residents, and me over the past thirty years. The obstructive efforts of then minister of the interior Aryeh Deri set the project back ten years. Even today, the residents of the village suffer discrimination. The Ministry of the Interior did not recognize us as a community in all respects for a decade, while neighboring Ma'alot enjoyed such recognition. The Israel Lands Administration prevented us from continuing to expand the village; and the Ministry of Education, as well as other ministries, did not assist us. The government seems to do all it can to hamper progress.

Nonetheless, when I glance out the window of my office,

Founding a Village

I see Tefen and Kfar Vradim blossoming, with numerous factories, in an area that was mostly desolate thirty years ago. In this area Jews and Arabs are living in close proximity, participating in its educational systems and industries.

CHAPTER 9

THE GREAT BREAKTHROUGH

ISCAR started out in 1952 in our small home in Nahariya, with me as the sole manager, worker, and salesman. Later, the first two employees joined me. Today, in the framework of the IMC Corporation (now part of Berkshire Hathaway), there are more than twelve thousand five hundred people working at ISCAR in Israel and abroad. This success in gradually growing from a tiny family workshop to huge factories in Israel and the world, and the sale of the company to Warren Buffett would not have been possible without the work and dedication of thousands of employees at ISCAR.

Among all of them, Yossi Pano was truly unique. He came to me as a skinny youth during ISCAR's second year. Who imagined then that this teenager, who actually wanted to be a pilot, would ultimately bring ISCAR its greatest success story?

Yossi Pano: Basic Concepts

Cutting tool: A steel rod or bar with a piece of hard metal attached to its end by silver soldering in a corresponding indentation. This piece of metal is sharpened with a diamond to make an edge that can cut all sorts of metal.

THE HABIT OF LABOR

Hard metal: Metal made of tungsten (wolfram) powder in a carbon shell, which is consolidated with a binder material (cobalt) and undergoes a process of high-pressure compression and sintering at a very high temperature. Hard metal was first developed at the Krupp steel factories in Germany and was called *widia* (short for *wie Diamant*, "like diamond") because of its hardness, which was compared to the hardness of a diamond; this enables it, after molding, to cut very hard metals. It is commonly known as tungsten carbide or simply carbide.

Chipping: Cutting and removing chips from metal to mold it into the desired form and dimensions. Using cutting tools of hard metal, this is the most common method of metalworking for producing precision forms for parts in all types of modern industry. Modern machines reach a precision of 0.01 millimeter (a tenth of the width of a hair) thanks in part to the enhanced durability of cutting tools.

The great success of ISCAR, which became an important international leader in its field, begins with the story of the Self-Grip small parting tool and continues with the story of the HeliMill multi-purpose milling blade and many other revolutionary breakthroughs in the field of metalworking. ISCAR, it should be noted, focuses on industry for industrialists; you will not find our tools on the shelf at the hardware store. Our products are primarily designed for use as essential tools in metalworking. Automobile and aeronautic plants, factories producing electronic products with high metal content, and the shipping and arms industries—all these and many other

The Great Breakthrough

industries require extremely strong and durable tools capable of cutting steel with great precision.

In this specialized arena a relatively small number of international companies compete against one other. ISCAR has established itself as a leader due to the good reputation of its products and its strict adherence to contractual conditions and timetables. The company has continually developed, expanding markets, exports, and production. In 1975, ISCAR's worldwide sales totaled about $5 million. Nonetheless, there was a feeling that we were not making progress. This feeling disappeared when the Self-Grip was invented.

In the metalworking tool industry, there are very few real inventions. Most companies copy one other, producing identical products or making minor alterations. The invention we introduced to the international market in 1976 was brilliant in its simplicity. The other manufacturers in the world mumbled in amazement, "Why didn't we think of this?" Giant companies, whose annual turnover was thirty times larger than ours and which had looked at us with derision, started to get nervous.

Until the 1970s ISCAR did not have a large range of unique products and did not carry much weight in the international market. Our development activity was not advanced. We had a milling tool called Iscamill, but it was already quite old. Newer and more efficient versions of this sort of tool had appeared. But the company had accrued knowledge and experience over the years in producing tools from hard metal—particularly in tools for cutting metal.

If you are thinking now of a sort of traditional knife with a blade and handle, please throw aside that image. Instead, imagine a flat sheet of steel, rectangular, with a small and sharp piece of harder metal attached to one of its ends. This can be visual-

THE HABIT OF LABOR

ized as a steel jaw with a tooth, and this tooth—which professionals call an insert and which is made of the hardest of metals—is the knife's cutting edge. In our industry, the quality of the tool is measured by its precision, the depth of cut it can perform, its strength, and its durability.

One of the problems we encountered was that the inserts we produced wore down quickly. The small and narrow cutting edge could not bear the whole load of cutting metal over time, and could not contain the full strength of the heat generated during the work. There was a vicious circle here. On the one hand, the heat generated when the blade met the metal increased over time, partly due to the bending of the metal chip created during the cutting. On the other hand, as the blade became hotter, this chip became thicker and the metal being cut became softer. Thus, as the heat increased, the blade's precision decreased and the flaws became more numerous.

The chips produced during the process of metalworking are one of the most difficult problems. They are peeled from the metal, curl, and become entangled, become thicker from the heat, clog the machines, cause temperatures to rise through friction and bending, impede their own removal and disposal, and can also become a real risk of injury to the worker if they fly out from the machine.

Another weak point of the tool was the connection between the insert and its steel base, the root connecting the jaw to the tooth. How do you prevent the tooth from moving? Traditionally, the insert was welded to the steel base, but the welding would weaken and fall apart, especially if two different metals like steel (the softer one) and hard metal were connected. Later we tried to attach the insert to the base with a special clamp, but the problem was not solved. Then we developed large inserts with a recess drilled for a screw, but even this did not help much.

The Great Breakthrough

Yossi Pano knew that whoever succeeded in curing the cutting tools from these weaknesses would hit the jackpot. In his spare time as a technical manager and cost accountant in 1973, he developed a new version of a parting tool we called the Cut-Off whose unique feature was to grip the insert, the cutting blade, and clamp it between two concave steel prisms, as in a vise. In 1975, we were awarded a US patent for this tool. The success of the Cut-Off was only partial, but it led to future successes.

In 1975 the Swedish manufacturing giant Sandvik displayed an innovative parting tool called T-Max at an exhibition in Paris; it became the star of the exhibition when its lathe cut a strip of railroad track. This development stirred our curiosity; Yossi wanted to design an alternative parting tool that would be capable of cutting various diameters of steel, with a narrow cutting width and considerable depth, and that would succeed in reaching 80 percent of the Swedish tool's performance and reliability. Yossi asked me to approve a budget for eighteen hundred inserts for experimentation. I said to him, "If we're already doing this, let's prepare two thousand inserts." And thus Yossi started working, circumventing the customary procedures of planning and production.

From his experience in the partial failure of the Cut-Off, Yossi drew two important conclusions: the first was to reverse the steel prisms clamping the insert at both sides from female to male, from a recess to a protrusion, in order to reinforce the steel construction, which was traditionally the weak link in the connection; the second took into account that since the conventional means of reinforcing the steel were not sufficiently durable in heat, and the screw hindered deep cuts, it was necessary to shift the load to the insert itself because it is harder and stronger than the steel that is clamping it. The solution was found in designing the base for the insert, the root, like a cone-shaped wedge imbedded in the steel. In the new structure, a light push was sufficient to affix the insert in place. The pressure created when starting the metal cutting work only tightened its grip on the steel instead of weakening it. This was the "self-grip" concept that gave the tool its name.

But the successful embedding of the blade in the socket without the aid of a screw solved only one problem; the problem of the chips still remained. Yossi tried to control the thickness of the chips, to make them thinner so that they would not hinder the cutting work. He experimented with unconventional designs of parting tools with small recesses or protrusions. He designed dozens of models of inserts with a chip breaker, but without real success. One day, nearly in despair, he used brute force on the grinding wheel he was using to sharpen an insert. He later tried the sharpened insert during work and, finally, the chip he had hoped for emerged from under the experimental parting knife: thinner, rolled up, dense, and small, like a watch spring.

"I felt like Archimedes when he jumped out of the bathtub," Yossi said when he rushed to tell me about the success.

And thus a new invention was born, a revolutionary development in the history of metalworking tools. The solution that Yossi discovered, almost by chance, in the correct grinding of the insert (which later underwent a series of improvements) changed ISCAR and opened the world for us.

The name Self-Grip describes the blade's revolutionary ability to hold itself with great stability in its steel base without welding, screwing, or clamping. In fact, we later learned that in 1886 a patent was registered in the United States on the principle of self-tightening, but no one could have dreamed then of the advanced technology with which it could be implemented.

The Great Breakthrough

When the Self-Grip was presented to us, we still did not realize its huge marketing potential. On the contrary, some of our best people doubted whether the new tool could be sold at all without the screw attached to its base; after all, the world only bought parting tools connected to their bases by a screw. There was even a senior manager who suggested, in all seriousness, that we attach a fake screw (whose purpose would be only psychological) to each insert base of the Self-Grip.

The Self-Grip was displayed for the first time at a trade show in Japan in October 1976 and stirred attention. After the exhibition, Yossi continued to improve the product, changing angles and ratios. But it was amusing to discover years later that a Japanese manufacturer, who was so impressed by the performance of the initial Self-Grip product he saw at the exhibition, had produced it with all of its original shortcomings.

In 1977 we submitted Yossi's candidacy for the Rothschild Prize, awarded to those who contribute to industrial development for exporting. ISCAR's marketing volume was then about $7.5 million a year. But in the form for submitting his candidacy, we wrote that the product he developed had an annual sales volume of $4 million, a huge sum for ISCAR at the time. The reality far surpassed our boldest dreams, however: in 1978–79, our export sales of the Self-Grip reached about $5 million and continued to grow. The Israeli patent rapidly conquered the markets, became the company's primary economic engine—about 70 percent of the exports and about 80 percent of the profits—and led to great expansion of ISCAR. New branches opened in various countries, and ISCAR started to become a familiar name everywhere.

We witnessed its full power in the practical demonstrations of the Self-Grip for prospective customers, for example, when Yossi came to demonstrate the tools we specially built for

THE HABIT OF LABOR

the American Motors Corporation (AMC) for grooving camshafts. Everyone was astonished. Until then, AMC's grooving process took two and a half minutes per unit, but five more minutes were required for removing the processed part in the lathe from the many chips that got entangled around it and for collecting the chips in a special container. When Yossi conducted a demonstration of our Self-Grip, the tiny chips curled up and disappeared. When the local lathe operator saw there were no chips, he called his manager in frenzy. "No chips!" the manager shouted in amazement. It was a real revolution.

Within a year or so our work was directed at manufacturing and marketing Self-Grip products to meet the demand, which grew exponentially. I became concerned about a slowdown in developing other products, for a range of products is essential in a company like ISCAR. Therefore, I asked Yossi to leave all of his other roles and focus on a single mission: to design and develop a variety of products. He began sketching tools of different sizes for face grooving and prepared an initial catalog of dozens of steel clamps and insert grips, as well as inserts of various widths.

We looked at the extensive proposal and decided to narrow it to focus our activity on increasing our penetration of export markets. We removed products that we were less proficient in making or were producing at only an average standard and concentrated instead on what we really excelled in making. Someone who wants to be a good musician cannot focus on string instruments in general; he must choose between a cello and a viola and reach the highest level of achievement with his chosen instrument.

The new tool Yossi designed was the Cut-Grip, whose uniqueness was in precise grooving, with an insert that cut on both of its ends. For this purpose the Self-Grip was not sufficient, and it was necessary to return to the traditional screw to attach the blade to the steel so that it could withstand the hard action of penetrating the steel and moving in it. Moreover, the cutting tool of the Cut-Grip reached extraordinary sizes. A blade Yossi made to demonstrate cutting a steel pipe 9 meters in diameter (354 inches) was 600 millimeters long (24 inches), with a peak height of 150 millimeters (6 inches) and a cutting depth of 300 millimeters (12 inches). This type of cutting action previously took three and a half days. With ISCAR's tool, the pipe was cut after four and a half hours, with two and a half tons of chips piled up on the sides.

    Yossi also developed an effective chip breaker for the Cut-Grip, and in 1983 this product stirred great interest at an exhibition in Tel Aviv. The load of orders and production of the Self-Grip made it impossible to also begin to manufacture the new product, however; it was only in 1985 that Eitan decided not to delay production and assigned the responsibility to our Microdent factory, which until then made grinding inserts for the Self-Grip. Some doubted whether Microdent would be able to perform this mission, but the factory and its manager, Haim Cohen, proved able and the new blade soon hit the markets.

    This was not before we had a pleasant surprise. The Cut-Grip, which was designed to cut a groove in metal, is also capable of cutting to the side due to its great stability. This feature, which is not characteristic of similar tools, gives it durability against the side forces of the penetrated metal. In the area of grooving, we had faced many competitors, giant corporations with great advantages in the markets. Many parting tools could also be used in a limited way to cut into the sides. But to enter to a depth of three or four millimeters with a blade and cut to the sides, and then penetrate deeper and again cut to the sides, and to do all of this with great precision—this was quite unconventional. ISCAR had once again created a revolution.

THE HABIT OF LABOR

Indeed, in ten years ISCAR's sales grew more than tenfold, from $5 million a year in 1975 to $52 million a year in 1985. In 1990, ISCAR was seen as one of the world's leading manufacturers for metalworking companies, with sales of $165 million. The clearest sign of success was the blitz of imitations; many competing manufacturers unabashedly began to copy our unique products. Although this flattered our team pride, the copies could detract from our exclusivity in this market and hurt our profits, and the various means of protection—patent registration, lawsuits, and the like—were slow and insufficient.

We continued to work on additional developments. In 1990 ISCAR presented another revolutionary product: the HeliMill milling tool. The field of milling and drilling tools is several times larger and broader than the field of parting and turning tools. Amir Satran, an engineer at ISCAR, developed a spiral milling tool that could perform various functions at speeds four times faster than regular cutting tools. The revolution, in terms of the world of metalworking, was only the beginning. In 1987, ISCAR's exports in the field of milling tools totaled about $1 million, but three years later, in 1990, we reached $20 million thanks to the HeliMill. The product's development was still at an early stage, and more advances awaited it.

CHAPTER **10**

INDUSTRIAL PARKS: A WAY TO ENSURE THE FUTURE

How could it be that on a former goat pasture in the Galilee each industrial worker manufactures and exports more than $200,000 worth of goods per year? How is it possible that on this same hill about 10 percent of the State of Israel's industrial exports are produced by 1 percent of Israel's population, with an annual turnover of about $2 billion, comparable to the entire Jerusalem region?

The answer lies in the Tefen Model, which has generated more than two hundred factories and companies in Israeli industrial parks, producing a level of exports similar to industrial zones in the United States, the European Union, and Japan. The Tefen Model is a successful economic initiative that focuses on five overlapping circles: export industries, technical and entrepreneurial education, community development, cultural initiatives, and coexistence **Export industries,** the Model's first circle, are important for several reasons. They strengthen a country's economy and also foster understanding and ties among trading partners throughout the world. They create jobs, attract foreign investment, and direct a society's energies into positive, future-oriented initiatives.

THE HABIT OF LABOR

The Model's second circle, **technical and entrepreneurial education,** is the mainstay of industry. Israel's relative lack of natural resources has actually been a blessing, forcing it to turn instead to its major asset: its human resources. A dynamic economy rests on a skilled workforce. Because Israel has not yet reached its potential in this field, education remains one of my primary concerns. To this end, in some of my parks are technical schools for high school pupils and adults, training for professional teachers and an institute for training Meisters (master craftspeople); I am partnering with Europe's foremost research institute, the Fraunhofer Institute, for promoting practical academic research in the field of robotics and materials here in Israel. I have also introduced the techniques of a dual system in which one studies in a classroom for part of the time and employs what he or she has learned as an apprentice in industry for the remainder of the time.

My industrial parks provide an incubator space for emerging companies. There, budding entrepreneurs have the services they need to build strong export-oriented enterprises, e.g., a post office, an employment office, patent attorneys, and a congenial atmosphere where they can welcome their customers.

The third component of the Tefen Model is **community development.** My industrial parks are located close to some of the highest quality communities in Israel, such as Kfar Vradim, Lavon, and Omer, Tefen, and Tel Hai. These communities—some of which I built myself—are vital in attracting talented employees to the parks' firms. Hopefully, similar communities will be built and will flourish adjacent to the other industrial parks.

Culture is also an integral part of the Tefen Model. A workplace with attractive buildings, well-manicured lawns, sculpture gardens, art museums, concerts, children's activities, and community events, demonstrates without words the creative force that industry embodies. All of my seven parks have cultural components that help to eradicate the no-longer-valid image of industry as a low-level and dirty endeavor.

The last circle, **co-existence**, is also of great concern to me. Since the beginning of ISCAR, I have had an integrated workforce. My aim has always been to find the best person for the job, regardless of his or her ethnic background, religion, age, or gender. That just makes good business sense. There is also no better way to foster trust and understanding than to bring Israel's various sectors together in the workplace.

While the Tefen Model is a new approach, the basic idea of an industrial park is not. I strongly believe that one can achieve success by taking an existing idea and simply improving on it. The initial concept of an industrial park, in fact, appeared long before my birth. In the mid-1860s in the German town of Hoechst, near Frankfurt, an aniline dye company created a factory and housing for its workers. It assumed a different and more modern form several decades ago, when Western Europe underwent reindustrialization. In the Ruhr Valley in Germany, they looked for new opportunities for unemployed workers. The initial industrial parks were built in outlying regions, where they created vocational schools to train people to become highly skilled industrial workers.

This idea of industrial parks germinated in my mind during the strike by textile workers in Beit She'an in 1976, which repeated itself at the Kitan Dimona factory and reached a tragic peak in its closure and the subsequent firing of the factory's long-time employees in 1985. I thought that what was happening was scandalous, and that employees deserved economic and personal security and a high quality of life.

My aim was to demonstrate that even in a far-removed setting it was possible to develop sophisticated industry that could compete internationally. The industrial park would have a center with a dining hall shared by all of the factories in the park, like a kibbutz dining hall—a place where workers, sales personnel, and managers would eat together, with the camaraderie of people working for a common goal. Thus, the country's periphery would be as attractive and efficient as its center.

In 1979, as a member of the Knesset, I formulated the idea in an initial motion titled "A Proposal to Convert and Rehabilitate Failing Factories." The bill aimed to prepare Israeli industry to meet the challenges of the coming decade and to improve the image of industry. Changing this image is perhaps more important for us Jews than for any other people due to the centuries of discrimination in Europe that forbade us to become skilled craftspeople or to join guilds. To implement the transition, I proposed establishing ten industrial parks throughout the country. Each such park would include three components: a training center, an industrial area, and a services area.

The training center would include a school for adults seeking to acquire an industrial vocation and a technology center to provide advanced training for industrial workers. The industrial area would be built around the training center and would comprise industrial buildings of two hundred to a thousand square meters each. Young entrepreneurs would rent space in these buildings with leased equipment to lighten the burden of their initial investment. Seasoned industrialists would help the beginners in manufacturing, marketing, and other matters. And when they reach a production volume of $1–1.5 million after three to five years, they would be encouraged to leave the park for larger and more independent facilities.

In this way the industrial park would provide incentive to entrepreneurship in industry, would prevent many of our children from fleeing overseas with their talents, would bring back Israeli emigrants, and would help to secure the future of industry.

To date, each of my seven industrial parks is based on the Tefen Model. Arie Dahan has managed this challenging project for the past twenty-seven years.

TEFEN INDUSTRIAL PARK, 1984

The Tefen area, formerly under the jurisdiction of the Druze Regional Council Ma'aleh Hagalil, was earmarked in the early 1980s to provide employment for the mountain ridge communities. The government-owned Industrial Buildings Corporation managed the land, flattened its contours, and built infrastructure including paved roads. When I visited it for the first time, there was a lone factory for producing batteries, Vulcan, that was polluting the environment with lead. I leased the land from the state, and in 1982 I moved the ISCAR factory in Nahariya to Tefen, creating modern buildings to house it with the help of my late friend, the architect Moshe Zarhi.

I then started to plan my first industrial park across from the ISCAR complex. Together with South African–born architect Harry Brand, we designed the first industrial park: a large center and twenty small and clean industries among lawns, trees, a sculpture garden, and a museum. The combination of the natural landscape with art, modern architecture, and industry enhances the quality of life for those who live and work in the area. The idea arose in a conversation with Amos Kenan, who helped demonstrate the creative aspects of industry.

Industrial work, which demands precision and beauty as well as craftsmanship of the hands and mind, is parallel to artistic creation. Amos suggested that we build a sculpture garden

THE HABIT OF LABOR

that would blend in with the natural setting and the buildings. In this way we created a completely new environment that combines serenity, culture, beauty, and a space for work and creative activity.

In those days the government even helped us, though it was a short period of support that quickly ended. The park was placed under the administrative purview of the ministers of trade and industry, finance, and labor. We set forth criteria for the entrepreneurs accepted for this first and all subsequent industrial parks: the quality of their product, its standard of production and market promise, and a clear business plan.

At the beginning of 1982, following a year and a half of construction, we laid the cornerstone for the Tefen Industrial Park. The park opened in 1984, with fifteen start-up enterprises. Soon thereafter, Chaim Herzog came to visit us; he had just become the sixth president of Israel in March of that year. Son of the chief rabbi of Ireland, Herzog was seventeen years old when he left Ireland to join the nascent Jewish state in Palestine. In World War II, he served as a tank commander for the British Army in Germany; he became a distinguished military leader here in Israel before opening a legal practice.

In addition, I brought American lecturers to teach the entrepreneurs and others from the region—highly respected professors of business, such as the late Richard Rosenbloom from the Harvard Business School; Edward Roberts, the David Sarnoff Professor of Management of Technology for the Sloan School of Business at the Massachusetts Institute of Technology (MIT); and, more recently, Jean-Pierre Jeannet, who served for many years as a professor of business at Babson College. With others I also organized an exhibition of industry in the Galilee. We included the Galilee communities in all these efforts to transform our region.

Industrial Parks: A Way to Ensure the Future

The first enterprise that entered the park was Adimek (today Tefen Metal Casting). It was joined by three other enterprises, all of which today are large, successful companies: Patrus, which manufactured fine glass tubes for the Intel factory; USR, a company for electronic components; and KP Electronic Systems, which has international annual sales of about $10 million.

Stepac L.A., which Israel Ben-Tzur and his wife Shosh started at Tefen in 1993, provides an interesting tale of the surprising path entrepreneurship can take. Israel and Shosh, who were trained as a psychologist and a mathematician, respectively, had spent some years living in Los Angeles, where they founded a company that made medical products. On their return to Israel they started another company, CARERITE sterile packaging.

One of their staff members once put cucumbers in one of the sterile bags and then forgot the package was there. Weeks later, when she opened the bag, the cucumbers were still quite fresh. The Ben-Tzurs had the packaging material tested, and what resulted was a new product that became very successful worldwide: Xtend, a special line of wrapping that prolongs the shelf life of fresh produce, each product slightly different to conform to the type of fruit or vegetable that it is protecting.

Recently the Ben-Tzurs sold that firm and have started a new company called BT9. They have headed in an entirely new direction, one that uses highly sophisticated equipment to track produce from before it is even harvested to the store where it will be sold. This end-to-end cold-chain management solution promises to save millions of dollars in protecting food from spoilage and will also be used for other sensitive products such as pharmaceuticals.

OTI, a company producing smart electronic cards, also started out in the Tefen Industrial Park and is now a large factory

THE HABIT OF LABOR

in the Tzahar Industrial Zone in the Galilee. Later came Micro Tools, which succeeded in the international market with its mechanical tools and very small and precise electronic parts; this enterprise later became part of ISCAR and expanded its range of products. Kobi Ben-Zvi also started his enterprise, PMS, at Tefen. The company specialized in manufacturing computerized systems with artificial intelligence technology, primarily in computer software for the insurance firms of large hospitals in the world. Ben-Zvi is a native Israeli who went to the United States, succeeded in his field, and returned home after persuading his parent company to establish PMS Israel.

We strive to have a range of products at the park. A Druze woman named Gamila Hiar (who is known as Savta Gamila, or Grandmother Gamila) from the nearby village of Peqei'in has been in the park for nearly a decade now, producing her very successful line of herbal skin-care products called Gamila's Secret with a minimum of machinery. She employs dozens of women from the area who produce items that are sold in countries throughout the world. In creating this business she was able to convince her son Fuad to return from the Netherlands, where he was serving as a guard for El Al, the Israeli airline. Thus industry becomes a vehicle for family reunification.

The other entrepreneurs at Tefen are also originals, full of a desire to succeed in their mission. Over the years, only one enterprise folded, and that was due to a dispute between the partners. A wide range of new export businesses has developed there, from the simplest products (silk prints, jewelry, industrial graphic design, soaps, and photography) to products employing the most advanced technologies, such as SanDisk, whose flash memory cards are used in cell phones, digital cameras, and other devices.

Industrial Parks: A Way to Ensure the Future

The industrial park soon came to nurture not only products but also culture. The Open Museum opened its doors to visitors in 1984, and our exhibition hall opened in 1987 with an impressive exhibition of works by the famous artist M. C. Escher. Ami Shavit was asked to assume the initial management of the museum, and then my good friend, the late Amos Kenan subsequently managed the museum for about five years (1982–87); he was followed by the poet Natan Zach for one year, and he was succeeded for the next two years by the late Annie Goldberg. Today Ruti Ofek serves as the museum's curator and is responsible for all of the parks' museums, sculpture gardens, family education programs, and cultural events.

Tefen has become a haven for all residents of the region and a respected center in our art world. We have mounted hundreds of exhibitions, and tens of thousands of visitors from around the world have come to see them.

In London, Amos Kenan found an impressive sculpture by Yitzhak Danziger, *The Victim*, considered a seminal work in the short history of Israeli modern art, and brought it to the Tefen Industrial Park. From Paris we brought sculptures from Israeli artists such as Achiam, Shlomo Zelinger, and Yehuda Neiman who, though living overseas, continued to create works that were purely Israeli. This was another way to bring Israeli émigrés back to their native land.

Paintings, drawings, and engravings by Uri Lipshitz pertaining to industrial work; environment sculptures by Itzik Shmueli (placed opposite ISCAR, on the road linking Kfar Vradim and the industrial park); and works by Yisrael Hadani, Menashe Kadishman, Izhar Patkin, Buky Schwartz, Yehiel Shemi, Yigal Tumarkin, Ofra Zimbalista, and many other artists are also displayed in the park.

History also draws visitors to Tefen. The Museum of the

History of German-Speaking Jewry was a project that Yisrael Shiloni (formerly Hans Herbert Hammerstein) initiated in his home in Nahariya. With the able help of Ruti Ofek, the museum moved from Nahariya to the Tefen Industrial Park, and the Association of Central European Immigrants also joined this project several years ago. Almost all the items in the collection are donations. People are proud to see the items displayed that their families brought with them from the German-speaking parts of Europe.

One exception, however, is a purchase I made in 2005 of a rich collection of works from the artist Hermann Struck—etchings, oils, aquatints, diaries, and correspondence. Struck was a religious German Zionist who first visited Israel in 1903 and then settled in Haifa in 1922. His work spans scenes of early twentieth-century Europe to the early days of Jewish immigration in Israel and profiles the landscape and the people—both the humble and the well known. Among the collection are portraits of Albert Einstein, Sigmund Freud, Gerhardt Hauptmann, Theodore Herzl, and Leonid Pasternak.

Another major addition arrived this year: An original one-room dwelling that housed new immigrants was moved from Nahariya to its permanent site at the back of the museum. (Miriam and I lived in a similar house in our early married life.) Now furnished with vintage household items, it affords a glimpse into the humble lifestyle of the then new immigrants.

TEL HAI INDUSTRIAL PARK, 1992

For my next park I found a site at the extreme northern reaches of the country to continue populating the Galilee with industry and entrepreneurs. But perhaps my nostalgia with regard to the place, Tel Hai—where I served in the Palmach's Yiftach Brigade

Industrial Parks: A Way to Ensure the Future

and was with Miriam during the days of the War of Independence forty-two years earlier—was also a decisive factor. Here we created a forum of export manufacturers from fifty-two private enterprises and kibbutzim in the Galilee that immediately adopted the idea.

I wanted a road to be paved from Alonim, at the edge of the Lower Galilee, to Tel Hai to shorten the travel time. I dreamed of building an industrial park every forty kilometers along the new highway though, naturally, not everything came to pass. My old connection with the local kibbutzim, from Yiron to Kfar Giladi, helped. I received the land from Kfar Giladi and the Israel Lands Administration. The park was built according to the Tefen Model, including the integration of landscape, culture, advanced technologies, and a sculpture garden.

Eli Lamberger, my second wife's father, was a member of Kfar Szold and an amateur photographer, and he helped to build the Museum of Photography at the site. The museum opened with a retrospective exhibition of Micha Baram's photographs, and it continues to mount exhibitions that enjoy high critical acclaim.

The first eight years at the Tel Hai Park were very difficult; the Katyusha rockets fired from Lebanon chased away the entrepreneurs. Prosper Azran, then mayor of Kiryat Shmona, who portrayed his city as "miserable," also hindered the attractiveness of the park.

Today the industrial park at Tel Hai houses ten enterprises that provide work for hundreds of people. One of our most successful parks, it is doubling its area and encouraging young people from the Galilee to enter the field of export industry. It includes BMC, one of the world's top software companies, which started in Houston, Texas. Its staff, a microcosm of Israel—Christians, Circassians, Druze, Jews, and Muslims—has grown fourfold in the past eight years. BMC supports an enrichment program for disadvantaged youth in nearby Kiryat Shmoneh. Also active in the park is Melanox, a firm that designs silicon chips. Life Technology (formerly called Etrog and now located in its own facilities in Kiryat Shoma) uses gel with electricity to analyze DNA. In 2006, it launched a new product, the iBLOT, which has a wide range of applications, from mapping the genetic basis of corn, to developing additional food supplies, to forensic police work.

Nearby Tel Hai College offers courses in such important fields as biotechnology and electronics and provides a constant flow of interns who are trained for jobs in the park. The college started a work placement initiative called "The Best for Industry" that subsidizes the employment of students during their final two years of study. Over the past two years, some 90 percent of graduates from the computing studies program have been recruited by companies in the Tel Hai Industrial Park. The program is now expanding to other fields of study.

OMER INDUSTRIAL PARK, 1995

In 1995 we turned our sights to another peripheral area of Israel, the Negev, and built our fourth industrial park at Omer near Beersheva. The park cooperates on numerous projects with nearby Ben-Gurion University, and many of its workers reside in the beautiful town of Omer, whose mayor Pini Badash has been a strong ally.

The park began on a twenty-three-acre site with 21,000 square meters of industrial space, and the requisite museum, sculpture park, and well-landscaped grounds. It was so successful that several years ago we embarked on an expansion to provide another 45,000 square meters of flexible industrial space.

Industrial Parks: A Way to Ensure the Future

As we expected, the park filled up with a wide range of companies. More than thirty companies occupy the park today; these include the innovative Medigus, a medical device firm specializing in endoscopic procedures that has developed in the park over the past decade. Also operating there is Albatronics, a company that provides complete turnkey hardware and software system design, and ECI Telecom, a global company providing turnkey solutions for network challenges. Vishay Intertechnology, one of the world's largest manufacturers of discrete semiconductors and passive electronic components, is currently transferring its operation to the Omer Industrial Park. Also in the park is Freescale Semiconductor Israel, a subsidiary of the global company Freescale Semiconductor.

LAVON INDUSTRIAL PARK, 1998

Three years after the park at Omer opened, we launched another industrial park at Lavon, which is fifteen minutes south of Tefen. Alongside the park, on a bluff overlooking the cities of Karmiel and Deir al-Assad, I purchased and revived the remains of a failing community. The noted landscape architect Shlomo Aronson (who was trained at Harvard University's Graduate School of Design) drew up the plans, following which ten years of intensive work and a considerable sum of money were invested to build, populate, and operate the residential community of Lavon. We were fortunate to have a good partner in this enterprise, the Misgav local authority. Today, about a hundred families live in Lavon, and development work is underway for seventy-two additional residential units.

Lavon's bustling factories are examples of how one can succeed in taking an existing product and simply making it better than that of the competition. In 1993, I founded Plasel at

Tefen and then moved it to Lavon when the park opened. Its workforce of eighty specializes in the manufacture of high-quality injection- and blow-molded plastic products. Efrat Ben-Horin, who has more than twenty years of experience with the firm, now serves as its president and CEO. Plasel exports its products—items such as packaging for cutting tools—worldwide. About four years ago, we started to engage in blow molding. We supply the baby bottles for Born Free, a company started by "three concerned dads" that became very successful worldwide for its alternative to plastic bottles with the harmful chemicals BPA and PVC. Plasel uses advanced technologies, such as the unique manufacturing process called in-mold labeling, that allow a company's labels to be inserted into the product itself.

In 1996 a former student of mine, Guy Cohen, joined me in starting Metalicone, and now serves as its CEO. Its workforce has grown from 14 to 180 employees: 150 in Lavon and 30 in our plant in Muggensturm, Germany. It specializes in high-precision metal parts production: printing drums, forging dies, and machine-tool spindle parts, and also serves as a subsupplier for various other applications where highly accurate parts are needed. The firm is now exploring new products in the fields of both medical and aircraft parts. Metalicone received the "seal of approval" early on, when firms in Switzerland—the nation that epitomizes quality—became its first customers. Last year it was awarded the Prize for Quality and Excellence, which is patterned after the Malcolm Baldridge National Quality Award in the United States.

In 2000 my grandson Oren Harpaz entered the park, founding Colibri Spindles, whose current workforce of thirty designs, manufactures, and markets patented air-bearing spindles; these are the driving force in metalworking and some other types of machinery. Like the bird that bears their name, Colibri products float on air, reducing friction and prolonging the life of machines. Recently Oren's team created a new product: the Spin Tool, which can be used within regular machinery when higher speeds (up to 60,000 rpm) are needed.

Another of my students, Guy Brokman, established a new firm, Plasel Molds, from something that that we had originally started at Plasel—the making of exceedingly precise molds. The process actually began as part of our training program, as these very demanding molds serve as a superb challenge for those striving to excel in the mold-making field. Plasel Molds devotes 95 percent of its work to the intricate molds that are used in the manufacture of drippers for the drip irrigation market. India, a nation with limited water resources, purchases a great number of these molds. Under Brokman's leadership the firm is also the first in the world to gain expertise in a new method called powdered metal technology, which uses new substances to create cavity inserts of great complexity and repeatability that could not be produced efficiently by other metalworking processes.

DALTON INDUSTRIAL PARK, 2006

The Lower Galilee was the location for our fifth industrial park. In a spectacular region near Gush Halav with views to Mt. Hermon, Mt. Meron, the Sea of Galilee, and the Hula Valley, barren lands are giving way to modern industry. The Dalton Industrial Park, which opened in the summer of 2006, comprises twenty-five acres. Among its initial innovative industries were a water purification company and a firm that has developed a method of analyzing diamonds to maximize their cut value. ISCAR has also established a rapidly growing company, MasteRound, there for grinding solid hard metal. This firm works closely with the Zur Lavon Training Center to recruit and train the local population to work in the company. All of the one hundred employees at MasteRound are local residents.

One of my best memories from Dalton comes from an event held there several years ago. As with all of my industrial parks, Dalton has an integrated workforce that utilizes the talents from the various sectors of our society. Events are scheduled regularly at the park, and everyone is invited. One summer evening Lynn and I were there, and we greatly enjoyed seeing different groups perform while their families applauded their work. Muslim girls danced the *dabka* and performed ballet, a professional Circassian troupe performed their traditional dances, and young Jews sang popular songs. For both of us, it was a vision of what this country can be if its people can overcome their fears of one another.

NAZARETH INDUSTRIAL PARK, 2012

Ten years ago I wanted to build an industrial park in the Arab city of Nazareth. As I will discuss more fully in chapter 14, my earlier attempts to build such parks within the lands of the Palestinian Authority and in Jordan failed due to political reasons—most notably, the Second Intifada, which created an atmosphere of mistrust in this region. Of all the countries in the Middle East, only Turkey collaborated with me in building a successful industrial park. These two factors spurred me to begin building the park in Nazareth.

The only place I could build the park was just below Mount Precipice, where there are several hotels and not much open land. As in the past, my main obstacle was the Israel Lands

Industrial Parks: A Way to Ensure the Future

Administration (ILA), which demanded that I purchase the land on Mount Precipice at land prices for hotels. I refused; I would not pay for an industrial park, from which I make no profit, as I might for a hotel. The bargaining continued for eight years, with the mayor of Nazareth, Ramiz Jeraisy, holding firm with me in this battle until the ILA agreed to assess the land at the lower industrial land price.

Mount Precipice, also known as the Mount of the Leap of the Lord, is a Christian holy site. According to Luke 4:29–30, the people of Nazareth did not see Jesus as the Messiah and attempted to hurl him from the mountainside. However, "passing through their midst, he went away." On May 14, 2009, Pope Benedict XVI landed by helicopter at the future site of my Nazareth Industrial Park, where I had a chance to speak with him briefly. He later led a Mass in Nazareth in which forty thousand people participated.

Shawki al-Khatib, then chairman of the National Committee of Arab Mayors and former mayor of Yafia, who is an engineer and Technion graduate, started working as the project director in early 2009.

Al-Khatib toured the existing industrial parks, spoke with entrepreneurs, and learned the subject thoroughly. Harry Brand (who designed the first industrial park at Tefen), his daughter Eila Brand, and landscape architect Amir Mueller (whose father, also a landscape architect, worked with Brand at Tefen) have planned a beautiful building and grounds. The twelve-thousand-square-meter (more than one-hundred-twenty-nine-thousand square foot) structure opened in December 2012.

The park's first occupants include Amdocs, whose integrated workforce has taken an entire floor for its operations, and Alpha Omega, a local Nazareth firm that develops state-of-the-art microelectrode recording equipment for neurosurgery and advanced systems for neurological research. Its equipment is sold to about a hundred hospitals throughout the world, including the Mayo and Cleveland Clinics. In February 2015 we also created a school for jewelry there. Our partners in this endeavor are Orna and Isaac Levy, who own the Yvel jewelry factory in Motza. Also assisting us in this effort was Sigrid Kopittke, director of the Goldsmith and Watchmaking School in Pforzheim, Germany, a city that has been known for its jewelry industry for three hundred years. The park is also housing an organization called MEET that was started by Israeli students at MIT. This educational program, which brings talented Arab and Jewish high school students together to study computer programming for three years, has become so successful in its ten years of operation that it has expanded its Jerusalem-based activities to the Galilee. Through our regularly scheduled concerts, this new building also serves as a community gathering place; it has an auditorium that can seat 180 people, as well as a café that can accommodate about 75.

I am told that I should be proud of these industrial parks and all that they contribute to the social and economic fabric of Israel. Yet I am still troubled by one question: Why aren't there at least another dozen such parks in operation throughout the country, boosting Israeli exports by billions of dollars? Many new immigrants would find suitable places of employment in these industries. Many young people would seek their future in local industry. The logic is so simple that it is hard to comprehend why policy makers do not see it.

People in the Galilee have finally started to believe in industry. Today, at Kibbutz Kfar Szold, there is a factory that manufactures radiators for refrigerators with exports of about

Industrial Parks: A Way to Ensure the Future

$30 million per year. Good factories have also been built in Baram, Shamir, Kfar Blum, Sasa, and Yiron, among other places. And the industrial parks that I mentioned earlier at Bar-Lev and near Rosh Pina and Shahknin continue to produce products for export. I do not have a direct part in all of these, besides the general inspiration in demonstrating that it is possible to establish successful export industries in the Galilee.

I have invested between $10 million and $22 million in each of my six industrial parks in Israel, with money I have earned from ISCAR and other enterprises. The investment should reach a break-even point only after a decade or two of activity. But I also make a substantial investment in education, quality of life, and art, for which I do not really see a profit. Nonetheless, the problems are there and the opportunities are there—so I take action.

Well-rooted industry is what stabilizes the Israeli economy. Today a relatively small population in the Galilee and in the Negev manufactures a substantial share of Israel's export products. In other words, a small part of the state's population, living on its periphery, is making a major contribution to the state's annual export levels. The industrial parks, though too small in number, continue to generate business and jobs for professional workers and managers who export high-quality Israeli products. Consider this: 30 percent of the labor force in Western Europe works in industry, while no more than 15 percent of Israelis are industrial workers.

And if all of the wrong decisions by the leadership are made between Tel Aviv and Jerusalem, while the real Zionism is being done on the periphery, the question becomes, where is the center, and where is the periphery? And which of them truly ensures the continuation of our existence here?

THE HABIT OF LABOR

GEBZE INDUSTRIAL PARK (GOSB TECHNOPARK), 2005

In the 1990s, when Israel had sound relations with Turkey, I started thinking that Turkey could be my first offshore industrial park project. It seemed to be a way to strengthen ties between our two nations and to help advance Turkey's future as well. In 1995, when I accompanied then president Ezer Weizman on his state visit to Turkey, the idea captivated the governor of Izmir, Kemal Naharazoglu. Later, when he became the personal secretary of the president of Turkey, Naharazoglu helped to promote the idea among his country's leadership.

Turkey's president Suleyman Demirel came on a state visit to Israel in 1999 and toured the Tefen Industrial Park with me. Afterward the opposition leader, Bulent Ecevit, also paid a visit to Tefen. Both of them showed great interest in the concept of industrial parks, and the path was opened to us.

At first we tried to build the park in the Izmir area, near the city's airport, but this did not materialize. Then Naharazoglu put me in touch with people at the Organized Industrial Zone of Gebze (GOSB), with whom I subsequently entered into a partnership. We brought in two local universities, Sanbanci University and Kocaeli University, as secondary partners.

We laid the cornerstone for the park in 2003, and it began operating in the last quarter of 2005. Today, under the able administration of Betsi Boeno and professor Emre Aksan, it houses about a thousand people in its ninety companies or research and development departments. Most of the companies are high-tech enterprises, but there are also factories producing automobile parts, car safety systems, rubber accessories, and robotics. MTM Pazarlama, located in the park, is Turkey's first hologram manufacturer. ISCAR also opened its own branch in

Industrial Parks: A Way to Ensure the Future

Turkey near the park, with a factory and sales agency.

The focus of the park is directed more at development than export manufacturing due to the requirements of Turkish law, which stipulate that the firms within the park must be related to the courses of study at the universities. The project is successful, all of its partners willingly cooperate, and the Turks are very proud of it – justifiably so, as it won an award in 2015 as the best Turkish industrial park.

In 2003 I was asked by the previous prime minister of Turkey to be a member of a new committee called the Investment Advisory Council to provide guidance on developing industry there. Along with a few other members like James Wolfensohn, who then headed the World Bank, I was an active member for about five years. If the geopolitical circumstances that later developed do not undermine this trend, I expect Turkey to become an important exporter, including in the field of metalworking. The Turks have a large metal industry with great potential, and they have recently enjoyed considerable success in producing automobile parts for major global corporations. I hope very much that the relationship between Turkey and Israel will be restored, and that such development will help to bring greater tranquility to the Middle East.

CHAPTER **11**

ON ENTREPRENEURSHIP

An entrepreneur is one who takes total responsibility for creating something and selling it to people who are interested in buying it.

I believe that an entrepreneurial spark is present in every person and that it simply needs to be awakened. Perhaps I have had an advantage. Part of my own success story lies in the Jewish tradition, which is strong in learning how to survive and to take risks.

But one needn't be Jewish to launch a successful firm, of course. When I talk to budding entrepreneurs, here are the points that I usually make:

- Follow your heart and invest your time and resources in a product that you love. If you are excited about what you are making, it will hold your interest and you will be well equipped to interest your customers in it.

- Be stubborn. You will probably not succeed in your initiative by the end of the first year, nor perhaps even by the end of the fifth year. If you believe in your product, you should continue, despite temporary set-

THE HABIT OF LABOR

backs. The proof of success is to make it to the stage where you have repeat customers.

- Be frugal when you begin. Don't invest in fancy offices or equipment at the start. Your funds should be used to improve your product and to hire the best people that you can. And don't add staff members until you definitely have a need for them.

- Don't think you have to invent something entirely new. Most products (including my own) start out as a slight improvement over an existing item. Find something that interests you and make it a little bit better.

- Once you have a good product, make sure that it is delivered when promised. This is a cardinal rule. Your customers are relying on you, and this is one important way that you can keep their orders coming.

- Show up on time for meetings. This sounds obvious, but it is amazing how many people don't follow this rule. You will lose customers if you do not respect their time.

- Study your competition. You should know your competitors' strengths and weaknesses by heart.

- Listen well to your good customers. Find out if they are loyal because of the product itself or the way you present it; both are important bits of information. Listen even more carefully to your disgruntled customers; they will tell you ways that you can improve your product or your service. Then, be sure to follow their advice.

On Entrepreneurship

- Take some risks, and in so doing recognize that you will have to endure some failures to really understand your business. It is not the mistakes you make that matter but what you learn from those mistakes.

- Be honest in all your dealings—with your staff, with your clients, and with your subcontractors. As Warren Buffett would tell you, "It takes twenty years to build a reputation and five minutes to ruin it. If you think about that, you'll do things differently."

There's no magic to any of these suggestions. They are a prescription for success in life, not just in entrepreneurship.

During Israel's early years we aspired to have one thousand pilots who would ensure the state's security. This aspiration has been achieved, for the most part, and while security is still at the top of our agenda, Israel now also needs a thousand additional entrepreneurs to build advanced industries so that our future will depend not only on our military strength.

I am speaking about initiative, about fresh thinking and the desire to compete. The struggle is about the industrial export of a product you believe in and have studied thoroughly. It is a product for which you are sure you will find markets abroad.

Let's say that you decided that you want to manufacture and sell soap made from olive oil. You begin by studying the product, its components, and its different varieties. Perhaps you will discover that about two hundred different manufacturers of this product are active in the market and that ten of them are very successful in sales, and that of these ten there are two leading manufacturers. Perhaps subsequently you will learn more, by temporarily marketing the product of another manufacturer before starting to manufacture a product yourself. Perhaps you will later decide that you cannot manufacture a product that is better than those already on the market. Even then, do not give up, just as it is not prudent to immediately shoot for the stars. Almost any product will need to be tailored once you know more about your customers' needs.

Research and development are not the whole story. During the first thirty years of ISCAR we did not produce a new product of our own. We specialized and became more technologically advanced and competed with existing products until we were good enough to begin the second stage of original development and then to aggressively pursue international markets.

Let's take the example of the Republic of Ireland that became known as the Celtic Tiger. Until about thirty years ago, it was a backward and poor nation, with its economy primarily based on agriculture. Then its government decided to establish modern industry that would export products globally. With the help of their Irish brethren in the United States, they developed ties between the government and private economic stakeholders, changed the direction of education, built excellent vocational schools, and lowered corporate taxes to 15 percent to attract investment in the state and to provide stability for manufacturers. As a result, the Republic of Ireland was transformed from one of the poorest countries in Europe to one of the most prosperous.

The Irish economy grew at rates much higher than the European average, while rapidly transitioning from agriculture to industry. The per capita gross domestic product surpassed that of the rest of Europe. Those in the Irish Republic called upon their neighbors in Northern Ireland to cease fighting and to join them in developing both parts of the island. Another important reason for the success should also be noted: the government in the Republic of Ireland was stable and did not change its rules and laws every few days.

On Entrepreneurship

I fear that the Israeli economy is concentrated too much on the high-tech sector and not enough on industry and basic production. It is estimated that each new manufacturing job generates five others in the economy. Many high-tech enterprises closed during recent periods of crisis, and the important knowledge and technology developed in Israel was sold to other countries.

Denmark also has something to teach us. In November 2002, its Copenhagen Declaration set forth the aims of the Copenhagen Process. The goals focused on enhancing vocational education and improving its effectiveness throughout Europe. Included in the mission of the Copenhagen Process is the promotion of vocational teachers and their continued development.

Far-off Singapore, the large port on the tip of the Malay Peninsula, also has something we can emulate. This island ministate won its independence about fifty years ago, and its population, like Israel's, was mixed—native Malays, Chinese, and Indians; all of them shared a strong desire to succeed. They lacked land and water, so they decided to expand their commercial port and their industrial capabilities. They selected a successful attorney, Lee Kuan Yew, as prime minister, and he was a tough executive. Singapore established vocational schools based on the German model, and began to sell port services and tourism. The country transitioned to selling products, and then expanded production and marketing.

The Singaporeans realized that their success was liable to stir strong envy on the part of their large northern neighbor, Malaysia, so they signed agreements to purchase water from Malaysia and to provide work in local services and factories for half a million Malaysian workers.

I was invited by the Singapore government to help find ways to educate people and mold them into industrialists. Singapore is a sophisticated state that created realistic solutions for itself, transformed shortcomings into advantages, prevented confrontations, and reduced poverty.

Singapore encouraged and nourished entrepreneurship, the initiative that is a gamble, at least during the first stage. Most entrepreneurs want to prove something to someone—to a father, to a wife, to friends. Entrepreneurs are like creative artist: restless, driven relentlessly by determination to realize their ideas. After succeeding, an entrepreneur might lose interest in his or her enterprise and then will deliver it into someone else's trusty hands, to then begin something new.

CHAPTER **12**

LIFE'S UNEXPECTED TURNS

The year 1983 was one to celebrate. ISCAR's annual sales reached $32 million. The first industrial park opened in Tefen. Kfar Vradim was already two years old and had several hundred residents.

But 1983 also held one of life's unforeseen twists, and it happened right at the start of the year. On January 4, I drove to Caesarea to deliver a lecture for Bank Leumi executives. It was a rainy afternoon, and as I turned right at the exit for Caesarea, the car skidded and crashed into a truck.

I was taken to Hillel Yaffe Medical Center in Hadera, unconscious; the doctors feared for my life. I had suffered a concussion, four major fractures, and various other injuries. I do not remember a thing from those days, but a doctor who accompanied me to Rambam Hospital in Haifa said a few days later that I had asked them, in blurred consciousness, not to operate on me. At Rambam the doctor delivered me into the hands of Dr. Moshe Feinsod, who knew me. The CT scan revealed an injury with considerable bleeding in the left side of the brain, in the area that controls speech; there were also signs of cerebral edema. Every effort was made to avoid operating, which would have damaged brain tissue. The treatment included medication aimed at lowering blood pressure, together with medication to "calm" the brain—all under close monitoring. Within a week or two my state of consciousness started to improve and the speech impediments began to dissipate.

Eitan, who was in Hong Kong, spent a day and half in flights and hurried to the hospital. He then went to ISCAR and informed the employees that the work would proceed without change. He asked that no one sit in my place in the dining hall or in my office, and that no one park in my reserved parking spot.

During the first two difficult weeks following the accident, Eitan was able to summon his special ability to function for many days with practically no sleep, which he had acquired during his continuous work on the front lines in the Yom Kippur War. He would replace Miriam or Ruti in watching over my bed at night, and in the early hours of the morning he would arrive at the ISCAR branch in Haifa a few minutes after the gates opened, take a shower, make himself a cup of coffee, and race to the factory. Every few days he would gather the workers in the central hall and give them a report on my condition.

They tell me that when I was lying unconscious in my hospital bed, I constantly tried to get up while still in a coma. So the nurses tied me down. One time, still unconscious, I got up on my feet, with the bed tied to my back. Apparently my desire to return to work and home was so strong that it gave me this power. When I completely woke up, after about two weeks, I demanded that the doctors allow me to return home.

Dr. Feinsod would come to my home to examine me because I refused to return to the hospital. Gradually I returned to life, but with a faulty memory and speech problems. I slowly recuperated without any operations. For the next three months, no one knew how I well I would recover from my injuries: perhaps I'd be partially or completely disabled, with problems in thinking and speaking. Yet I was sure that I would return to my former self; I was careful to increase my physical activity gradually, and strictly followed a regimen of physiotherapy and speech therapy.

Eitan's transition to managing ISCAR was not simple. He was not familiar with the rules and dynamics of a large factory, which were completely different from those of the relatively small factories he had managed. And there was no one from whom he could learn. He carried on his shoulders the ultimate responsibility for the hard metals and Blades factories in Nahariya, for his factory in Shlomi, and also for Kfar Vradim, which was still in the midst of construction. But the need to cope with problems is the best teacher, and Eitan learned well. "This included," he would tell me, "the ability to discern who at ISCAR was exploiting the situation and who was a serious and loyal friend." After I recovered he admitted that he was scared to death of the responsibilities and, even more, of making mistakes.

Eitan set out to double ISCAR's production and began to reorganize the company without adding workers. He also continued to establish the facilities in the Tefen area; a few months before my accident, in November 1982, we had inaugurated the new ISCAR factory there—ISCAR Tools—with 180 workers who had transferred from Nahariya. The work continued day and night, and ultimately Eitan met his goals with the help of the workers. He improved efficiency, computerized all of the departments, and doubled output.

As soon as April 1983, three months after the accident, I started to return to my old self, with the help of speech and physical therapy. Soon after I was allowed to spend several hours a day at the company. Six months passed before I fully recovered. On the first day I returned to work, Eitan said to me, "Dad, I did the best I could and kept everything clean and orderly. Here are the keys." After six months of exhausting work, he set off to Japan with a friend for a vacation.

When he returned, I said to him, "You did a nice job. Why don't you join the company?" Eitan had planned to return to his factory in Shlomi and concentrate on acquiring small and failing companies, resuscitating them, and then selling them at a profit. But he was willing to change his plans. In a smooth transition he transferred the management of his independent factory in Shlomi to Haim Cohen, and then set out to survey the scene at ISCAR.

Eitan learned that he was unable to receive information quickly enough from the computer. So he gathered several of his contemporaries, who today comprise the management echelon at ISCAR, and together they worked to improve efficiency. The result was ISCAR's entrance into twenty-first-century technology: an effective computer system, robotics in the factories, and an emphasis on advanced marketing and development.

When my decision to hand over the management of ISCAR to Eitan became known, many people expressed doubts, openly or implicitly. Some close friends said that he was too young, too much of a "playboy," that his only experience was in managing a small factory, that he was not yet ready for the enormous complexity of a large array of factories. But I knew my choice was correct. The company had always been a part of the life of the Wertheimer family.

"This is your opportunity to take responsibility, and to love the actual taking of responsibility," I told Eitan. "I will not supervise you or tell you what is good and what is bad. You will need to make the assessments yourself. You will find the truth yourself, and the truth regarding ISCAR can be found with the customer and with those working with you." Years later, Eitan himself said in a newspaper interview, "For five years, Stef did not say a word to me, good or bad. 'Find out yourself.' At first, I had no criterion to judge what was correct or not. At each stage, I told him in advance what the plans were, but he did not interfere. Today he is involved in what he wants. We run after him because he has lots of experience and logic. He knows exactly what he wants, learns at a crazy pace, innovates and is rejuvenated all the time."[14]

Eitan formed an outstanding management group of people his age, all of whom grew up at ISCAR next to the machines. Some of them are graduates of Zur-Nahariyah, which demonstrates the importance of a vocational school that enables its graduates to succeed. This group of friends has spent a considerable part of their lives together—in airplanes, in hotels, and in meetings in various places around the world—with the goal of expanding markets and aspiring for more.

Eitan never exercised supreme authority but instead respected those working with him; he employed a flexible administrative structure. Of the many people who helped to ensure ISCAR's development, he found that those who had studied at Zur-Nahariyah met every international standard of excellence even though they lacked a degree in engineering. He and most of his team were autodidacts with a strong desire to learn. This is the spirit in the ISCAR-IMC management group at the start of the second decade of the twenty-first century: everyone works with the same mind-set. These people are good friends, and they are experimenting and searching, each with expertise in a particular field (planning, manufacturing, or marketing); they have a sound approach toward the future.

The current president of ISCAR, Jacob Harpaz, was born in 1951 and grew up in Kiryat Bialik, near Haifa. He studied

---

[14] Inbar, op. cit.

mechanical engineering at the Technion. In 1973 we asked him to help establish a development department at ISCAR. As he started working at the factory, while still in his last year of studies, the Yom Kippur War broke out.

Harpaz was a tank commander. His half-track was hit near the Suez Canal, and despite suffering an injury himself, he pulled a wounded comrade from the tank and dragged him for many kilometers to safety. For this action he was awarded the Medal of Distinguished Service. He spent over a year in hospitals, undergoing a series of complicated operations after losing the sole of his foot and sustaining other injuries in battle. During that year, when his physicians permitted, and between operations and completing his studies, he would come to the factory to continue his work.

Harpaz began his career at ISCAR working in developing coatings, hard metal materials, chip breakers, and other production technologies. One day I overheard him arguing with one of our salesmen, who claimed there were problems in selling ISCAR products. "My friend, you simply don't know how to sell," Harpaz said. "The new products require technical understanding, and your sales methods are outdated and no longer appropriate!" I asked him if he really believed what he said. When he answered yes, I told him that he should immediately leave the development department and go into marketing.

He became the technical person in ISCAR's marketing division. With customers, who were still primarily local at that time, he would demonstrate the tools and solve technical problems. Due to his talents, many customers remained loyal to ISCAR. When we came out with our unique parting products and exports began to expand, Harpaz was sent on his first overseas trip, to customers in France and Belgium. "I didn't even know how to put on a tie," he jokes.

Life's Unexpected Turns

Danny Goldman has been involved in some of the company's most crucial decisions in the past decade and serves as the CFO of ISCAR and IMC. He became a certified public accountant after graduating from the University of Haifa, and while doing his internship at the Income Tax Authority, he noticed a newspaper advertisement that read, "Help Wanted: Accountant." This brought him to ISCAR more than twenty-five years ago; he started out by introducing advanced computer systems at the headquarters and in all of ISCAR's worldwide branches.

In 1997, when South Korea suffered a serious economic crisis, ISCAR decided to acquire TaeguTec, a competitor that faced bankruptcy. Goldman was sent to conduct the negotiations, and today, TaeguTec-ISCAR is a successful part of IMC. Danny was also involved in the acquisition of more than twenty other companies around the globe, including Ingersoll and Tungaloy and, of course, the two-part deal with Warren Buffett.

Haim Cohen, IMC's vice president for operations, has worked in our group for more than forty years, starting as a lathe operator after he finished his studies at Zur-Nahariyah. When I had my car accident, Haim was appointed manager of Microdent; under his direction, the company doubled its number of employees, its output, and its revenues.

In the snowy winter of 1992, the roof on one of the buildings at Microdent collapsed and destroyed many machines. The next year, Cohen supervised the construction of the Microdent campus at Tefen—five large buildings on a plot of twelve thousand square meters, with advanced equipment and innovative technology.

In October 1994 Eitan asked Cohen to hand over the management of Microdent, whose annual exports had grown to about $50 million under his leadership, and assume his current position at ISCAR, where he is responsible for the operation of factories in Israel and abroad: the construction of facilities, the introduction of advanced technology and equipment, the recruiting of personnel, and investments. He now spends about one week per month in Japan, operating the giant Tungaloy company acquired by IMC and converting it to the group's "character" and work style. He devotes much of his time to thinking about the future, especially in preparing cadres of new managers. Our managers today are fifty to sixty years old on average and will be yielding their positions to younger managers during the next decade.

The 1980s was a decade of tremendous growth. At the Tefen Industrial Park in 1985 there were already 25 entrepreneurs. In 1986 Kfar Vradim, in its fifth year, was home to 700 residents; Eitan and his family, and Miriam and I, also built our homes in the village. In 1987 there were 850 employees at ISCAR and sales had reached $86 million, 93 percent of which was in exports. The turnover of ISCAR Blades, which already employed 350 workers at the time, reached $32 million, all for export. In 1987 the school for young entrepreneurs opened at the Tefen Industrial Park in collaboration with the efforts of the late professor Richard Rosenbloom from Harvard Business School and professor Edward Roberts from the Massachusetts Institute of Technology. This was my first real step in establishing an academy for entrepreneurship in industry.

In 1988 we acquired part of Discount Investments' holdings in ISCAR. Shlomo Lahat, Dan Tolkovsky, and their colleagues, who had been good partners for us, retired from the bank. Their replacements, with the exception of the long-serving Yaakov Eshel, were bankers who were only interested in sure profits; they did not understand the spirit that guided ISCAR. In time the company became 100 percent ours again. That same year, we also reacquired the Duracarb company we had built in the Netherlands in 1962 but had sold several years later.

After stepping down from the management of ISCAR, I still served as its chairman for the next fifteen years. Of course, I received regular reports and was occasionally asked for advice and "to address the big picture," as Eitan defined it.

I now had more time to realize the big dreams that had been pushed aside somewhat: working on new industrial parks, revitalizing our vocational education system, expanding the Tefen area, and thinking about the future of Israel and the Middle East.

Throughout the years, after we were able to afford it, Miriam would pull me away from work and take the whole family to the Swiss village of Flims. She made this vacation sacred: it was family time only. We devoted the vacation to hiking, reading, solving puzzles, or engaging in sports.

I would bring fresh rolls from the local bakery for breakfast. The baked goods were excellent, so a business deal resulted from this. We persuaded the local baker, Paul Schertenleib, to come to us in Nahariya after he retired, and there he helped us start the Lahmi Bakery and Pastry Shop. Miriam designed Lahmi to her taste, with European elegance, and later expanded it into a café at the site of the Astor Hotel in Nahariya. She was a partner in the business and would work there every day, closely supervising its operation.

When the three older children grew up and left the house, we looked for a suitable place for Yiftach, and he went to live in Kfar Tikva. At age forty-eight, Miriam began to study art and photography at the University of Haifa and participated in choirs and evenings of folk dancing. She was also active on the culture committee in organizing events in Kfar Vradim. Through all the years, she also continued to be involved in what was happening at ISCAR and at Blades, and she always kept abreast of goings-on in the families of workers. She helped to organize the communal dining hall, choosing the tableware and preparing the menus. She knew how to constantly engage herself, as if she felt that time was pressing, yet she still had time for our children and grandchildren.

In October 1988, I drove Miriam to the Rambam Hospital in Haifa after she experienced several days of stomach pains. Despite a battery of tests, the physicians were unable to provide a diagnosis and asked her to return in a week. Our family physician, Dr., Biterman, examined her and instructed that she immediately be hospitalized. That very evening a Dr. Stambler operated on her. The children and I waited at the hospital; the expressions on the physicians' faces when they emerged from the operating room told us in a direct and dreadful way how serious Miriam's condition was.

The discovery of cancer was a terrible shock. After all, Miriam had always been the picture of heath and vigor; she was an outstanding athlete, exercised regularly, was strict about proper nutrition. And only a month earlier we had all spent a wonderful vacation together in Switzerland. She had been so joyful there, full of life and activity.

The doctors estimated that she had only a month or two to live, but Miriam fought her battle for six months, and with great courage. She asked to leave the hospital and live in the house at Kfar Vradim that she had designed and nurtured, that she loved so much. Upon the physicians' recommendation, a professional caregiver, Hudar Bisan, accompanied her. The doctors did much to ease her pain, and Hudar, a young Druze man from the village of Jatt, was an outstanding caregiver: calming, supportive, and a wonderful conversationalist; he became a real member of the family during the six months he stayed with us.

Life's Unexpected Turns

I left all the work at the company and the industrial park to others, detached myself from all other pursuits, and remained by Miriam's side at home. I faced a cruel, incurable situation, which could not be changed—regardless of how hard we might fight against it.

Since we never concealed anything from each other, I wanted to inform her about her condition, but the children asked that I not do this. After her death, Eitan told me that he believed she knew what her condition was all along, but that she decided not to allow anything, except for life, to enter the room. "Mom decided that illness is in the mind, not in the body," he says. "We all pampered her during that period, preparing food she liked, reading newspapers to her, and reporting to her on what was happening in theater and music. It was important for her to remain up-to-date. We continued to make plans for the future and to tie up loose ends."

Miriam and I spent many hours together during this period. We talked about the two of us and about our children and grandchildren. We had a beautiful life together, a full life, a life of action. Her strength waned and her weight also steadily declined, but she, an optimist by nature, never revealed or even hinted that she was aware of her condition. She was convinced she would succeed in overcoming any adversity and did not even complain that she was suffering from pain. "Mom never believed in pain—and the 'end' did not interest her. She always believed, absolutely, in life," Ruti says. And indeed, Miriam always maintained a good mood. Just once she nearly got caught up in despair and said, "Enough! Leave me alone! Enough with all these treatments!" But she immediately regretted saying this and noted, "Everything is so beautiful outside. Soon the spring will come and everything will bloom in lots of colors—and I was speaking nonsense."

The children were full partners in taking care of their mother with great devotion and love. Each of us helped the others to be stronger. A month before her death, we took her—in our arms because she was unable to walk—to a hill in Tefen near the industrial park, and Eitan showed her where we planned to continue building ISCAR and Kfar Vradim. He also showed her the film Moti Kirshenbaum made on how Tefen would look in the year 2000. Miriam was there with her four children, five of her grandchildren, and me, and she was happy despite her weakness.

Until the last moment she remained optimistic and confident that she would recover. On the last night, she and I watched a new video. Then we made a date to drink coffee together at breakfast, but she did not live to see the morning.

All of us knew, for many difficult months, that this bitter day would come—and still, when it came and when all of the children and grandchildren gathered around me in silence, it was very hard. Yiftach was unable to understand the meaning of his mother's death. "But when will she return?" he asked again and again. "I've lost a friend," our grandson Erez said.

Since Miriam's death I haven't been able to stay much in our home in Kfar Vradim, the home she loved so much. I preferred to live in the old house, in Nahariya, near the beach, and later in Kfar Shmaryahu. I now live with Lynn in Tel Aviv. Miriam left a deep imprint on each member of the family and on all her acquaintances. Once a year we celebrate her birthday at a small family gathering. On the anniversary of her death we visit her grave; dozens of family members and friends talk about her and honor her memory.

CHAPTER **13**

EXPANDING MARKETS

Since 1982, ISCAR has grown by 20 percent a year on average, both in sales and in profits. Its profitability has been double that of similar companies in the industry. From a relatively unknown company that accounted for only several percent of a small market, ISCAR has become the world's second largest company in this market.

Twenty-two years before the deal that transferred 80 percent of ISCAR to Warren Buffett, I stepped down from the management of the company and Eitan took over. He managed ISCAR with great success before handing over its management a few years later to Jacob Harpaz, who is continuing with its success. Though I was no longer managing ISCAR, I was at the company nearly every day and was involved in everything that was happening. But my mind, heart and schedule were devoted to my other initiatives: vocational education and the building of industrial parks, among other projects.

Despite the skepticism of many, Eitan made a huge investment in automation, computerization, and robotics at the factories. Since there was a constant shortage of professionals as a result of the closure of most of the vocational schools, we were forced to look for other solutions to deliver our products on time. We found that automation does the work of people very well, as well as work that people are unable to do. We sent people for training overseas and formed a department for assembling robots and adapting them for the production machinery according to our requirements. We accomplished this great technological revolution on our own.

Today large robots at ISCAR do the work, in a clean hall with conveyor tracks. A mobile robot moves between them, collecting the small cutting tools, which are made out of powder metal and look like star-shaped nuts. They are then sintered at very high temperatures. The mobile robot also adds metal powder to its "colleagues" when their containers become empty. It once took three hundred workers to do this work. Today about a dozen robots do the job. In the corner of the hall, there is still a machine that in the distant past would press the hard metal powder, with manual labor, into small sheets. It was the first (and least expensive) machine I brought from America in 1956.

Harpaz shifted the emphasis and best personnel from production—where the robots did excellent work—to the development, marketing, and sales departments. Marketing is no less important than production and technological development; after all, what will you do with a unique product if there are no customers for it? We worked for many years to expand our branches and global sales network. There were places where we failed again and again—in the United States, for example, when unsuitable people were chosen to manage our branches there.

By 2006, ISCAR had expanded to include seventy-five subsidiaries that spanned nearly the entire globe. While twenty-five years ago we depended on local agents around the world who sold our products among many in their range of offerings, today most of ISCAR's marketing efforts are based on subsidiaries that are under our full ownership, with sales personnel who are all ISCAR employees.

Expanding Markets

The workers in all the locations are primarily local as a matter of principle and not only because they have easier access to local customers. We did not want to give Israelis an excuse to settle overseas. ISCAR's high-quality products, our sales and marketing personnel, and their unique method of marketing have generated great success for our companies in world markets, and they ultimately led to the deal with Warren Buffett.

What makes a good marketing and sales person? Someone who markets all the time and expands his circle of customers, selling more products to more customers. A good marketing person believes in his or her ability to contribute something beneficial to the customer. A good marketing person has developed an understanding of the buyer's psychology, and knows what the buyer's decision depends upon and thus creates a real advantage for that buyer. He or she quickly passes along the customer's comments and requirements to the manufacturer to make revisions. A supremely important principle is this: that customers receive their orders at exactly the scheduled time. A good salesperson identifies with the product, knows how to build a name for it, and knows its advantages. He or she will always do better marketing with a high-quality and unique product that offers advantages. A good salesperson also knows that he or she is free to make decisions and set sales policy, and that he or she has the full backing of the company in doing so. A good salesperson is also someone who is proficient in both the technical/practical and marketing aspects of the product.

ISCAR's uniqueness lies in the innovativeness of the products and the continual updating of production: multipurpose products, and products that make work easier, remove nuisances like metal chips, shorten processing times from an hour to ten minutes; in short, revolutionary products. A good marketing person succeeds in convincing the skeptical consumer of

THE HABIT OF LABOR

these advantages.

Japan was a huge marketing challenge. It is a country that had shaken off the destruction it had brought upon itself in World War II and by the 1980s had transformed itself into one of the world's great industrial powers. Japan's success was designed to prove to the Americans that Japan did not lose the war—that the war, in fact, was still continuing, but the instruments of war had changed. While fifty years ago postwar Japanese industrial products conjured up the sense of cheap imitations, for the past thirty years their high quality has been recognized. Japan's effective weapons are now its giant manufacturing companies like Honda, Kyocera, Mitsubishi, Sony, Toshiba, and Toyota. Its image in the world—and, consequently, its own self-image—is determined by its ability to manufacture products that are in demand in other countries. Today, export products are the true diplomats.

We considered it a victory when ISCAR started to manufacture products for the Japanese market. But we decided to take real steps only after the market conditions in Europe and the United States became more difficult. In 1978 it was clear that in Japan there was great potential for our products. A team was sent to a large international exhibition there, but ISCAR's booth did not sell even a single item. The reason? We traveled there without learning about the place, its people, the mentality, and the nature of the market.

We thus started to conduct research on markets and possibilities, objectives and competition. We checked what the market looked like, how many competitors were operating there, which local companies had serious marketing capabilities but lacked products in our field, and what profit these companies would expect to receive if we proposed to them that they sell our products at a reasonable price.

Expanding Markets

In 1980, I traveled to Japan to look for a good distributor and a way to penetrate the market there. I sought a connection to a large local company that specialized in products from hard metal, but not the same products that ISCAR produces. Thus we could offer our goods, with the exclusive features we developed, as complementary products.

I went to several such companies, but I cannot say that I was an ideal salesman on this trip. As I was demonstrating our cutting tools, the very worst thing happened: the tools broke. Perhaps I was not fully versed in our products, which had become much more advanced, and I certainly was not proficient in all of their possibilities. For me this was yet another lesson in how important it is to be prepared.

Fortunately, my subsequent meeting with Kazuo Inamori, the chairman of the board of the giant corporation Kyocera, was more successful. Kyocera was a perfect fit for us: a company whose annual turnover was about $2 billion, a manufacturer of a broad range of products (from Yashika cameras to computer chips and tools made of a special ceramic material), and whose production lines did not include our type of products, though it had a small division for manufacturing cutting tools.

I was told the meeting would last twenty minutes, but the conversation continued long past the allotted time. It seemed that good chemistry developed between us. Perhaps Inamori, like I, had built his life's enterprise with his own hands. In any case, the wall of foreignness fell and at the end of the conversation he said to me, "Okay. I am willing to try to sell your products. In two weeks, I am opening our annual exhibition of products. If you can prepare for me an attractive catalog in Japanese by then and send me the products, I would be very happy."

In the very polite business language of the Japanese, this was a test: Inamori wanted to check whether I could meet his demands under an almost impossible deadline. At the same time, he asked his people to check the product in question, the Self-Grip.

We worked like crazy for two weeks—and we succeeded. I sent Jacob Harpaz to Japan to ensure that the demonstration would not fail this time. Harpaz also discovered a new, exciting, and confusing world in Japan. He gave a comprehensive lecture in English about our Self-Grip to Kyocera's manufacturing and development personnel, explaining how it is produced, its potential, and its practical use. Every so often, he asked, "Clear?" And only at the end it became clear to him that none of his listeners spoke English. And a translator who was quickly summoned turned out to be a French language translator. Harpaz explained to them with hand motions and various sounds; he moved on to the demonstration on the factory floor, dressed in a special work uniform in accordance with the strict Japanese work procedures, walking around in socks in the work area covered with hot chips because they could not find shoes that fit him. But the demonstration of the Self-Grip's capabilities was very successful this time.

Kyocera decided to try to sell the Self-Grip in Japan, and our revolutionary blade was displayed at the company's big exhibition. But even during the first day, Harpaz realized that ISCAR's booth was not drawing any attention. By evening not a single blade had been sold. Harpaz decided to report to the sales booth himself the next day.

The reticence that seem to be typical Japanese characteristics vis-à-vis foreigners quickly dissolved as Harpaz stopped visitors at the exhibition and enthusiastically demonstrated the possibilities of the Israeli tool. The change was amazing. The booth filled with visitors, the Self-Grip became the hit of the day at the exhibition, and sales rose at a dizzying pace.

Expanding Markets

Despite the breakthrough, unanticipated problems later arose in ISCAR's Japanese initiative. Complete shipments of our products were returned to us from Japan with polite comments—sometimes about the quality, but mainly about the packaging. They completely rejected our packaging—the expensive and attractive version we were proud of—because a different type of packaging had been agreed upon.

We had thought that Kyocera's packaging demands were a fleeting whim and had ignored them, but our shipments began to return to us in huge quantities, with precise comments. Harpaz, who was already familiar with the special character of the Japanese, went back to visit Kyocera once every two months. He warned us, "Guys, if we want to sell successfully in Japan, we need to comply with their demands. They want the standards that were defined and approved."

Another ISCAR delegation set off for Japan, this time a group of production and control personnel, to persuade the Japanese that they were wrong. Our people sat across from their people for a long conversation and were sure they had succeeded in convincing them. At the end of the conversation the head of the Japanese team said, with typical courtesy, "That was interesting, but if you want to sell to us, please do what we request."

ISCAR's personnel were thus compelled to work harder on the products, on quality control and packaging, in accordance with the Japanese requirements—and this helped. Fewer products were returned, and the mutual satisfaction increased with the sales. A fortunate by-product of this was that ISCAR's standards became stricter and our image in the industrial world advanced even beyond the high level it had enjoyed before.

ISCAR operated in Japan as a department in the cutting tools division of Kyocera, which became one of Japan's three leading companies in this field. We supplied about a quarter of our output to this division, and the sales grew from year to year. In 1995, ISCAR established an independent subsidiary in Japan that began to sell our entire range of offerings there and became well known for its innovative and smart products. A few years ago we purchased Tungaloy, which allowed us to greatly increase our presence in Japan.

Through his documentary films, my friend Moti Kirshenbaum had an important role in the efforts to persuade the Japanese. Moti, one of the pioneers of Israeli television, is among the most talented, original, and cerebral filmmakers and interviewers in Israel; he has produced and directed dozens of documentaries and is an Israel Prize laureate. For more than a decade Moti was part of the ISCAR family: a friend, adviser, and filmmaker who helped to lead ISCAR into the twenty-first century.

We first met after the Yom Kippur War at a symposium in Jerusalem. A few months later, we met again at the home of Amos Kenan, at a gathering of creative people. I tried to mobilize support for the Council for Productive Zionism that I had founded at the time. I proposed that Moti make a film about ISCAR and about industry in general, but not an advertising or propaganda film; I told him that he would have a free hand in the film's creation.

Moti said that he was not familiar with industry and that it did not appeal to him as a filmmaker, but he asked for some time to consider the proposal. After Amos Kenan published "Industry Is Beautiful," his series of articles in *Yedioth Ahronoth*, Moti called and said, "If we make a film, it has to be in the spirit of Amos's articles."

He started to film at ISCAR, at Blades, and at the sites of our other industries; he visited ISCAR branches around the world, and also the EMO international exhibition for metalworking in Hanover, Germany, accumulating thousands of meters of material. His film *Industry Is Beautiful* made an immediate impact.

I felt that we should utilize the video for marketing, as it would make it easier to show people in the industry things they do not usually get to see: cutting angles, the behavior of the insert (the sheet) during the cutting or milling, the way the chips emerge. The video could demonstrate the clear advantages of our products to prospective customers, from up close, in the actual act of cutting the metal. "I come from the world of 'fudging,'" Moti said to me. "It's a world of television work in which, with good editing, effects, music and correct narration, you can sell bad material. But here, with these products, nothing external can help sell an ISCAR tool if it is not good and true."

In Moti's films the mesmerizing beauty of the blade cutting the metal like butter, with great precision—the beauty that has fascinated me since my childhood—was revealed very persuasively. After all, the little tools we manufacture are part of the foundation for the industry of the modern world. It was suddenly possible to see how much intelligence and experience goes into a tiny blade, the size of a person's fingernail, with all of its applications, and how this tiny blade overpowers the hardest steels. The industry professionals began to take the videotapes home, to show them proudly to their families and, for the first time, imbue them with some understanding and interest in their line of work.

Of course, a video alone is not sufficient. But it can open doors and arouse curiosity; prospective customers who saw the videos became very eager to try the tools. Moti left Israel Television and recruited Eli Buenos to help him (and to replace Moti at ISCAR when he returned to television work), and they started to make videos that covered each type of ISCAR product. The dozen films they made on the products were reproduced in fifteen different languages and were sent to ISCAR branches throughout the world. Positive results were quick to follow, and as a result various competitors started using video for instruction and promotion of their products.

Exhibitions and trade fairs are the major arena for showing products. ISCAR displays its products at about a hundred international exhibitions each year. The central exhibition, EMO, is held every two years in Paris, Hanover, or Milan. Many hundreds of manufacturers in the field of metalworking display their products in huge halls: machines, lathes, mills, drills and parts, cutting tools and other metalworking tools. Europe is the most important area in the world in this field; America is in second place.

With the conviction that an industrial Israel must be part of this world to maintain its existence, we make a point of participating in each exhibition. ISCAR assembles a large pavilion every two years at EMO despite the considerable expense this entails, and the pavilion attracts a stream of industry professionals. We come with dozens of ISCAR personnel from Israel and from our global branches, and sometimes also with students from our courses.

All of the latest innovations appear at these exhibitions. Everyone dispatches emissaries to the competitors' pavilions to see what new products they have developed. Everyone collects data and brochures, watches films about new products, compares and checks. Sometimes a visitor furtively slips a blade from the display into the pocket of his jacket. Industrial espionage works overtime at these shows.

The exhibitions are like colorful fairs. There is great commotion; waitresses serve rivers of beer, mountains of steaming sausages, cakes, and coffee, all free of charge. The food and drink are an inseparable part of this professional game. Every self-respecting pavilion looks from the outside like a combination of a café and hardware store.

Expanding Markets

The competition is severe. ISCAR (today the IMC group) faces many companies in the world. The largest of them is the giant Swedish company Sandvik, which erects the largest pavilion at the exhibitions. We find ourselves in open, direct competition with dozens of its products.

The theft of intellectual property is a serious problem in the industry and the meticulous registration of patents, an expensive and cumbersome process, is not very effective. If the manufacturer who steals your idea changes even a tiny detail, the law will not recognize it as patent infringement. Therefore, the speed at which the inventor can sell his innovative product—before his imitators begin to manufacture and market it themselves—is really critical. This period of sales exclusivity is what determines success. ISCAR, long before the Buffett deal, won many rounds in these exhibitions, with its revolutionary Self-Grip, Top-Grip, HeliMill, and other exclusive tools, and these successes led to our most significant breakthrough in the world market.

A correct reading of the world map transformed ISCAR from a manufacturer with marketing representatives and sales branches in various countries into a large corporation of local companies in different countries, thus overcoming the obstacle of foreignness in places outside of Israel.

In 1998 ISCAR acquired the South Korean company TaeguTec. This marked the beginning of a process of acquiring knowledge for the automobile industry. In 1999 we opened our factory in India, which set new standards for industry in that country. In 2000 we acquired the German-American company Ingersoll, which provided not only automotive technologies but also access to its customer base in this field. We started supplying our cutting tools to companies such as Chrysler, General Motors, Mercedes, and others. This also opened the markets of the heavy metal industries to us: manufacturers of ships, boats, airplanes, machines, and other industries.

During the first years of the twenty-first century, ISCAR acquired several small companies in France, Italy, and Spain, each one specializing in a different technology and all of them contributing to the capabilities of our expanding product range. The small companies were exposed to ISCAR's large customer market, so they grew very rapidly.

In 2006, on the other side of the world, ISCAR acquired a small Japanese company, which also mainly provided a specific technology, and two years later ISCAR acquired Tungaloy, one of the leading companies in Japan in the metalworking industry.

CHAPTER **14**

A NEW KIND OF EXPORT: THE TEFEN MODEL

After the Israeli industrial parks proved to be successful, I wanted to export this idea to the entire Middle East. I tried to interest several neighboring countries to join me in establishing industrial parks based on the Tefen model.

The poverty and conflicts that have characterized parts of the Middle East for decades bring problems that endanger not just this region but the entire world. I felt that I had something to contribute to solving the long-standing issues of this area. The Tefen Model creates opportunities for the more enlightened states in the region—especially those not endowed with oil wells, which are looking to enable their citizens to earn a decent living. This path would lead the states of the Mediterranean and the old Levant to the threshold of Europe and the Common Market. The model offers new and optimistic, yet pragmatic, directions of thought.

A strong desire for peace with our neighbors motivated me to bring this concept across our borders. If history had been a bit different, successful industrial parks for export would today be operating in not only Israel but also Jordan and the lands of the Palestinian Authority. They would be providing employment to thousands of people, raising the standard of living, enhancing education systems, and leading to the expansion of infrastructure—roads, water, and electricity.

I wanted to focus on the Mediterranean region. After all, it is my home, and it is here that I made my start as an exporting industrialist; my first agents and partners outside of Israel were in Greece, Italy, Spain and Yugoslavia. But I decided that the original target—the Mediterranean basin—was too extensive, at least as a starting point, and that I should focus only on some of the countries adjacent to or near Israel.

In late 1995, I traveled with Eitan and several others to Jordan to propose the idea of the industrial park to King Hussein. He received us very cordially, apparently upon the recommendation of Yitzhak Rabin. We spoke about the idea, and we sent delegations to one another to learn more. A very capable Jordanian-Palestinian decided to partner with us. Later, he went to Washington, DC, with me to advocate the concept.

Some years earlier, I had recruited businessman Shmuel Dankner as a partner, and we met with Yasser Arafat, who was enthusiastic about the idea and was willing to have our partner from Jordan serve as his representative. I presented the idea to Rabin, proposing that we take about three square kilometers on each side of the border and create two industrial parks. The Palestinian park would be built at a place called al-Shoka adjacent to the newly constructed airport at Dahaniya, just two-thirds of a kilometer across the border from the proposed Israeli site at Kerem Shalom. We would declare this entire area a free trade zone.

Saadi al-Krunz, then minister of industry and chairman of the Palestinian Industrial Estate and Free Zone Authority, signed a memorandum of understanding with me on March 11,

A New Kind of Export: The Tefen Model

1999, to promote the Israeli-Palestinian Industrial and Trade Park Project. Two Israeli prime ministers also committed themselves to the project: Benjamin Netanyahu signed a letter to that effect on February 4, 1999, and his successor, Ehud Barak, signed a similar letter on September 13, 1999.

I took this opportunity to once again engage Harvard University's Graduate School of Design to assess the areas we had designated for the joint industrial parks. In May 1999 Lynn Holstein and Carl Steinitz returned, this time with professor Alex Krieger, then chairman of the school's Department of Urban Planning and Design and six students from the school for an on-site study (known as a studio) that included a visit to the proposed sites. The student group comprised several students from the United States, one from Chile, one from Egypt, and one from Israel.

It is hard to believe in today's current political environment, but the spirit of the Oslo Accords prevailed then, so much so that the studio's published study *Towards a Joint Palestinian-Israeli Industrial Development in al-Shoka and Kerem Shalom* stated the belief that the area around the Sufa Crossing in Gaza "could evolve over time into a coherent, even integrated, area." Their findings indicated how integration could be achieved in the future through subsequent developments in infrastructure or common areas that could unite the two parks.

Indeed, in 1999 Harvard professors and students shared our vision for this area. "So, one can imagine this region to be central one day to both the Israeli and the Palestinian industrial areas, linked to the growth along the border areas, and to nearby residential and social areas," they wrote. "This is our future town model: imagine a convenient location to work and to live, because of easy access to the workplace, to transportation corridors, to places of enjoyment, and the many activities that make for a desirable community."[15]

That was indeed my dream, and I wanted to see it implemented not only in Gaza but throughout the lands of the Palestinian Authority as well as in Jordan and Turkey. A string of industrial parks, offering solid technical training and job opportunities, could change this entire region. It could foster political, social, and economic stability; raise gross domestic product (GDP); create a better way of life; afford greater accessibility to global markets; and enhance democratic forms of government in the region. The price tag was a mere $20 million— eight times less the cost of one fighter jet. (The controversial F-35 fighter jet can cost up to $169 million, while the price for a Eurofighter Typhoon is not much less: $159 million.)

---

[15] Harvard University Graduate School of Design, *Toward a Joint Palestinian-Israeli Industrial Development in al-Shoka and Kerem Shalom: An Assessment of Location and Future Planning Flexibility* (Cambridge, MA: Harvard University Graduate School of Design, 1999), p. 23.

CHAPTER 15

A NEW MARSHALL PLAN FOR INDUSTRIALIZATION OF THE MIDDLE EAST

I have always admired the former US secretary of state George Marshall and his enlightened plan to rehabilitate the devastated countries of western Europe following World War II. In 1947 Marshall introduced an assistance program to give these nations the tools for reestablishing themselves, especially by restoring advanced industry. Marshall had anticipated what would develop into the Cold War between the West and the communist Soviet Union, and he sought to strengthen potential allies among the countries receiving assistance under his plan.

The Marshall Plan was in the spirit of the Schuman Declaration instituted in 1950 by the French foreign minister Robert Schuman (upon the recommendation of one of his aides, Jean Monnet). The Schuman Plan aimed to reconcile postwar France and Germany by creating a supranational community. Schuman proposed uniting the two countries' resources of steel and coal and jointly monitoring their development. In this way the states of Western Europe—the nucleus of what would become the European Union—were able to prevent conflicts among countries in the region.

In December 2000 Lynn made aliyah (formal immigration to Israel). She had been approached by the Israel Museum for a position in Jerusalem, but ultimately she decided to work with me. With her American background, she seemed the right person to direct my new initiative, which sought to gain support from the US government for a string of industrial parks for Israel's friendly neighbors.

In October 2002 Lynn and I completed the basic outline of a report, *The New Marshall Plan for Industrial Development of the Middle East*. The plan envisions one hundred industrial parks in the region, to be built over a period of seven to ten years.

It seemed to me that the United States would benefit from such an initiative and could potentially interest some of the more prosperous European countries—those that it had helped to revive after World War II with its generous funding—to join in this effort, as well as some of the prosperous Arab Gulf states.

I saw many benefits that could result. First, the plan would help to lessen world terrorism. Although it can be argued that the perpetrators of the 9/11 attack on the United States were well educated, it cannot be denied that poverty and lack of opportunities create a Petri dish rich for terrorism. Second, it would foster political stability in the oil-rich regions of the Middle East, thus ensuring the free flow of oil to the West. Third, such a program of industrialization would create enhanced trade opportunities for the West: once the Middle East became productive in industries other than oil, it would need expertise and machinery to become a vital economic power. As this development unfolded, the region would become an important new market for the West. Fourth, America and its allies in this cause would achieve a remarkable foreign policy victory by working in tandem to solve the issues that plague the Middle East.

A New Marshall Plan for Industrialization of the Middle East

And the region itself, of course, could benefit enormously from such a project. The dramatic increase in jobs could elevate the gross domestic product of the countries; create a better way of life; and foster political, social, and economic stability. By creating a strong middle class, the initiative could well serve as a foundation for ushering in more open, democratic forms of government. Cross-border initiatives such as regional infrastructure projects of energy, transportation, water, and communications, could become more common, as could joint private enterprise ventures. Perhaps most important, this program could provide hope for a future in a region that has been sorely lacking in this commodity for some time now.

I proposed Jordan as the first pilot project because the leaders of the Hashemite Kingdom are eager to transform their country into a modern and productive state, and Aqaba had recently been designated as a center for industry. I also had a Jordanian partner who was eager to join me in making a better future for that nation. We felt that the success of the first industrial park in Jordan would serve as a prototype, leading to its expansion in other Middle Eastern countries. I calculated that a budget of $20 billion would be required to implement the New Marshall Plan.

Lynn suggested that we take the plan to Washington, DC, and so began an initiative that led to ten visits to the American capital. We felt that we needed five different elements to bring this new plan to fruition: (1) American backing for the concept; 2) an initial display of support—perhaps $20 million to test the pilot project in Jordan; (3) American willingness to convince other countries to share in the initiative; (4) support from the business community in terms of orders and possible startup operations in Aqaba; and (5) a powerful and respected figure to spearhead the effort in the American government.

Oded Eran, a professional Israeli diplomat who knows both Washington and the Middle East, helped us in outlining the program initially. He suggested to Lynn that we meet with the six committees on Capitol Hill that could help with our effort. These consisted of three Senate committees—the Foreign Relations Committee, the Subcommittee on International Operations and Terrorism, and the Appropriations Committee. In the House of Representatives we were to meet with the heads of the Committee on International Relations, the Subcommittee on Foreign Operations, and the House Appropriations Committee. We met with every one of them, some of them repeatedly.

Our first trip took place in late February and early March 2002. It began with a talk I gave to a large audience at the Harvard Club of New York. There I presented the new challenge facing the wealthy countries. I asked for trust in light of my fifty of years of developing successful industrial enterprises for export that employ some ten thousand workers (Arab, Druze, and Jewish residents of the region) and my twenty years of successful experience in building six industrial parks that by that time had engendered and nurtured about 150 companies. I explained that all this was concentrated primarily in the Galilee, in a relative small area of Israel, and had brought about $2 billion in export profits to the state—about 10 percent of Israel's industrial exports. I outlined the anticipated achievements of the plan.

On July 24, 2003, at the invitation of the late representative Henry Hyde, who then chaired the House Committee on International Relations, I had the opportunity to present my plan at an all-day hearing before the forty-nine members of this committee. The hearing was titled "Economic Development and Integration as a Catalyst for Peace," and included several other speakers, such as former Senate majority leader George

A New Marshall Plan for Industrialization of the Middle East

Mitchell (who had helped to resolve the conflict in Northern Ireland and had produced the Mitchell Report on the Arab-Israeli conflict only fourteen months earlier); Akel Biltaji, chief commissioner of Aqaba; the economist Hernando de Soto; and Rima Hunaidi, one of the thirty Arab experts who wrote the scathing United Nations Development Program report on the status of the Arab world. Mitchell underscored the need for an economic solution to bring about peace in the Middle East; Biltaji supported my plan for the pilot project in Jordan; De Soto linked the lack of development in the Arab world to the absence of a property system; and Hunaidi outlined the dire situation in the Arab world in matters such as education, poverty, illiteracy, and women's rights.

The response to my statement was positive, as it was invariably in the many meetings that we had in Washington. On Capitol Hill we met dozens of representatives from the House, most of whom who seemed eager to help. I am particularly grateful to several of these congresspersons, three of whom represented the state of California. Jane Harman, who had visited me in Tefen just before we embarked on this initiative, met with us nearly every time we came to Washington. Perhaps she understood the situation better than some because her industrialist husband Sidney, who was then executive chairman of Harman International, had offered to create a factory in our park-in-the-making in Aqaba to produce the metal parts for his sound equipment products. He was not alone in making such a commitment; a number of other international firms had also agreed, including Daimler Chrysler and Gildemeister in Germany, Ingersoll Cutting Tools in the United States, and TaeguTec in South Korea.

Howard Berman, who also represented California, also met with us repeatedly and made a commitment to help. Even in 2008, when I met him here in Tel Aviv, he continued to say that he would push this initiative through Congress, advising me not to hire anyone in Washington. "We'll do it," he said. Another California representative, Darrel Issa, who established a successful automotive security company before becoming elected, also understood the concept immediately and supported it. When I told him that I was looking for orders for products we hoped would be made at the proposed Aqaba industrial park, he suggested that I contact Ford Motors, which is headquartered in the metropolitan Detroit area, which has the largest Arab population in the United States.

Congressman David Obey, who served as the ranking member of the House Appropriations Committee, told us that we needed a financial institution to implement the proposed New Marshall Plan, a Bretton Woods type of entity.[16] He also stressed that the Jordanian government must be involved; to succeed, the plan had to be a government-to-government initiative.

On the other side of the Hill we met with dozens of senators, including Joseph Biden of Delaware (now the vice president of the United States), Arizona's Jon Kyl, New York's Charles Schumer, Pennsylvania's Arlen Specter, and Nebraska's Chuck Hagel. Senator Hagel (who served as the US secretary of defense until his resignation in November 2014) told me, "I agree completely with your analysis. I've been saying the same thing. Take a look at my recent op-ed piece in the *Washington Post*. It speaks of the importance of not losing the next generation of Arabs." He then told me that he and senator Joe Lieberman had been working on a major piece of legislation focusing on economic and social assistance for the Middle East.

---

[16] The Bretton Woods Conference (formally known as the United Nations Monetary and Financial Conference) took place in 1944 with the purpose of organizing the international monetary system across industrialized nations.

A New Marshall Plan for Industrialization of the Middle East

We broadened our efforts in Washington. Lynn found out who we should meet with in not only the US government but also the private sector and the academic world; she scheduled dozens of meetings for us in these arenas. We met with those in power, such as Elizabeth Cheney, deputy assistant secretary of state for Near Eastern affairs, who appreciated the need to further economic opportunities in our region but was focusing her efforts on empowering women in the region. We met with Richard Armitage, deputy secretary of state and, at the Pentagon, with Douglas Feith, under secretary of defense for policy. Armitage assigned Ted Mann and Clark Price from the US embassy to follow up on my initiative; although he could not promise funding, he did imply that some State Department funds might be available. Feith felt that Israel was making a big mistake to continue to take funding from the United States.

We used the time well. On our trips, we would arrive early in the morning from Israel, check into our rooms at the Willard Hotel, and then immediately head for meetings that would often continue through the evening. A typical day might find us at eight or ten meetings, at the offices of USAID, the Department of Commerce, and onto Capitol Hill, then to the Washington Institute, the Brookings Institution, and the World Bank. My secretary, Esti Balitsky, would sometimes chastise Lynn for scheduling too much into one day. But I didn't mind; I wanted to see as many relevant people as we could.

We sought a prominent spokesman for the initiative and invited suggestions. Two names kept coming up: George Schultz, who had held cabinet posts under presidents Richard Nixon and Ronald Reagan; and James Baker III, who served in the administrations of presidents Gerald Ford, Ronald Reagan, and George H. W. Bush. Other names that were suggested included

THE HABIT OF LABOR

then secretary of State Colin Powell, former secretary of state Madeline Albright, congressman Henry Hyde, former secretary of defense Bill Cohen, and former national security adviser Brent Scowcroft.

In the end I decided to work with two individuals who were well versed in how to shepherd concepts like this through the decision processes in Washington. Former Senate majority leader George Mitchell and former congressman Robert Livingston joined us in the final six months in the attempt to make the plan a reality.

In January 2004 about three hundred people made their way on a cold and rainy morning to Tefen for a conference that Lynn and Erez Navon had planned to discuss the New Marshall Plan. Lynn introduced the dozen or so speakers, which included George Mitchell; former congressman Robert Livingston, who chaired the House Appropriations Committee for four years, and former congressman Anthony J. Moffett from the United States. Turkey was represented by Ali Babacan, then minister of state in charge of the economy, and Tosun Terzioglu, the president of Sabanci University. Representing the Palestinian Authority was Dr. Abdul Malik al-Jaber, then managing director of the Palestinian Industrial Estate Development Management Company. Jordan's minister of planning and international cooperation, Dr. Bassem Awadallah, was scheduled to attend, but at the last minute Jordan dispatched a lower-level official, Dr. Bilal Bashir, to the meeting.

The day had significance in that we hoped to educate the Israeli public about this plan. It was also the day that we planned to sign the document that Mitchell and Livingston needed to ensure the appropriations for the pilot project in Jordan. But to our surprise, Dr. Bashir said that he had no authority to sign the document, and a signature from the Jordanian government was

A New Marshall Plan for Industrialization of the Middle East

required. There was speculation that Jordan feared that by obtaining the requested funding for the Aqaba industrial park it would forfeit its annual allocation from the United States. Perhaps there were other reasons. I suppose we will never know, but this signaled the end of our campaign to usher industry into Jordan.

It was disappointing, for sure. But this was a time when the reservoirs of trust were particularly low in this region. The Second Intifada, which began in September 2000, was still ongoing; it did not end until the following year. And America's war in Iraq had begun less than a year earlier. Perhaps David Obey was correct in saying that we should have involved the Jordanian government all along. It was a pity that this climate of heightened mistrust undermined a project that would have made a significant impact on Jordan's future.

Given the current geopolitical unrest, it is clear that Israel cannot lead such a process right now, but the United States and the European countries that it rehabilitated with this approach sixty years ago could. They could deter an arms race and start to change the atmosphere of hatred and violence in the Middle East. If the West extends assistance, in another fifteen years the region could have an affiliation with Europe, achieving rapid advancement in its standard of living, in industrialization, and pursuing sound relations among nations that are in conflict today.

I am not giving up. I continue to travel the world and meet with leaders past and present, such as former German chancellor Helmut Kohl and former US secretary of state Henry Kissinger, to try to interest them in the plan. I first met with Kissinger in 2008, when he came to Israel for the sixtieth anniversary of its creation as an independent state. Some months later Lynn and I also met with him in his New York City office.

THE HABIT OF LABOR

After he examined my plan he said to me, "Listen, throughout my life I have been engaged in making peace in your region and in the entire world. I never imagined, as you have, that creating places of employment and livelihood for the residents of war zones could help solve the problems of their countries and promote peace." He was impressed by the plan, and said that that in principle he regards it as part of the solution for war-stricken regions.

CHAPTER **16**

THE DEAL

The year 2006 saw a major development for ISCAR: the much-publicized deal with Warren Buffett. About a year before the deal was signed, I learned that my son Eitan, Jacob Harpaz, and Danny Goldman were considering the idea of a possible buyer-partner. In 2006 they had the first meeting with Warren Buffett. "This meeting and the ensuing transaction were the experiences of a lifetime for me, as a finance person," Danny says. "I felt like a player from [the soccer team] Hapoel Raanana playing on the field of Real Madrid!"

Buffett invited them to lunch—hamburgers and mashed potatoes—at his usual restaurant at a mall in Omaha, Nebraska. Of course, the deal was not concluded at that meal. "The whole transaction with Buffett is a fascinating story of a buyer who did not want to buy from a seller who did not want to sell," Danny explains. ISCAR was then enjoying great success, and there was no reason to sell it. On the other side, Buffett did not want to make an exception to his practice of not investing outside the United States. But after they got to know one another better, the deal developed.

The deal played a part in Israel's relative economic prosperity and ability to withstand the global crisis, while it also helped to boost the value of the shekel and Israel's reputation as a center for investments in industry. It is a milestone in Israel's economic history.

As has been noted, years before this I had gladly handed over the management of ISCAR to Eitan and Harpaz, and both of them had proven themselves to be outstanding managers. Thus I did not think to question their decision. I had devoted much of my life to developing and industrializing the Galilee, and ISCAR was our starting point, center, great success story, and flagship. I had always believed in the potential of the company and its people, and we had always refrained from playing with it on the stock market.

Financial profit was not the key to ISCAR's sale. We wanted to ensure that ISCAR could continue to grow, and we saw Warren Buffett as the person who could help achieve that. Earlier I had found good international partners with whom we could develop and who could help us expand our products in the global market. This was the case with the American company Adamas in the 1950s and the establishment of the factory in the Netherlands in the 1960s. In the 1970s, it was the giant American company TRW. In 1995 we had brought Pratt and Whitney into a partnership with Blades, and later also added Rolls-Royce as a partner. The search for a suitable partner represents the difference between a purely financial approach and an industrial-marketing approach that also assists in creating new jobs.

In truth, the money—$4 billion for 80 percent of ISCAR—was not the most important consideration for us in this deal. What concerned us was the continued Israeli production, in the Galilee, by Israeli hands and with an Israeli brain, within an advanced and competitive world.

Among all of the potential partners I was very pleased with the choice of Warren Buffett. He is today considered the leading investor in the world. We are about the same age, and while his life involves monetary matters and I came from manual

The Deal

work at machines, we have a lot in common in our worldview. Buffett started out in the 1960s by purchasing Berkshire Hathaway, a failing textile company, for $22 million. He transformed it over the years into his holding company. Its estimated worth is about $140 billion today and incorporates about a hundred leading companies in various fields. A financial genius, Buffett has remained a man of simple ways, modest and honest. Bill Gates, who regards him as the figure who has influenced him more than anyone else, has said that the most important lesson he learned from Buffett is the importance of decency. In the midst of the global economic crisis, which started in the United States, Buffett was mentioned as a prospective secretary of the treasury for the administration of president Barack Obama, but he politely rejected the idea.

I liked the fact that Buffett does not operate in the stock market as a speculator but as an investor. He does not look for a rapid profit but instead for stability and growth potential in the companies he acquires. He has said that he buys businesses, not stocks, they are businesses he wants to own forever. Incidentally, Buffett decided to acquire ISCAR even before visiting Israel because the strength of the company could be seen from its financial statements. In addition, the fact that he made an exception—for the first time—to his practice of not investing in companies outside of the United States and acquired 80 percent of ISCAR's shares testifies to ISCAR's world stature.

For us, the deal was more than a tribute to the unique value of the company I had founded fifty-four years earlier with an old lathe in our two-room apartment in Nahariya. I would like to again thank all of ISCAR's workers over the generations who helped us reach this important moment, and to achieve this in the Galilee. I am also convinced that the deal is a tribute not only to ISCAR but also to Israel's industry and economy in general.

THE HABIT OF LABOR

When Buffett visited Israel, I accompanied him on his tour of ISCAR. He is warm, intelligent, and friendly, and not at all arrogant despite his standing; he is also a quick study. He was impressed by ISCAR's history, by the principles that have guided us, by its stability and growth over the years, and by the people who are part of it. He agreed in advance to let us continue to manage ISCAR and lead it forward with our staff of managers and workers.

I believe that what attracted Buffett was not primarily ISCAR's financial value and economic potential but the unique character of the company, its special culture of work, production, quality, motivation, and good labor relations. The deal was signed on May 5, 2006, in Omaha, Nebraska, in Buffett's "kingdom," and was covered extensively by the international media.

The story did not end there. In May 2013, seven years after we concluded the first agreement, he bought the remaining 20 percent of ISCAR. The company's valuation had doubled in that time, so the purchase price for the remaining shares was $2.05 billion. In an interview with the Israeli publication *Globes* Buffett was asked how unusual it is for a company the size of ISCAR to double its valuation in seven years. He noted that ISCAR is "an exceptional company," and that he was "with the right people, the right business, and the right country." He also promised that the company would remain in Tefen, and thus ended an important chapter in my life.

CHAPTER **17**

SUMMING UP, AND A LOOK TO THE FUTURE

I immigrated to Israel as a refugee from Germany, a boy ten and a half years old, several years before the outbreak of World War II.

At school in Tel Aviv I felt, looked, and sounded foreign. I also did not Hebraize my foreign name. I was expelled from school because of discipline problems, so I set out to learn a vocation. I fell in love with metal and metalworking.

In the Palmach I felt for the first time like a native son of the Land of Israel, part of a cohesive group with a shared national objective. After I fought alongside my friends for the establishment of the State of Israel, I continued to work for it as a civilian in its young weapons industry.

I was self-employed, and tried to support my new family in the Galilee with an occupation that I loved: working with hard metal. Hard work, full of dedication and love, led to personal success and prosperity. I founded and managed a company that continually produced, sold, and expanded. I also saw myself as an educator for the young workers in my factory, helping them to develop their talents and abilities. From the outset I understood that the export of excellent products to world markets would bring us economic strength, stability, and well-being.

Twice I feared for the future of Israel: first, when the president of France, Charles de Gaulle, imposed an arms embargo on us in 1967, on the very eve of the Six-Day War, and then during the

THE HABIT OF LABOR

Yom Kippur War. At the state's request I founded a large factory to supply essential parts for aircraft engines, and I decided that it was vital for the state to settle the Galilee and industrialize it.

After the companies I founded—ISCAR, Blades, and others—grew and created markets in the world, I wanted to make use of my experience for the benefit of the state and the Galilee. I built, with many other good people, a new and independent community in the Galilee. I built an industrial park there that saw the growth of many companies and provided thousands of jobs. Today that region is filling with magnificent export industries that are bringing billions of dollars to Israel.

I realized that we must also include in these initiatives the other groups who share the land with us—Arabs, Circassians, Druze, and those who immigrated to Israel as part of the Jewish Diaspora. Side by side, with equality in duties, rights, and opportunities, these people work as managers and skilled workers in manufacturing, research, design, and international marketing.

I have often swum against the tide. When the state's vocational education system collapsed, I founded vocational schools with other partners, and the graduates of these schools became skilled workers, managers, and entrepreneurs. In 1975, when the country was brought to a standstill by strikes, I promised prime minister Yitzhak Rabin, on behalf of the managers and workers in our factories, that we would not strike. That same year, we ourselves paid the income tax of the workers in our companies for three months to serve as an example for others in encouraging industrial workers.

All my life I have tried to help create a better state for all of us. Today I am trying to help the entire Middle East become more advanced, productive, and peaceful through my New Marshall Plan, designed to mobilize the world's wealthy countries to build many industrial parks.

Summing Up, and a Look to the Future

But, like a little boy, I want more. Not for me, but for the state and all of its residents. And for the countries of the region: more peace, more work and production, more vocational education, more exports, more security, and a higher standard of living.

Among all of my successes, I also count some major failures: for example, the failure so far in implementing industrial parks as a model and solution, both in Israel and internationally. Or the failure to put vocational education in Israel on an equal footing with academic education to create the skilled reserves we so urgently need for a high-quality export industry.

After all, the Zionist idea is really an attempt to transform Jews into a people like all peoples; not so much a "chosen people" as normal people that overcome their fears from years of exile; a nation of people that chooses vocations that can ensure stability in the land rather than itinerant people who are fearful for their existence. Israel must change from being a military or agricultural power, as it was during a period when there were few people and much land, to a small industrial power. The state's early substantial investments in agricultural research and development yielded great technological advancements, which led to a situation in which only 2 percent of the workforce provides for all of the state's food needs (except for grains). There is no land, and particularly no water, for more than this. Defense, which provides a livelihood for a large part of the population, will need to change when our neighbors also realize that the solution is not in national and religious struggles but in pragmatic processes for changing their world, their ways of life and thinking—in building infrastructure for employment, in education, and in raising the standard of living. Industrial parks and vocational education are some tools for changing the future.

THE HABIT OF LABOR

I created the Foundation for Education, Work and Entrepreneurship for Industry in November 2010 with the aim of furthering my vision for these areas, particularly the Galilee and the Negev. The subject that most worries me is the emigration of our children out of Israel due to their choice of professions for which we have few jobs here. I am also worried by the depth of alienation that has grown among some of our citizens, such as the ultra-Orthodox Jewish sector and the Arab sector. In these sectors, the rate of employment is particularly low. There is also a low sense of partnership, and certainly of pride, in the state we have created here. How do we change all of this? How do we generate hope instead of despair, work instead of frustration and anger? How do we bring the various groups closer together without imposing a specific lifestyle on them?

I do not have all of the solutions, but I believe strongly in the therapeutic power of work in general and of industry in particular. The foundation we started, which is managed by Danny Goldman, ISCAR's highly esteemed CFO, is an instrument for fulfilling this goal: by promoting vocational education, it is designed to assist universities, as well as the army, in training the young generation for full and satisfying lives of creative work in Israel—and not just *luftgesheft* (pie in the sky).

The foundation's focus is on education, skills, entrepreneurship, industry, community development, and culture – those same areas that drive the Tefen Model.

The foundation's activity will not be limited, of course, to the industrial parks; it will be active in initiatives that promote its objectives, such as the project to train ultra-Orthodox youth for work, which we launched with Rabbi Dovid Grossman in Migdal Ha'emek, or the new industrial park in the Arab city of Nazareth, where we hope to inspire a new generation of both Arab and Jewish entrepreneurs. We also have a project to train

Summing Up, and a Look to the Future

teenagers in industrial vocations prior to their army enlistment. My foundation is designed to promote a healthier, more cohesive, more productive, and more stable society in the Middle East. This is my great hope.

What do I want from the future?

I want the Galilee and the Negev to prosper, to be filled with communities, with industrial parks and enterprises, and to be freed from their peripheral isolation. I want a rapid transportation artery to connect them to the center of the country.

I hope that in another decade or so, the northern border with Lebanon and Syria will be open. A series of industrial parks, theirs and ours, will operate along both sides of the border and mark the beginning of a new era. Industry is also peace. Christians, Druze, Jews, and Muslims will build, operate, manage, and work—together or separately, as they choose—in factories in the Negev and the Galilee with borders open to our neighbors to the north and with Jordan and the State of Palestine. Industrial parks will be built throughout the Middle East, and the citizens of these nations will work in them, in knowledge-intensive export industries, as well as in the tourist industry and in agriculture, in comradeship and with a sense of a shared objective. The conflicts will be left far behind as a bad memory.

An industrialized and advanced Israel cannot succeed alone; it must become integrated into the region in which it lives. Because if we succeed alone, the disparities between us and our neighbors will grow wider, and the envy, hatred, and sense of foreignness among us will only intensify.

The change will occur if we and our neighbors can learn from the mistakes of the past and also learn from the countries that have achieved independence and stability, such as Finland, Ireland, Singapore, South Korea, and Taiwan—small countries

THE HABIT OF LABOR

surviving among giants. As in our region, some of them have a history of wars, occupation, destruction, backwardness, and poverty. In the not-too-distant past they were weak and agricultural states supported by others. With the help of industry and targeted education, they applied creative and productive thinking and set out to compete in the markets of the world. This region, too, can achieve a better and more promising future if we only learn to develop our entrepreneurial and productive human resources.

Economic interdependence will also lead to peace—not only an end to the wars, but also the beginning of a new life in which land, water, and natural resources are not the source of the state's powers. Instead, these powers will derive from sound social organization, education, and technological innovation that can engender a life of shared economic interest for an entire region in the global market.

Jews and Arabs must replace the enmity of today with the competitive partnership of tomorrow. Israel must also maintain its deterrent power and its Jewish majority, while granting democratic rights to the minorities and opening its gates to the Jews of the world when they realize that Israel is the homeland of the Jewish people.

I am eighty-eight years old as I write these words. I do not plan to depart from this earth anytime soon. I am healthy, physically and mentally, and full of curiosity and a desire to contend with reality—just as I was two generations ago.

But, I tell myself, at least I have tried. I have really tried. I learn from the lessons that come from my failures. Perhaps there will be sophisticated readers who smile and say, "This is the naive Stef and his simplistic *idée fixe*, which he has constantly preached for sixty years." I indeed hope that a bit of innocence still remains in me; I am aware that these ideas are

Summing Up, and a Look to the Future

simple. Perhaps it will yet be proven how essential it is to implement them for the future of the state and its people.

People often ask me, "Stef, what is your formula for success?" as if everything can be summed up in a sentence or two. And I respond, "I don't know. Perhaps it is simply to want something good and to get up in the morning and work to achieve it!"

ACKNOWLEDGMENTS

To Miriam, of blessed memory.

To my children, my grandchildren and my great-grandchildren.

To my dear Lynn, who came at just the right moment in 2000 to help me conceptualize and further the Marshall Plan. Our chance meeting in 1996 led to a fruitful working relationship that eleven years later turned into a shared life. I am very grateful for both, as well as for her extensive work on this version of my autobiography.

I prepared a list of acknowledgments that grew to include many hundreds of names, and even then I was afraid that I might be forgetting someone. Therefore, I do not have the space here for all of those I need to thank personally for their help, support, friendship, and advice over the course of the long journey and in all of the wars, struggles, achievements, attempts and failures.

Gratitude is due to the friends from my childhood and teenage years; to my friends from the ranks of the Palmach, the place that shaped me more than anywhere as a person and as an Israeli; to my colleagues at HEMED and the Israel Military Industries; to the initial workers at ISCAR, at Blades, and in all of the companies we founded; to all those who lent a hand in building the first industrial park in Tefen and the parks and schools that followed; and to my creative friends in industry, writing, and art. Alas, many of you are no longer with us.

My thanks also go to the thousands of employees of ISCAR, Blades, and our other factories both in Israel and abroad; to the people of the industrial parks in Israel and Turkey; and to the friends and associates without whose faith, support, and love this life story would not exist.

My thanks and appreciation go to all those who helped in preparing this book, and particularly to Yitzhak Ben-Ner, who followed my story for over twenty years and to George Eltman of the Deborah Harris Agency, who helped to shape the final version of this book with his intelligent questions and good humor. Thanks too to Deborah Harris, who found a publisher for the English version, Peter Mayer, who really understood what I have tried to say in these pages.

TIMELINE

1654   First Jew takes up residence in Kippenheim.

1793   Wertheimer family known to reside in Kippenheim.

1850   Opening of the Kippenheim Synagogue.

1871   Peak of Kippenheim's Jewish population at 323.

1909   Tel Aviv founded.

1917   Balfour Declaration.

1926   Stef Wertheimer is born, July 16.

1933   Adolf Hitler elected chancellor of Germany.

1935   Stef's parents begin preparations to leave Germany.

1936   Stef and his family depart from Kippenheim, December.

1937   Stef and his family arrive in Haifa, February 10.

1938   Kristallnacht, a night of Nazi terror against the Jews in many places in Germany, November 13.

1939   World War II begins in Europe.

           Stef is expelled from the Tel Nordau School.

1940   SS deportation of remaining Jews in Kippenheim, October 22.

1943   Stef spends six months in Bahrain as a civil employee of the British Royal Air Force.

1945   Stef joins the Palmach.

1947–49   Israel's War of Independence.

THE HABIT OF LABOR

1948 State of Israel is established.

Stef and Miriam are married.

1952 Stef founds ISCAR.

1956 Partnership with the New Jersey firm Adamas.

Sinai War.

1962–64 Stef begins his first foreign venture in Weert, Netherlands.

1964 Stef starts his first education initiative, the Zur-Nahariyah Vocational School. It operates until 1985.

1969–95 Partnership between TRW and ISCAR.

1971 ISCAR begins US operations in Clifton, New Jersey.

1976 Yossi Pano's revolutionary product, the Self-Grip, debuts at a trade show in Japan.

1977–81 Stef serves in the Ninth Knesset as member of the Dash party.

1979 Anwar Sadat makes his historic speech before the Knesset.

1983 Stef is hospitalized after a car accident; his son Eitan takes over the management of ISCAR

1984 First residents move into Kfar Vradim.

Tefen Industrial Park opens.

1989 Stef's wife Miriam dies.

1991 Stef receives his nation's highest honor, the Israel Prize.

1992 Tel Hai Industrial Park opens.

1993 Jacob Harpaz becomes CEO of ISCAR

1995 Omer Industrial Park opens.

1997 Blades factory opens in Xian, China.

ISCAR acquires the South Korean company TaeguTec.

Timeline

1998 At Lavon, Stef opens his new industrial park, a residential community, and a new vocational school.

1999 Partnership with Rolls-Royce begins.

2000 IMC acquires the German-American firm Ingersoll.

2002–4 New Marshall Plan campaign in the United States.

2005 GOSB Technopark in Gebze, Turkey opens.

2006 Warren Buffett purchases 80 percent of ISCAR.

Dalton Industrial Park opens.

2008 ISCAR acquires Tungaloy in Japan.

2012 German president Joachim Gauck presents Stef with the Order of Merit, Grand Cross (Grosses Vedienstkreuz), the highest honor bestowed on a civilian.

Nazareth Industrial Park opens.

2013 Warren Buffett purchases remaining shares of ISCAR.

LIST OF PRIZES, AWARDS, AND HONORARY DEGREES

1962
Kaplan Prize for Israeli export.

1962
Kaplan Prize for initiative and dynamism in establishing a factory for blades for aircraft engines.

1976
Rothschild Prize for industrial development and export progress.

1983
Good Industrial Design Citation for Self-Grip innovation, Stuttgart Design Center.

1986
Named Distinguished Friend of ORT on ORT's fortieth anniversary.

1990
Israel Marketing Prize, Israel Export Institute/Israel Manufacturers' Association.

1991
Friend of Haifa University.

Rothschild Prize for product innovation and export.

International Industry LEAD Award, Society of Manufacturing Engineers (SME), United States.

Israel Prize for contribution to society and the state.

1992
Honorary doctoral degree, Technion.

Hugo Ramniceaunu Prize in Economics, Tel Aviv University.

1994
European Achievement Award, ASM International, Amsterdam.

1995
Export Prize, Israeli Ministry of Economy, awarded for excellence in export.

1996
Entrepreneur of the Year Award, Entrepreneurial Center, Tel Aviv University.

Humanitarian Award, B'nai B'rith International.

Outstanding Citizen Award, Council for a Beautiful Israel.

1998
Appointed as member of Harvard University's Committee on University Resources.

Honorary doctoral degree, Ben-Gurion University.

1999
Appointed as honored member of the engineering faculty, Tel Aviv University.

2000
American Machinist Award for "the creation of an innovative cutting tool, as well as for his contribution to the independence of Israel during the years 1950-60 to 2000."

Yigal Allon Award.

List of Prizes, Awards, and Honorary Degrees

2001

Honorary doctoral degree in humane letters for lifetime achievement, Jewish Theological Seminary of America.

Israeli Metal and Electricity Union Award.

2003

Named one of Fast 50 Champions of Innovation by the American business magazine *Fast Company*.

2007

Lifetime Achievement Award, Dun and Bradstreet.

2008

Buber-Rosenzweig Medal for "his vision of peace through industry for the Mideast," German Coordinating Council of Societies for Christian-Jewish Cooperation.

European Foundation for Culture Award, awarded in Strasbourg for the contributions of the Museum of German-Speaking Jewry in the Tefen Industrial Park.

Henrietta Szold Award for "success in nurturing Israel's industrial development and promoting crucial foreign investment," Hadassah.

Honorary doctoral degree in engineering, Polytechnic University/New York University.

Lifetime Achievement Award, Silicom Ventures.

2009

Honorary doctoral degree, Bard College.

Honorary doctoral degree, Brandeis University.

Honorary doctoral degree, Weizmann Institute of Science.

Verdienstmedaille (Medal for Merit) of the Landes Baden-Württemberg, awarded for service in the field of industry to that region of Germany.

2010
Oslo Business for Peace Award, "the highest distinction given to a businessperson for outstanding accomplishments in the area of ethical business."

2012
Man of the Year Award for 2011, Israel-Turkey Business Council.

Order of Merit, Grand Cross (Grosses Vedienstkreuz), the highest honor bestowed on a civilian, presented in Jerusalem by German president Joachim Gauck for special service to the Federal Republic of Germany.

Outstanding Leadership Award "in recognition of his outstanding service to the State of Israel and to its industry and economy . . . and for his exceptional leadership," University of Haifa.

Platinum Book Award for the sale of forty thousand copies of Stef Wertheimer, *Man Next to the Machine*, Organization of Book Publishers in Israel.

2013
Honorary degree, Jewish Institute of Religion, Hebrew Union College.

Honorary degree, Rupin Academic Center.

Honorary Master of the Chamber of Crafts of the Stuttgart Region.

Honored in recognition of his role as a visionary and dreamer, Bible Lands Museum, Jerusalem.

Life Achievement Award, Israel-America Chamber of Commerce.

2014
Deming Cup for operational excellence, Columbia University Business School.

INDEX

7 Industries, 108

Achiam, 163
Adamas Carbide Corporation, 63, 64, 67, 222
Adimek (Tefen Metal Casting), 161,
Agranat Commission of Inquiry, 118
Aharonchik (Aharon Donagi), 34, 39, 40
AKA packaging plant, 19
Aksan, Emre, 174
Albatronics, 167
Albright, Madeline, 218
Ali Baba and the Forty Lawyers, 117
aliyah, 111
Allen family, 3
Allon, Yigal, 38, 42, 43, 110, 121, 130; as minister of education, 80; as minister of labor, 114
Aloni, Shulamit, 117
Alpha Omega, 171
"Alternative Futures in the Western Galilee, Israel," 110
Amdocs, 171
American Motors Corporation (AMC), 152
Amit, Meir, 118, 122, 129
Arab sector, and unemployment, 85
Arab-Jewish Center for Economic Development, 86
Arab-Jewish Course for Industrial Entrepreneurship and Management, 85
Araf, Elias, 60
Arafat, Yasser, 208

Arazi, Oded, 31–34, 57
Arens, Moshe, 130
Armitage, Richard, 217
Aronson, Shlomo, 167
Asheri, Avraham, 95
Atidim, 107
Atom Platoon, 32
Auerbach (camera repairman), 22
Aufbau, 16
Awadallah, Bassem, 218
Azran, Prosper, 165

Babacan, Ali, 218
Babcock and Wilcox Company, 67
Bachman, Gidon, 16, 18
Badash, Pini, 166
Baker III, James, 217
Balfour School, 27, 45
Balitsky, Esti, 217
Bar-Lev, Haim, 114, 121, 136, 137
Barak, Ehud, 209
Baram, Micha, 165
Baron of Flour, 5
Bashir, Bilal, 218
Begin, Menachem, 121, 129
Beit Shemesh Engines factory, 99
Ben-Gurion University, 166
Ben-Horin, Efrat, 168
Ben-Nun, Yochai, 118
Ben-Tzur, Israel, 161
Ben-Tzur, Shosh, 161
Ben-Zvi, Kobi, 162
Benedict XVI, 171
Berkshire Hathaway, 51, 101, 145, 223

Berman, Howard, 215
Berman, Yitzhak, 129
Biden, Joseph, 216
Biltaji, Akel, 215
Bisan, Hudar, 192
Biterman (Dr.), 192
Black Saturday, 35
Blades Technology, 98, 190, 192, 202, 222, 226, 233, 234
Blau-Weiss, 24
Blumenthal, 16
BMC, 165, 166
Bochbut, Shlomo, 139, 141, 142
Boeno, Betsi, 174
Born Free, 168
Bosmat, 78, 79, 89, 106
Brand, Eila, 171
Brand, Harry, 159, 171
Brandeis, 79
Breyer (pilot), 28
Brokman, Guy, 169
BT9, 161
Budget Restraint Law, 119
Buenos, Eli, 203
Buffett, Warren, 51, 101, 145, 179, 189, 221–24

Carboloy, 68
CARERITE, 161
Carlson, Robert J., 99
Celtic Tiger, 180
Cheney, Elizabeth, 217
Citizen's Rights Movement (Ratz), 117
Cohen, Bill, 218
Cohen, Guy, 168
Cohen, Haim, 153, 186, 189–90
Colibri Spindles, 168–69
College for Entrepreneurship, 82
Copenhagen Declaration, 181
Copenhagen Process, 181
Council for Productive Zionism, 130, 202
Cut-Grip tool, 152–53
Cut-Off, 149

dabka, 170

Dagan, Anat, 87
Dagan, Yehezkel, 63, 73
Dahan, Arie, 159
Daimler Chrysler, 215
Dalton Industrial Park, 2006, 169–70
Dankner, Shmuel, 208
Danziger, Yitzhak, 163
Das Leben unseres Kindes (Wertheimer), 11
DASH (Democratic Movement for Change), 118–22, 128–29
Davidka, 38–39
Dayan, Moshe, 130
de Gaulle, Charles, 96
Deganya kibbutzim, siege on, 38, 40
Demirel, Suleyman, 174
Democratic Movement for Change. *See* DASH
Dendrinos, Panos, 67
Deri, Aryeh, 142
Discount Investments, 71
Dohan, Belu, 62, 63, 73
Donagi, Aharon, 34, 39, 40
Drayer, Ed, 64
Dreifuss, J. J., 18
Dreyer, Ed, 63, 68, 71
Dubnikov (teacher), 21
duel education system, 89
Duracarb, 74, 191

Eban, Abba, 75
Ecevit, Bulent, 174
ECI Telecom, 167
Einstein, Albert, 1
Eisenstadt, David, 81, 87
Eitan, Rafael ("Raful"), and education 82
El-Op, 25
Eliav, Arie Lova, 124
Emil (lifeguard), 18
EMO, 202, 204
Eran, Oded, 214
Erez, author's grandson, 8, 194
Erich (cousin), 3
Erna (Aunt), 2
Eshel, Yaakov, 71, 190
Eshkol, Levi, 74–75

Index

Eyal, Shmulik, 140

F-15 aircraft, 119
Fanne (Aunt), 2, 10
Feinsod, Moshe, 183, 184
Feith, Douglas, 217
Feller (principal), 17, 21
Fischer, Stanley, 85
Forest City Materials, 76
Foundation for Education, Work and Entrepreneurship for Industry, 228
Fraunhofer Institute, 156
Free Zone Authority, 208
Freescale Semiconductor Israel, 167

galuti, 31
Gamila's Secret, 162
Gates, Bill, 223
Gebze Industrial Park (GOSB Technopark), 174–75
Generals Project, 83
Georgy family, 29–30
Geva, Aryeh, 31
Gildemeister, 215
Ginsburg, Abraham, 83, 84
Gleichman, Moshe, 65
Globes, 104–5, 224
Goldberg, Annie, 163
Goldberg, Chava, 25
Goldberg, Emanuel, 22, 25, 28
Goldberg, Sasha, 70
Goldman, Danny, 189, 221, 228
Goralnik, Yisrael, 80
Gordon, A. D., 77–79
Greenberg, Avner, 110
Greenberg, Noam, 110
Grossman, Dovid (Rabbi), 86, 228
Gush Etzion, 38
Gut Company, 30

Hadani, Yisrael, 163
Haganah Museum, 40
Haganah, 18, 25, 30, 34, 35
Hagel, Chuck, 216
hakafot, 24
Halperin, Ernst, 16

Haredim, 85–86
Harel, Yossi, 36
Harlinger Café, 17
Harman, Jane, 215
Harman, Sidney, 215
Harpaz, Jacob, 187–89, 195, 196; and Japan, 200–1; and Warren Buffett, 221–22
Harpaz, Oren, 168–69
Harvard University's Graduate School of Design, 110, 167, 209
hasaka, 24
HeliMill milling tool, 146, 154, 205
HEMED, 34, 39, 40–42, 46, 47, 113
Hermann (Uncle), 2
Herzog, Chaim, 160
Hess, Manfred, 83
Hiar, Gamila (Savta Gamila, or Grandmother Gamila), 162
Hirsch, Seev, 85
Histadrut labor federation, 18, 118, 127
Holstein, Alizah, 110
Holstein, Lynn, 12, 110–11, 209, 211–14, 217–19
Hunaidi, Rima, 215
Hussein (King), 208
Hyde, Henry, 214, 218

iBLOT, 166
IMC, 101, 145
Inamori, Kazuo, 199–200
Industrial Buildings Corporation, 159
Industry Is Beautiful (Moti), 203
"Industry Is Beautiful," *Yedioth Ahronoth*, 202
Ingersoll, 101, 189, 205, 215
Institute 3, 42, 46, 47, 49
Investment Advisory Council, 175
Iscamill, 147–48
ISCAR Blades, 98
ISCAR Metals, 101
ISCAR, 51, 52–76; and first Arab employee, 60; and first catalog, 66; and first shares, 63; and Israeli Defense Forces, 113; and jet

engine blades, 96–101; and Yom Kippur, 113
Israel Defense Forces (IDF), and Palmach, 42; and education, 82; and ISCAR, 113; and Ruti Wertheimer, 107
Israel Lands Administration (ILA), 138, 142, 165, 171
Israel Military Industries, 36, 47, 49, 50, 53, 113, 233
Israeli Metals Committee, 95
Israeli-Palestinian Industrial and Trade Park Project, 209
Isratech, 72, 95
Issa, Darrel, 215

Jaber, Malik al-, 218
Jeannet, Jean-Pierre, 160
Jeraisy, Ramiz, 171
Jewish Fate, 14
Jonas (Uncle), 2

Kadishman, Menashe, 163
Kagan, Rachel, 46
Kaplan Prize, 100, 110
kashrut, 6
Katyusha rockets, 165
Katz-Oz, Avraham, 130
Katz, Yerachmiel, 95
Katz, Yisrael, 122, 129
Kaufman, M. M., 18
Kaufmann Milling Company, 18
Kenan, Amos, 130, 131–32, 159; and "Industry Is Beautiful," *Yedioth Ahronoth*, 202; and *The Victim*, 163
Kennametal, 68
Kfar Vradim, 110, 130, 133–43, 190, 194
Khatib, Shawki al-, 171
Kippenheim: description of, 1; Jewish cemetery in, 7; Jewish settlement of, 4; and Nazis, 13; synagogue of, 8
Kirshenbaum, Moti, 130, 194, 204; *Industry Is Beautiful*, 202–3
Kishurit, 109, 136

Kissinger, Henry, 219
Kitan Dimona factory, 157
Kocaeli University, 174
Kohl, Helmut, 219
Kopittke, Sigrid, 172
KP Electronic Systems, 161
Kretschmann, Winfried, 90, 91
Krieger, Alex, 209
Krunz, Saadi al-, 208
Kyl, Jon, 216
Kyocera, 199–201

Lahat, Shlomo, 71, 190
Lahmi Bakery and Pastry Shop, 191
Lamberger, Eli, 109, 165
Lavon Industrial Park, 1998, 167–69
Law to Regulate Manpower, 119
Leder, 17
Lehi Group, 30
Lehman, Erich, 8
Leibinger, Berthold, 90
Levy, Isaac, 172
Levy, Orna, 172
Levy, Otto, 71
Levy, Stella, 130
Life Technology (Etrog), 166
Likud Party, 120–21
Lipshitz, Uri, 163
Livingston, Robert, 218
Logos bookstore, 17
Lowe, Jud, 4

M2, 40, 41
Maharam, etymology of, 5
Mann, Ted, 217
Maof, 82
Mapai, 18, 115, 117, 118
Mappus, Stefan, 90
Marco Polo, 15
Marshall Plan, 111
Marshall, George, 211
MasteRound, 170
Mattes, Hartmut, 90
Max (Uncle), 2, 15
May, Karl, 12
Mayer, Andreas, 61
Mecanis Company, 67

Index

Medigus, 167
MEET, 172
Meir of Rothenburg (Rabbi Meir Ben Baruch / Maharam of Rothenburg), 5
Meir, Golda, 114
Melanox, 166
Metalicone, 168
Micro Tools, 162
Microdent, 153, 189
Misgav Local authority, 167
Mitchell, George, 214–15, 218
Moffett, Anthony J., 218
Molina, Raul, 67
Monnet, Jean, 211
Moser, Elisabeth, 90
MTM Pazarlama, 174
Mueller, Amir, 171
Museum of Photography at Tel Hai, 165
Museum of the History of German-Speaking Jewry, 164

Naharazoglu, Kemal, 174
National Committee of Arab Mayors, 171
National Religious Party, 119
Navon, Aryeh, 43
Navon, Erez, 218
Navon, Yitzhak, 130, 141
Nazareth Industrial Park, 2012, 170–72
Neiman, Yehuda, 163
Netanyahu, Benjamin, 209
New Marshall Plan, 111, 211–220
New Marshall Plan for Industrial Development of the Middle East, The, 212–13
Night of Bridges, 33
Nusbaum Café, 34

Obey, David, 216, 219
Oded group, 118
Oettinger, Guenther, 90
Ofek, Ruti, 163, 164
Omer Industrial Park, 1995, 166–67
Open Museum, 163

Operation Agatha, 35
Organized Industrial Zone of Gebze (GOSB), 174
ORT, 85, 87, 92
OTI, 161

Palestinian Industrial Estate, 208
Palmach, 18, 30–43, 225
Pano, Yossi, 55–56, 67, 68, 74, 145–46; and Self-Grip, 149–52; and Cut-Grip, 152–53
Parosh, 39–40
Patkin, Izhar, 163
Patria, 25
Patrus, 161
Penguin Café, 139
PIAT, 38, 40
Piron, Shay, 88
Plansee, 63
Plasel Molds, 169
Plasel, 167–68
Plesner, Maya, 88
Plesner, Ulrik, 88
PMS, 162
Posnanski (literature teacher), 17
Powell, Colin, 218
Prat, Dan, 87
Pratt and Whitney, 76, 99, 100, 101, 222
Price, Clark, 217
"Proposal to Convert and Rehabilitate Failing Factories, A," 158
"proto-Israeli," 31

Ra'anana (Eliyahu Sela), 34
Rabin, Yitzhak, 114, 119, 208, 226
Rappaport, Ernst, 34
Ratner, Jenka, 39–41
Ratner, Max, 76
Red House, 18
reinforced instruction, 84
Rice, 67
Richard (Uncle), 2, 64
Roberts, Edward, 160, 190
Rosenbloom, Richard, 160, 190
Rosenfeld, David, 87
Rouse, James, 140

Rubinstein, Amnon, 118, 122

sabras, 16
Sadeh, Yitzhak, 35, 41
Sakhorov, Yisrael, 36
Sanbanci University, 174
SanDisk, 162
Sandvik, 68, 149, 205
Santo, Edgar, 16, 18
Sapir, Pinhas, 72–74
Satran, Amir, 154
Scala record shop, 17
Schertenleib, Paul, 191
Schocken, Uli, 16
Schocken, Yosefa, 15–16
School for Meisters, 88, 91
Schultz, George, 217
Schuman Declaration, 211
Schumer, Charles, 216
Schwab (*hazan*, cantor), 6
Schwartz, Buky, 163
Schwarz, Beth, 101
Science Corps (HEMED), 34
Scowcroft, Brent, 218
Self-Grip, 55, 146–47, 150–53, 200, 205
Shalem Premilitary Preparatory Program, 87, 88
Shamir, Yitzhak, 130
Shapira, Yonatan, 116
Sharon, Arik, 138
Sharon, Dan, 83, 87
Shaul, Sasha, 113
Shavit, Ami, 163
Shemer, Naomi, 130
Shemi, Yehiel, 163
Shilo, Yael, 109
Shiloni, Yisrael (Hans Herbert Hammerstein), 164
Shinui movement, 116–18
Shire, Jerry, 64
Shmueli, Avner, 36
Shmueli, Itzik, 163
Sinai War, 64
Singer, Haim, 35
Six-Day War, 95
Slavin, Yosef, 37

Smooha, Ephraim, 55–56
Snecma, 97–98
"sock hats," 45
Soto, Hernando de, 215
Specter, Arlen, 216
Spin Tool, 169
Stambler, 192
Steinitz, Carl, 110, 209
Stepac L.A., 161
Stern Gang, 30
Struck, Hermann, 164
Swanson, Gloria, 63

T-Max, 149
TaeguTec, 101, 189, 205, 215
Tamir, Shmuel, 122, 129
Tapiola, 137
Technion, 70, 78–79, 82, 83, 84
Tefen Industrial Park, 1984, 159–164
Tefen Initiative, 136
Tefen Metal Casting (Adimek), 161
Tefen Model, 155–59
Tel Hai Industrial Park, 1992, 164–66
Terzioglu, Tosun, 218
Thompson (Captain), 28
Tibor Rosenbaum, 63
Tichon Hadash High School, 18
Tiger Hill, 25
Tolkovsky, Dan: and jet engine blades, 96–97; and DASH 118; retirement of, 190; and Stef Wertheimer, partnership with, 70–71
Tolstoy, Leo, 78
Towards a Joint Palestinian-Israeli Industrial Development in al-Shoka and Kerem Shalom, 209
TRW, 76, 100, 222
Tumarkin, Yigal, 163
Tungaloy, 101, 189, 190, 202, 206

USR, 161

Valfer, Fanne, 15
Victim, The, 163

Index

Vishay Intertechnology, 167

Wachenheimer, Hilde, 4
Wallach, Hermann, 2, 4, 6
Wallach, Ruth, 26–27, 30
Watad, Mass, 86
Weill, Kurt, 1
Weizman, Ezer, 174
Weizmann Elementary School, 104
Weizmann Institute, 19, 20, 25
Wellington, Ran, 86
Wertheimer IMC Group, 101
Wertheimer, Abraham, 2
Wertheimer, Benno, 7
Wertheimer, David, 2
Wertheimer, Doris, 2, 24
Wertheimer, Eitan, 100, 106–7, 221–22; birth of, 50; childhood of, 104–5; and Cut-Grip manufacturing, 153; and ISCAR, 184–8, 195; and school, 81
Wertheimer, Eugen, 6; and baking, 20; death of, 109–10; diary of, 8–10; and mill, selling shares of, 20; and Palestine, move to, 14–15
Wertheimer, Hermann (butcher), 2
Wertheimer, Hermann (metal market), 2
Wertheimer, Hirschel, 4
Wertheimer, Irit, 45; and ISCAR, 104; and margosa tree, 56
Wertheimer, Julius, 2
Wertheimer, Karolina, 6, 20, 110; *Das Leben unseres Kindes*, 11
Wertheimer, Leopold, 2, 7
Wertheimer, Miriam, 7, 19, 30–31, 38–40; and birth of Eitan, 50; childhood in Germany, 27; death of, 192–94; and early ISCAR, 71; and family life, 54, 56, 60, 103–6, 191; and kibbutz life, 47, 48; and Kristallnacht, 27; and Lahmi Bakery, 191; and naming of first factory, 52; trip to Palestine, 27; and politics, 115, 117; and Stef Wertheimer, marriage to, 45; and Stef Wertheimer, first meeting with, 26; and Yiftach, 108
Wertheimer, Paulina, 7, 11
Wertheimer, Poldy, 2
Wertheimer, Ruti, 105, 107–8
Wertheimer, Samuel, 7
Wertheimer, Selma, 2
Wertheimer, Siegfried, 7
Wertheimer, Sophie, 7
Wertheimer, Stef: and Yigal Allon, 43; and Auerbach, 22; and Baharain, 28–29; and Givat Brenner, 31–33; and car crash, 183–87; and demolitions, 35; and Ettenheim, anti-Semitism in, 13; and expulsion from school, 21; and Fabrique Nationale, 47; and father, relationship with, 10–11; on Galilee, 48; and Goldberg's optical laboratory, 25; and Gut Company, 30; and Haskala School, 23; and industrial parks, 133, 135–43; and Institute 3, 42; and ISCAR, beginning of, 51; and King of England, letters to, 23–24; and Knesset, 122–130; as lathe operator, 25; and run for mayor, 115; and Miriam, in Galilee, 38; and Miriam, marriage to, 45; and Miriam, first meeting, 26; and Nahariya city council, 116; and Nuremberg, trip to, 13; at optician's shop, 21; and Palmach, 31; and Israeli Egyptian peace talks, 127; as pilot, 37–38; and pilot course, 33; and British radar facility, 33; and RAF, 28–29; and Sten bullets, 36; and Yiron, 46; and Dov Yosef, letter to, 49
Wertheimer, Yiftach, 108–9, 191, 194
Wertheimer, Zvi (Peter), 2, 23
Westheimer, Ruti, 8, 105, 107, 108, 117, 184, 193
Wickman, 63

widia, 52, 146
Wolfensohn, James, 175

Xtend, 161

Yad Singalovski, 79
Yadin, Yigal, 118, 120–22, 129
Yedioth Ahronoth, 131–32, 202
Yedioth Hadashot, 66
yekke, 16
Yew, Lee Kuan, 181
Yiftach Brigade, 38–40, 164
Yom Kippur, 106, 113, 116, 118, 136, 184, 188, 226
Yoska (lifeguard), 18
Yugo Commerce Company, 67
Yvel jewelry factory, 172

Zach, Natan, 163
Zamberg, Mookie, 87
Zarhi, Moshe, 98, 159
Zarur, Eli, 61
Zeiss Contax camera, 22
Zelinger, Shlomo, 163
Ziegler, Avi, 87
Zimbalista, Ofra, 163
Zionism and Industry Initiative, 82
Zorea, Meir, 118, 119
Zur Barak, 92
Zur Lavon Training Center, 88, 90, 170
Zur Yam, 87, 92
Zur-Nahariyah Vocational School, 81–82, 85, 89, 187